The Newspaper

The Newspaper
An International History

ANTHONY SMITH

With 111 illustrations

THAMES AND HUDSON

This book is entirely dedicated to Benjamin Jessel,
Cavan Ash, Conrad Shawcross, Guillaume-Antoine Sylvestre,
Leo Crane and William (Rufus) Hardie.

© 1979 Thames and Hudson Ltd, London

Library of Congress Catalog card number 78-55193

Printed and bound in Great Britain by
Jarrold and Sons Ltd, Norwich

Contents

ACKNOWLEDGMENTS
I am indebted to the Leverhulme Trust Fund, whose generosity in the years 1973–5
enabled me to lay the foundations of my interest in press history, and to St Antony's
College, Oxford, where I resided during this period. My thanks are due to the Acton
Society Press Group for creating an 'invisible college' of people interested in the study
of the press, and to Jackie Lebe for typing the manuscript.

Dänischer Nachklang.   Schwedischer Fürgang.

Das ist /

Gründliche Erweisung /

Daß der Anfang deß jetzigen Schwedischen Kriegs-
wesens dem Dänischen / was die Ursachen anlanget / bey weitem
nicht gleich.   Dahero auch der Außgang / so viel die Billigkeit be-
trifft / nicht ersprießlicher zuhoffen.

Durch ei-
nen Aven-
turirer, so
an jetzo
Relation
vmbtregt.

Relation.
Relation.

Zur netwen
Zeitung
auß den
Pommeri-
schenGuar-
nisonen
angebracht

Gedruckt im Jahr Christi / 1631.

Origins and Definitions

In all societies there exist innumerable chains of information, rather like the food chains of nature, through which different types of knowledge pass by custom or by contrivance. Since the end of the Middle Ages, in the Western world, the printed form we call the newspaper has acquired an important role as the major link between many of these cycles, providing for a constantly growing audience large quantities of information drawn from countless different spheres. At the start the newspaper situated itself somewhere between the historian on one side and the diplomatic, financial and military courier on the other. In the information which it chose to supply, and in the many sources of information which it took over and reorganized, it contained a bias towards recency or newness; to its readers it offered regularity of publication. It had to be filled with whatever was available, unable to wait until information of greater clarity or certainty or of wider perspective had accumulated. The newspaper developed as an ephemeral object which had constantly to combine its audience's various interests and seize upon every economy offered by technical innovation in order to expand further.

This book will look at the way in which the object which we call a newspaper developed through the centuries and across the globe. The term 'newspaper' is of much more recent vintage than the actual phenomenon. In England, news was published in book form for nearly a hundred years before it came to be thought of not as a special department of history but as 'throw-away' material. In German the modern word *Zeitung* did not become the universal word for newspaper until about 1850; until then it could still mean information, message, communication, an item of news or a novelty. At first it was used only within the phrase *Newe Zeitung* as a sub-title of various publications, which started appearing after 1500, consisting of narratives of single events. In German, also, the word *Presse* from the year 1500 onwards signified the machinery of printing rather than the product, but gradually narrowed until it came by the nineteenth century to imply the collectivity of daily and periodical publishing. Germany is not an exception: in all the European languages the modern word for a newspaper has evolved only by fits and starts. The earlier words employed in this context were all derived from the methods by which news was collected or produced, or from the kind of information which was being provided. Certain publications were called 'advertisers' or, in German, *Anzeiger* because that implied their principal function, even though they also contained political and social information. The word 'coranto', in various spellings and in dozens of linguistic variants, existed in many countries of Europe in the seventeenth century, denoting a publication in which different items of news were run together end to end to

Opposite First stage in the evolution of the newspaper: the 'relation', published not periodically but as occasion demanded. This example told of the victory of Gustavus Adolphus at the Battle of Leipzig, 1631.

Getruckt zu Cölln hinder den Minrebrüdern/
bey Godtfridt von Kempen/ Anno 1596.

One of Michael Aitzing's six-monthly summaries of 'the most noteworthy events and happenings' of the year. The distinction between a newspaper and an almanac or history had not yet developed.

Freytags, den 1. Septembr. Anno 1730.

Numero I.

Der Königl. Pohln. Churfl. Sächsischen Residentz-Stadt Dreßden Wöchentlicher

Anzeiger oder Nachricht,

Dessen, was in- und außerhalb der Stadt zu kauffen und zu verkauffen, zu miethen und zu vermiethen, zu pachten und zu verpachten, wer Capitalia ausleihen, und solche erborgen will, wer Dienste oder Bedienungen, desgleichen zu einer Reise ein, oder mehr Compagnons suchet, wer nach Persohnen, so nicht zu erforschen, fraget, wer etwas gefunden oder verlohren, wer in abgewichener Woche begraben, getauffet und copuliret worden, wer von Frembden ankommen, oder abgangen, wenn Fuhr-Leute oder Schiffe ankommen, oder abgehen, wie hoch die Victualien in Tax gesetzet worden, und was sonst in gemeinen Leben zu wissen nöthig und nützlich.

Dreßden, zu finden auf der Schloß-Gasse in der Hilscherischen Buchhandlung.

Anzeiger, or 'advertiser' (which was its principal function), published in Dresden in 1730. It addressed itself 'to all those within and without the city who would buy or sell, lease or rent, lend or borrow', as well as carrying shipping news, notices of articles lost and found, of births, baptisms and burials and so on.

describe the events occurring within a given period of time. In the mid eighteenth century a *journal* was defined by Diderot as a 'periodical work, which contains extracts from a newly published book, together with details of recent discoveries in the arts and sciences'. A *gazette*, on the other hand, was, in the words of Voltaire in 1756, 'a relation of public affairs'. Yet by the end of the eighteenth century the meanings had shifted considerably, and in 1777 the first enduring daily paper in French, containing political as well as cultural information, called itself a *journal*. As a further complication, the Dutch published a *gazette* in the French language from 1688 to 1792 which they called the *Nouveau journal universel*.

From the first development of printing in the late fifteenth century there began to appear printed narratives of single news events. In 1540, in Vienna, Hans Singriener received a state privilege for the publishing of *Novitäten*, which really amounted to official proclamations. In Poland, as early as 1513, a *New Zeitung auss Litten und von den Moscowitter* ('news from Lithuania and concerning the Muscovites') had been published. In Paris there was a trickle of *occasionnels*, leaflets containing formal statements of governmental information, between 1488 and 1529; at least two hundred were issued, followed by a stream of more polemical and more popularly produced leaflets known as *canards*. At the end of the sixteenth century in Germany many printers were producing, irregularly, leaflets and pamphlets of political and other news: an Austrian immigrant to Cologne, Michael von Aitzing, sent out a series of reports on ecclesiastical and political matters between 1588 and 1593, and also printed, at six-monthly intervals, summaries of recent events under the general title *Relatio Historica*, which were sold at the great twice-yearly trade fair at Frankfurt am Main. There were frequent attempts too at almanacs which summarized the events of a whole year: the *Mercure français*, which started up in 1611, presented a summary of official and semi-official material but also borrowed liberally from the *canards* of the previous year, popularizing itself with sensational descriptions of floods and natural disasters, plagues and giants, comets and portents. Away in Hungary an itinerant German printer, Janos Manlius, produced a *Newe Zeitung aus Ungarn* in the 1580s, but this was already a century after King Matthias had produced in his *Dracola Waida* ('the Devil Prince'), begun in 1485, a summary of events which Hungarians sometimes claim to be the oldest news publication in the world.

The crucial distinction between such publications and the phenomenon of the newspaper is that in the latter a continuing relationship is set up between reader, printer and the originator of the information. As the publisher of one of the English corantos of the 1620s explained it: 'Custom is so predominant in everything that both the Reader and the Printer of these Pamphlets agree in their expectation of Weekly Newes, so that if the Printer have not the wherewithall to afford satisfaction, yet will the Reader come and aske every day for new Newes . . . I can assure you that there is not a line printed nor proposed to your view, but carries the credit of other Originalls, and justifies itself from honest and understanding authority. . . .'

One can discern four distinct stages through which news publishing passed before it finally achieved the regularity and frequency of publication

Newes out of Holland:

Concerning Barnevelt

and his fellow-Prisoners their Conspiracy against their Natiue Country,
with the Enemies thereof:

THE

Oration and Propositions made in their
behalfe vnto the Generall *States* of the vnited
Prouinces at the H A G V E, by the *Ambassa-*
dors of the *French* K I N G.

W I T H

Their Answere therevnto, largely and truely
set downe: And certaine Execrable Articles
and Opinions, propounded by
Adrian du Bourg, at the end.

VVherevnto is adioyned a Discourse, wherein
the Duke *D'Espernons* revolt and pernicious
deseignes are truely displayed, and re-
prehended, by one of his Friends.

LONDON:
Printed by *T. S.* for *Nathaneel Newbery*, and are to bee
sould at his shop vnder S. *Peters* Church in Cornehill,
and in Popes-head Alley at the signe of the Star.
1619.

Nathaniel Newberry's 'Newes out of Holland' does not attempt to conceal its propagandistic purpose.

and the diversity of content generally expected of a newspaper. The first was the publication of a single story, known in most European languages as a 'relation' or 'relacioun', an account written so long after the occurrence it dealt with that it often sufficed merely to mention the year in which the event took place. In 1619, for instance, one Nathaniel Newberry published 'Newes out of Holland: Concerning Barnevelt and his fellow-Prisoners their Conspiracy against their native country, with the Enemies thereof'. The full title of this pamphlet provides a detailed summary of the complete story and covers the whole of the frontispiece.

The second stage consisted of a continuous series of relations published in the form of a coranto; in England the pioneers and dominant figures of the genre were Thomas Archer, Nicholas Bourne and Nathaniel Butter, who brought out a number of such publications between 1620 and 1625. In 1625 the Court of Star Chamber suspended all publishing of foreign news, but the group started up again on a fully legal basis in 1638, when Bourne and Butter received an official monopoly covering the printing of news from abroad. The coranto was still not a periodical in the sense in which we would understand it. It appeared weekly (with gaps), but did not conceive of itself as an entity speaking to its readers in its own voice; instead, its title listed by name the countries of origin of the information offered. Thus there appeared on 30 May 1622 a coranto describing itself as *Weekly Newes from Italy, Germanie, Hvngaria, Bohemia, the Palatinate, France, and the Low Countries*. This front-page title would change from week to week. Very often one week's publication would begin by describing itself as the 'continuation' of the previous week's. The coranto was an invention of primary importance, for it attempted to provide an account of the whole world and to give its reader the feeling of comprehensive periodical knowledge of world affairs. The Dutch printed the greatest number of corantos, which they circulated in many countries and in many languages. Jacob Jacobsz, for example, working for the bookseller Caspar van Hilten, produced in 1620 a series in French, the first entitled *Courant d'Italie et d'Almaign*, providing a variety of military intelligence in two two-column pages.

The third stage in the evolution consisted of a form usually known as a 'diurnall', which provided a weekly account of the occurrences of successive days. Robert Coles and Samuel Pecke were the most prominent practitioners of the form in English, and their copy was largely drawn from the affairs of Parliament itself. Dozens of diurnalls poured forth in the 1640s as attention shifted from the Thirty Years War, which provided the main content for most of the news publications of Europe, to the domestic problems of England, then staggering towards civil war; most of them were described as *A Perfect Diurnall of the Passages in Parliament*, followed by the first and last dates on which the events described took place. The frequency of publication was dictated by the daily nature of the events related.

The fourth and final stage was the 'mercury', which like the others appeard in the form of a book, with a title-page and an imprint. The word 'mercury' had also appeared earlier in the sequence in the title of the *Mercurius Gallo-Belgicus*, a Latin publication going back to the late 1580s which provided in continuous form an account of the affairs of central Europe; its copies penetrated as far as England, though its main places of distribution were the great trade fairs of the Continent. The poet John Donne expressed his disapproval of the *Gallo-Belgicus* in an epigram: 'Thou art like Mercury in stealing, but lyest like a Greeke.' During the Civil War in England, mercuries appeared so thick and fast from so many different pens that it was possible to buy one every day of the week in London, including Sundays. The title of this type of publication was symbolic: the Mercury was a messenger who wrote his material in his own voice, a journalist trying to attract and maintain an audience for the cash it provided or for the political returns. Yet even with this form the underlying concept remained that of a book of news published section by section; the pages were numbered consecutively throughout the series from week to week until the hazards of war or censorship blotted out the publication's existence altogether.

Alongside the mercury there developed the 'intelligencer' (paralleled in Europe by the *Intelligenzblatt*), which had the aura of being slightly more formal or official than its contemporary. The *Kingdomes Weekly Intelligencer* emerged during the second phase of the Civil War (1648), but the most important product of the genre was undoubtedly the publication supervised by John Thurloe, Secretary of State under Cromwell, who employed Marchamont Nedham, the most famous mercurist of his generation, to bring out *The Publick Intelligencer, Communicating the Chief Occurrences and Proceedings within the dominions of England, Scotland and Ireland. Together with an Account of the affaires from severall parts of Europe.*

A Perfect Diurnall of the Passages in Parliament, a weekly publication which summarized events in Parliament during the Civil War.

With the intelligencer the news periodical began to cover a wider variety of subject-matter, showing a willingness to add new layers of information or entertainment whenever there seemed to be a demand for it and the supply was at hand. Although this stage was still fairly distant from the newspaper as the word is understood today, it presented most of the prerequisites. The seventeenth century saw the establishment of the technical and administrative framework for newspapers in Europe and even North America; the eighteenth then went on to create the newspaper in its complete

THE
KINGDOMES
Weekly Intelligencer:

SENT ABROAD
To prevent mis-information.

From *Tuesday* the 1. of *October*, to *Tuesday* the 8. of *October*, 1644.

THis week hath produced little matter of Action in our Armies, I shall therefore in the first place informe you, of something done for the Armies, & concerning them.
1. The Parliament have voted (since my last) a Committee to go down to the Army, whose advice is to be taken by the Commander, or Commanders in chiefe ; I think the like course is taken in *Holland* : There are some of the States of the United Provinces, that do accompany the P. of *Orenge*, whose concurrent advice he takes upon any designe, & he takes this for no deminution of his command ; and how needfull this is in our Armies, the Kingdom is sensible of, considering what ill instruments have lately bin in the Army in the West,
Gggg   which

The Kingdomes Weekly Intelligencer, semi-official in style and content, was published by the Parliamentary side in the Civil War 'to prevent misinformation'.

form, with daily publication and miscellaneous content. In 1708 one Dutch publisher even referred to 'this century of newspapers', though perhaps a little precociously.

One important aspect of early news publication is that it began not within a small local compass but as an instrument for describing events across immense geographical areas. In the societies of Europe it planted in the mind of the individual literate citizen the picture of a world of public events which he could never see or experience for himself. It placed his own society within the context of the continent and the world. In the East, however, this stage was not reached until the eve of the twentieth century.

When Fukuzawa Yukichi returned home from his long journey to the Western world in 1866, he described to his compatriots in Japan the functions of a newspaper, which, he said, could bring the world to the reader 'though he remains indoors and does not see what goes on outside, and though he is far from home and cannot get word from there'. Japan and

China in fact started to develop a kind of press at the same time as Europe, but had then marked time until Europe reinjected the idea. The information systems of the Far East were of a different kind, never designed to envelop the common reader in the knowledge of a world of public events.

The Chinese civilization was one of the earliest to have found it convenient to set up a systematic news-collection network across a large land mass. During the Han dynasty (206BC–AD219) the imperial court arranged to be supplied with information on the events of the Empire by means of a postal network similar to the princely message systems of the European Middle Ages, when the postmasters of the Holy Roman Empire were required to write summaries of events taking place within their regions and transmit them along specified routes. By the time of the T'ang dynasty (AD 618–907), the Chinese had created a formal handwritten publication, the *ti pao* or 'official newspaper', which disseminated the information collected through the message routes among the governing groups of society. Within the court itself, special forms of the *ti pao* – the *ch'ao pao* ('court newspaper') and the *kung-men-ch'ao* ('imperial court newspaper') – were employed. At a later stage of its development, during the Sung period (960–1278), the *ti pao* was made to circulate among the purely intellectual groups, and during the Ming (1367–1644) was seen by a wider circle of society. In the Ch'ing period (1644–1911), private news bureaux sprang up which composed and circulated official news in the printed form known as the *Ch'ing pao*, the very last example of which was published in Nanking as late as October 1928 as the *kuo-ming cheng-fu kuan-pao* ('official news of the Nationalist Government').

Even though the Chinese had produced the essential technical prerequisites of the newspaper in its European guise before the year 1500, the Chinese press was very slow to develop. Ink, paper, printing, moving letters and even metal type were used in China long before the first *relacioun* or *coranto* appeared in Europe, but the public, printed and periodical distribution of news did not begin until European traders and missionaries started foreign-language newspapers on the Chinese mainland, for their own purposes, in the nineteenth century.

The Japanese social and political system, unlike the Chinese, did not encourage the systematic circulation of news even within the administrative class. Indeed, news information concerning foreign countries was strenuously prohibited, so that although the Dutch brought the printing-press to Japan in the seventeenth century they were unable to introduce their highly developed news-publishing skills. With the institution of a new military régime or Shogunate in 1616, however, a new quasi-bourgeoisie grew up in the towns, encouraging the spread of fiction and creating a market for social news, and from the early years of the century there emerged a system of irregular publication of courtly gossip and social (often sexual) scandal. The single-page courtly gossip-sheet was known as a *yomiuri* ('newspaper') or *kawara-ban* ('tile sheet'), and was produced in colour by pressing paper against engraved and inked tiles or slates. The printed impression obtained in this way was very similar to that made by a woodblock. In later years movable type was employed. The *kawara-ban* was a subsidiary commercial activity operated by the businessmen who controlled the palanquin transport system of Japan. The carriers acquired the most suitable contacts and information as they moved around the roads of Japan, but there existed at the same time a semi-professional group of writers who actually wrote the papers, and their work was frequently censored by the authorities. Rice riots broke out every so often, and satirical comment in verse, circulated by tile-block printing, played on the Shogunate's fear, particularly strong in the late eighteenth century, of a latent insurrectionary power in the written word: all developments in cultural literature underwent official scrutiny, and, as in China, the organized periodical distribution of news had to await Western influences in the late nineteenth century.

The evolution of the press in the Far East, therefore, though it seems at first sight to be an exception, actually bears out a general rule: the newspaper developed interconnectedly throughout the world, as a form dependent on printing which emerged from the economic and political conditions of Europe and spread only in so far as those conditions spread to other societies. As we shall see, the newspaper did not appear 'spontaneously' in any society: the needs of trade and the economy forced the medium into one country after another. Many societies and governments wished not to have newspapers at all, and allowed them only when it became more inconvenient not to do so. The circuits of information upon which human societies are constructed came more and more to rely upon this simple, mechanically produced article which, once it existed, became inseparable from the business of government and economics. The newspaper depends upon its own special lines of communication, inward and outward, bringing information to it and taking the printed copies to the readers. These lines of supply were laid down over many generations, but seemed to 'jell' suddenly and simultaneously over a vast terrain at the beginning of the seventeenth century.

Chinese newspaper-seller, about 1880.

此中國送報之圖其人多係山
東人在京開設報房所有外省
摺奏及諭旨皆由內閣而發其
報房刷印送至各官宅鋪戶之
家每日一換按月給錢名曰送
報的

Neuer
Auß Münster vom 25. deß Weinmonats im Jahr
1648. abgefertigter Freud- und Friedenbringender Postreuter.

Ich komm von Münster her gleich Sporenstreich geritten/
Und habe nun das meist deß Weges überschritten/
Ich bringe gute Post und neue Friedenszeit/
der Frieden ist gemacht/ gewendet alles Leid.
Man läßt ihn freudig auß mit hellen Feldtrommeten/
mit Kesselpaucken Hall/ mit klaren Feld-Claretten.
Mercur fleugt in der Lufft/ und auch der Friede: Jo!
Ganz Münster/Osnabrugg und alle Welt ist froh/
die Glocken thönen starck/ die Orgeln lieblich klingen/
HErr Gott wir loben dich/ die frohen Leute singen.
die Stücke donnern und sausen in der Lufft/
die Fahnen stiegen schön/ und alles jauchzend rufft:
der Höchste sey gelobet/ der Friede ist getroffen/
fortan hat männiglich ein besser Jahr zu hoffen/
der Priester und das Buch/ der Rahterr und das Schwerdt/
der Bauer und der Pflug/ der Ochß und das Pferd.

Die Kirchen werden fort in voller Blüte stehen/
Man wird zum Hauß deß HErrn in vollen Sprüngen gehen/
und hören Gottes Wort: Kunst wird seyn hochgeacht/
die Jugend wird studiern bey Tag und auch bey Nacht/
Man wird deß HErren Ruhm auff Psalter und auff Seiten/
In Osten und in West/in Sud und Nord außbreiten:
die Saine und Paris/die Donau und ihr Wien/
der Belt und sein Stockholm sind friedlich/frisch und grün.

Der Friede kömt Gott lob mit schnellem Flug geflogen/
mit ihm komt alles Glück und Segen eingezogen/
Er bringet Friedenspost und güldne Friedenszeit/
der Krieg ist nun gestillt/ geendet alles Leid.
Spieß/ Bogen/ Schild und Schwerdt/ und Lanzen sind zerschmissen/
Gerechtigkeit und Fried sich miteinander küssen/
Wo Mars der Landsknechts Gott/ die Oberherrschafft hat
da herrschet Lasterschwarm/ und Tugend hat nicht statt.
Drum freuet/freuet Euch/ ihr hohen Potentaten/
und alle die ihr müßt den grossen Städten rahten/

Fortan wird Land und Sand und Dörffer nehmen zu/
und Herr und Knecht wird sein in angenehmer Ruh.
Es werden Fürsten nicht in Cantzeleyen schwitzen/
der Raht nicht in der Nacht mit schweren Sorgen sitzen/
und dencken/wo doch Raht wol herzunehmen sey/
damit betrucket werd deß Krieges Tyranney.
Man wird stäts seyn bedacht/wie rechte Sach mög bleiben/
Wie man/was unrecht ist/recht möge hindertreiben/
Man wird nicht so versehn was böses wird verricht/
wie sonst zu Kriegeszeit/doch ohne Lust geschicht.
Es werden Obrigkeit und Untherthanen wohnen
in Einigkeit und Fried: das gute wird man lohnen/
das böse straffen ab: Kurz/ es wird friede seyn/
im Rathhauß/in der Stadt/ wo man geht auß und ein.
Ihr Obern dancket Gott/ der Frieden ist gerichtet/
Ihr Untern lobet Ihn/ das wibigist geschlichtet/
Es lebt in Fried und Freud die Rahtsherrn und die Stadt/
Biß das was in der Welt und Sie ein Ende hat.

Auch Ich der Kaufleut Gott Mercur komm hergedrungen/
und hab mich mit dem Brieff durch Lufft und Lufft geschwungen/
Ihr Kaufleut seyt wolauff und habt ein guten Muth/
Ihr Handwercksleute auch/es wird alls werden gut.
Fort wird man sicherlich zu Wasser können handeln/
und ohne noth zu Land auff Messen ruhig wandeln/
die Wahren werden wol zu reissen abgehn/
die Läden und Gewölb voll lauter Käuffer stehn/
Man wird zu Tag für Tag den Seidenzeug außmessen/
und zu Mittag zur Müh nicht euren bissen essen/
Gewürz und Speçerey verkauffen wol mit Macht/
bey lauter Centnern wegwägen Tag und Nacht.
Der Schuster wird sein Geldt vor Schuh nicht können zehlen/
Den Schneider wird das Volck um neue Kleider quelen/
Der Breuer nimbt nicht ab/ der Becker der wird reich/
Der Kürschner füttert stäts/und feyret keinen Streich.
Es hitzen bey dem Feur die Schmid/ die Amboß schlägern/
Es tauren mich allein die armen Degenfeger/

Die haben nichts zu thun: Laßt Degen/Degen seyn/
macht einen Pflug darfür/und eine Pflugschar drein.

Ihr Bauren spannet an die starcken Ackerpferde/
klatscht mit den Peitschen scharff/die Pflugschar in die Erde/
Säet/ Hirschel/ Heidel Korn/ Hanf/Weizen/ Gersten auß/
Kraut/Ruben/Zwiebeln/Röhl/füllt Keller/Boden/Hauß.

Ihr Gärtner werdet dann zu Marckt können fahren/
und lösen manchen Batz auß euren grünen Wahren/
dann lehret ihr mit Lust seyn in ein Küchlein ein/
und esset alle die wol lescht den Durst mit Wein:
Juch/ Juch/ ihr seyt befreyt von tausend tausend Nöthen/
und schlaffet biß es tagt mit euren Bauren Greten.

Ihr Wirthe freut euch auch der Friede trägt euch ein/
Es wird die Stub und Stall voll Gäst und Pferde seyn/
Voraus die ihr wol ligt/ beym weiß und roten Hanen/ neu
beim Baum/ Bärn/ Engel/ Stern/ Wolf/ Lasse/ Thurnen/ Schwan/
beim Bitterhold/beim Creuz/ Gans/ Rindfuß/ Rädlein/ Tisch/
beim wilden Mann/ Kron/ Mond/ beim güldnen Ochsen/ Fisch/
Beim Ochsenfelder auch: Ihr krieget gute sachen/
Ihr wolt denn selbsten nicht/ die Zech Wirthlich machen/
doch glaub ichs gänzlich nicht: Nun es hat keine Noth/
Ein jeder gebe mir ein guts Botenbrodt.

Doch dieses alles recht mit beten und mit dancken/
daß keiner überschreit der Erbarkeiten Schrancken/
Es dancke alles Gott/es danck Ihm frü und spat/
was kreucht/ fleugt/ lebt und schwebt/ und was nur
Odem hat.

Gedruckt im Jahr nach der Geburt unsers HErrn Jesu Christi 1648.

Faksimile eines Flugblattes auf den Friedensschluß vom 25. Oktober 1648.

2

'The Occurrences All Together'
1600–1696

At the beginning of the seventeenth century a basic network of postal routes, printing capacity and local distribution was established in many parts of Europe. The religious wars of the century provided the climaxes which stimulated the demand for news. When, in 1620, the first corantos in the English language were shipped across the North Sea from Holland, the opening sentences exposed to view the strata of social habits, assumptions and institutions which made an organized press possible and necessary.

'Letters out of Nuremberg make mention that they had advise from the borders of Bohemia, that there had been a very great Battel by Prage, between the King and the Duke of Beyeren and many 1000 slaine on both sides, but that the Duke of Beyeren should have any folks with in Prage is yet uncertaine.' The text suggests a day-by-day flow of information across a huge stretch of Europe; moreover, it assumes the existence of regular contact between readers and writer, and that the readers' acquaintance with the subject is so great that even interim information on the conduct of an important military campaign will have meaning. The single item of news has evidently passed along an established chain and emerges from the pen of a known correspondent whose communications are expected by the editor. A complex machinery of organized services is presupposed. Yet only twenty years before the Amsterdam printer Pieter van den Keere composed this text, no such complex possibility existed. In the early seventeenth century, changes had taken place in the civil organization of European society, in its transport and communications, in the printing industry, in the structure and conduct of its diplomatic and administrative affairs, which made periodic publication of news viable. Behind those changes lay other long-term shifts, in family structure, in patterns of population, in consciousness of citizenship, which rendered the supplying of news valuable and desirable.

Throughout the western half of Europe, at the end of the sixteenth century, the conjugal family was firmly established; each new marriage implied the creation of a new household. Every young male would assume that the first task of his manhood was to establish such a unit. The retail shop appeared in most of the larger cities of Europe by the year 1600; it was often the property of a single man, not necessarily a craftsman selling his own products, but a man looking for goods to sell to other individuals like himself. Amsterdam, Paris and London had all by then reached the quarter-million mark in population, and by the year 1700 London was to double that figure. The city represented a concentration of activity, in which individuals confronted travellers and immigrants from quite different societies who traded or worked at crafts or fought as mercenaries or took

Opposite When the treaties of Westphalia were signed in 1648, bringing the Thirty Years War to an end, the joyful news was spread by flysheets such as this. Beneath a woodcut rich in symbol the story is told in heroic couplets.

A mounted messenger of 1590, one of many who carried handwritten budgets of news along the roads of late medieval Europe.

Itinerant seller of news-sheets, almanacs and popular literature, 1630.

refuge. Within such cities there arose the sense of a world of public affairs on which citizens could take intellectual and moral positions. The 'King's affairs' were now things of common concern. It was interesting to hear about the affairs of other countries, affairs which could have an important bearing on the possibilities of trade, on the rise and fall of dynasties, on the recruiting and demobilization of armies. What the first periodical publishers 'invented' was the idea of running together in continuous prose accounts of events occurring in different countries. The object of Thomas Archer, the bookseller who inaugurated the first home-produced book of news in English, was 'to place the occurrences all together . . . to muster the Newes, which belongs to the same place, as it were unto one armie'. The London reader experiencing the new interests and anxieties of his time could slake his curiosity on Archer's new publication, the idea for which was borrowed from the Dutch printers who were themselves trying to break into various European markets with their attractive new product, the gathering together of news into a printed miscellany published once a week.

Since the late Middle Ages a formal network of correspondents and intelligence agents had come into being across the bulk of the European continent, busily sending news of military, diplomatic and ecclesiastical affairs along a series of prescribed routes. The information was handwritten and passed along carefully organized chains, each item being labelled with its place and date of origin. Throughout the Holy Roman Empire there grew up major centres of news exchange in the same towns which monopolized trade in goods and the exchange of bullion and coin. Through Vienna came

Jacob Fugger of Augsburg, banker and financier. The gathering of news was an essential aid to his financial dealings.

dispatches from the Balkans; Augsburg processed news from Italy, Switzerland, southern Germany and the East (via Venice); in Cologne messages from France and the Netherlands converged, together with news from Britain, which came by way of Antwerp. Material from Russia and surrounding countries passed through Danzig and Breslau, while Hamburg was the arrival point for news from Scandinavia and the whole of northern Europe. By 1600 the demand for such information had reached the level at which it had become economic to find printed means for distributing it. Western Europe was by then well covered by this network, and places as far away as Hungary, Russia and Poland were being brought into the system.

Rival systems were springing up: business communities in the larger towns were building their own private links along well-trodden routes. Small private systems run by important banking houses like that of the Fuggers were consciously or unconsciously competing with the message-bearers of princes and governments; indeed, for many decades the House of Fugger supplied news to its friends and clients on a scale which rivalled that of many princes, and certainly supplemented their arrangements.

The postal system gradually separated from the news system as, one by one, governments set up common postal services available for general use. In Denmark the royal postal system was established in 1624; England's followed a year later. France had constructed a postal service as early as 1480, and the Sorbonne in Paris had its own academic postal network. But it was Emperor Maximilian I who created the first truly international postal system when he organized a regular route between Vienna and his distant dependencies in the Low Countries; within a few decades the north–south axis was similarly joined, making regular intercourse possible between Milan, Brussels and Amsterdam via the town of Worms. The family of Franz von Taxis, who had been appointed Chief Postmaster by the Emperor in 1516 and given the sole privilege of running the system in the Low Countries, grew wealthy on the proceeds and doubled the family name to 'Thurn und Taxis' when ennoblement finally came. Within a century the family business found itself in bitter competition in many parts of Europe; its agents were excluded altogether, for example, from the lucrative Danzig–Berlin route opened up in the middle of the seventeenth century. The postmasters were obliged to keep up regular services in all weathers, despite bad road conditions. Early newspaper journalists constantly blamed the posts for the lateness of news, for the absence of whole editions and for their own sloth, misadventures and incompetence, but in fact the Thurn und Taxis postal service sometimes covered 166 kilometres in a day, and tried to keep up an average guaranteed speed of 6 kilometres an hour in the mountains and 8–10 on the plains. Their agents could cross from Augsburg to Venice in six days, while the competing service run by the Augsburg city authorities took two days longer.

England was late in building a national road system. Not until the restoration of the monarchy in 1660 did the Turnpike Act provide for proper toll roads; until then local landowners were supposed to pay for the repair of the roads which passed their way. Certain reforms were put in hand in 1635 which improved the coverage of post towns and enabled wealthy travellers to move from place to place in stages of about twelve miles, guided by small boys familiar with both route and horses. Before that date, just four cross-country routes had existed, but the development of the European international postal system obliged a certain order to be imposed on the chaotic state of affairs in England. In the mid 1620s the Thurn und Taxis postal system connected with London via Harwich on Wednesdays, and a regular post left London every Thursday, taking messages along the four routes. Within London, transport started to develop only after 1635, with street-paving and the arrival of Captain Bailey's first stand for hackney carriages; Sir Sanders Duncombe's City sedan-chair service came later. Travel in England was detestable on the whole, the rigour of the experience relieved only by the noted comforts of the inns and hostelries.

In France, however, the transport system was more thoroughly developed, and messages moved in and out of Paris and the royal court with an admirable regularity. In 1630, when the first periodically published news began to circulate, an organization of royal despatch riders, *les grands courriers*, covered many minor as well as all major routes in the country. From Paris to Bordeaux or Lyons took just under two days, and the journey could be relied upon; the transmission times were not improved upon in a major way until the 1820s, when Chappe's aerial telegraph (a point-to-point signalling system) linked several hundred stations across the country.

The printing-press on which the first regular news publications were produced was a mildly improved version of Gutenberg's and Caxton's devices for 'moving letters'. It consisted, basically, of an oaken screw with a

An English printing office, 1619. 'In serving others', says the motto, 'we are worn away.'

horizontal iron plate or platen attached to its lower end, which rose and descended between two vertical posts held by a cross-beam. The 'forme', or page of type, was laid on a movable flat bed which slid under the platen; when the platen was lowered, sufficient pressure was exerted on the type to produce a printed impression. The letters were inked between each printing with a mixture of oil and lampblack applied with a printer's ball made of leather and horsehair, and each sheet of paper had to be positioned and secured by hand; if both sides of the sheet were to be printed, the ink would have to be allowed to dry first. No really important innovation occurred until Koenig's cylinder press was introduced in 1812, although in the eighteenth century Lord Stanhope's all-metal press in England and Didot's precision press in France offered many operating improvements: until then, each act of printing had involved nine separate physical actions, from inking to removing the wet sheet, performed by men who had to remain standing or leaning. Even this represented an improvement on the system designed by Gutenberg, since in about 1620 an Amsterdam printer, Willem Janszoon Blaeu, had added a counterweight to his machine which caused the platen to rise automatically after each impression; this simple adjustment increased the printer's productivity enormously, conceivably doubling the printing capacity of Europe.

One can only guess at the work-rate of an early-seventeenth-century printing-press; in Paris the printers began work at five in the morning and finished at eight or nine in the evening, and in this time a printing-house containing two presses could probably have printed between 2,500 and 3,000 copies of a two-sheet publication. (It is generally thought that one machine of the time could produce about 150 sheets per hour.) One must not underestimate the muscle-power and the costs entailed in type-founding (casting the letters in metal) and type-setting (composing the page) – it took a skilled man a whole day to set one page of the Gutenberg Bible, and only sixteen impressions of such a page were made in an hour – but news

21

A printing office in Nuremberg, 1676. One man checks a four-page printed sheet on the tympan, while the other passes inked pads over the type in readiness for the next sheet.

A printing shop of about 1600, showing all the processes involved from type-setting (left) to printing the sheets and hanging them up to dry.

Ioan. Stradanus invent.   Phls Galle excud.

publishing was a more slapdash affair than Bible printing, and setting times much faster. So much capital was locked up in the printing of books (the King James Bible, for instance, cost the printer £3,500 to produce) that printers were constantly looking for operations which would admit of a quick return; the political and penal risks frequently entailed in publishing news were offset by the prospect of a desperately needed flow of cash.

In each country of Europe a different system was employed for supervising the activities of printers. In Italy both Church and state had a hand in the censoring; in France every product of the press was subjected until 1789 to an absolute royal power of censorship under which the inauguration of any new genre of material required the granting of a fresh royal privilege. In England printing was subject, after 1586, to the jurisdiction of the Court of Star Chamber, which began its work by limiting the number of presses and the towns in which they might operate: only London, Oxford and Cambridge contained any printing activity at all, and in London there were just fifteen legal printing establishments by 1615 and still only twenty in 1637, the year in which the Star Chamber banned all periodical publication of news.

In Germany the legal position of the *newe Zeitungen* was clearer than that of their counterparts elsewhere: the Holy Roman Empire had brought the printing-press under control as part of the legal machinery set up by the Edict of Worms (1521). The authorities at the Frankfurt Fair were scrupulous in carrying out the rules, which were strengthened by further regulations proclaimed by Emperor Rudolf II in 1608. Publishing on German territory meant prior censorship as well as an obligation to acquire a special concession from Church or city authorities. The town of Erfurt, for example, punctiliously defined the categories of material liable to censorship in order to prevent any news publication escaping the law by disguising itself under a harmless-sounding title. In the early decades of the newspaper the dual control of Church and state was necessary, since only the former had the social power and organization to guarantee the system against evasion, while the city authorities had the immediate opportunity for physical supervision.

Despite controls physical and administrative, there were important changes taking place in the world of printing and publishing. First of all, new divisions of labour were taking place: type-founding became separated from printing; bookselling and publishing emerged as distinct though overlapping activities. In England, however, all the processes entailed in creating and distributing printed works were brought within the jurisdiction of a single organization, the Stationers' Company, a self-policing bureaucracy of printers, publishers and booksellers charged by the government with the task of ensuring the legality of all publications in exchange for a total industry-wide monopoly. The Company registered every work and exercised free right of search of all premises suspected of infringing its privileges. The Archbishop of Canterbury and his colleague the Bishop of London, constituting the High Commission in Causes Ecclesiastical, had the exclusive right to nominate new master-printers who, on nomination, would function within the procedures of the Stationers' Company. None the less, within the Company there existed men who did no printing at all, but merely sold books or collected together the capital to employ their colleagues to print and sell them. There were 'publishers' who wandered the streets of St Paul's looking for interesting merchants' letters from abroad, spicy and sensational descriptions of trials and misdemeanours, eclipses and natural disasters, or travellers with a good tale to tell. No copyright existed with the author once his manuscript passed into the hands of a registered member of the Company. 'If he get any Coppy into his powre', wrote George Wither in his *Schollers Purgatory* (*c.* 1625), 'likely to be vendible, whether the Author be willing or no, he will publish it; and it shall be contrived and named alsoe, according to his own pleasure: which is the reason, so many Bookes come forth imperfect, and with foolish titles.' The organization of a regular market for news publication did provide new opportunities for writers as well as for publishers and booksellers; it was well into the seventeenth century, however, before news-writing (as opposed to printing and publishing) became a separate profession.

The transition from sporadic to regular publication was very rapid, taking place within the space of very few years across a great geographical area. In 1597 Samuel Dilbaum, who had already produced annual news reports in rhyme, arranged with a printer at Rorschach on Lake Constance the publication of a monthly news-sheet, each edition of which appeared under a different title. In Strasbourg in 1609 the bookseller Johann Carolus brought out the monthly *Relation aller Fürnemmen und gedenckwürdigen Historien* ('relation of select and noteworthy happenings'), while in Wolfenbüttel the printer Julius Adolph von Soehne seems to have had the same idea at roughly the same time. A printer in Antwerp, Abraham Verhoeven, had started publishing his *Nieuwe Tydinghe* in 1605; it appeared sporadically at first, but gained in frequency until it turned into a weekly in 1617 and even reached three editions per week in the 1620s.

Verhoeven's privilege, obtained from the Archduchy of Albert and Isabella, Regents of the King of Spain, consisted of permission to print or engrave on wood or metal 'and to sell in all the territories of our jurisdiction, all recent news, victories, sieges and captures of cities which the said princes may undertake or win'. The publication was influenced in style by the French *occasionnels*: it was highly ornate, with engravings and even maps. A French edition of it appeared from 1610 on. In 1610 also the Swiss town of Basle started a weekly paper which concentrated on transmitting news from neighbouring cities, in several of which imitators quickly sprang up: these publications had a new and important designation, *Ordinari-Zeitung*, which was attached to scores of city papers for the next half-century.

It was in Holland and Germany, however, that the new medium took root furthest and fastest. The spread of weekly papers was partly imitative, partly the product of mutual causation: the contents of the early papers tended to be drawn from other, similar papers, and the more papers in circulation the easier it was for a printer in a newspaperless city to start one. Towns along the great trade routes were naturally the first in the field: Cologne in 1610, Frankfurt am Main in 1615, Berlin in 1617, Hamburg in 1618, Stuttgart in 1619, and a string of further towns in the 1620s, including Vienna itself in 1622. The tide continued until, at Leipzig in 1650, the bookseller Timotheus Ritzsch began to produce his *Einkommende Zeitung*

A Envvyfinghe der forten en plaetfen , hoe eñ in wat manieren zijn Pr. Excel. Mauritz van Naffouwen een proeve heeft. ghedaen om den Vlaemfchen dijck in te'nemen,ende de beduydinge met cyferen afgheteekent.

10 Zijn alle floupen met bootfchefellen van die van Antwerpen,wachtende op zijn Ghenade Graef Ernft fchepen,
11 Hier gaen te lande een deel Schippers ende Booriffefeli-n van Antwerpen , gaende-naer s'Heeren Staten volk-le te bef-h-b--en.

27 Sloupen daer Schippers,Viffchers,ende Bootfgefellen in waren van die vande ftadt.

Afbeeltinghe watter gefchiet is den

verfterete/de welcke fo dapper op t'bo lrbã Graef Ernft d>ongen/ hoetwel onfe fchepen vãroo:loghe haer beft dedë met fchietẽ) dãffe tlant moften verlatẽ: eñ die/mãe flou-

('incoming news'), the oldest daily publication in the world; a decade later he brought out another commercial paper in which the news was more complex and multi-sourced, the *Neu-einlauffende Nachricht von Kriegs- und Welt-Handeln.* ('latest news of wars and world affairs'). The Dutch were even more prolific; the connection with the House of Habsburg (and therefore with Spain) and the seafaring basis of the Dutch economy meant that Amsterdam and other cities of the Low Countries had well-worked links across Europe and the known world. Before 1626 there are known to have been 140 separate news publications in Dutch; the first to be published periodically was Caspar van Hilten's *Courante uyt Italien, Duytslandt &c*, which soon appeared in various other languages, including English and French. In Spain the *Correos de Francia, Flandres y Alemánia*, started in April 1621 by Andrés de Almansa y Mendoza, used the Dutch papers as its model. The printers themselves moved across the Continent looking for new towns in which concessions could be obtained for periodicals: two emigrant Germans, Melchior Matzan, a printer, and Joachim Moltke, a bookseller, managed in 1634 to acquire the royal concession for Copenhagen and gave Denmark its first regular news.

The Swedes were spurred by the journalistic activities of the Low Countries to produce periodicals appropriate to their special military role in

Front page of Abraham Verhoeven's sporadic coranto *Nieuwe Tydinghe*. The engraving shows the river battle in which Prince Maurice of Nassau captured Antwerp from the Spaniards in 1605.

Ordinari Post Tijdender/
Anno 1645.   N. 4.

Extract Skrifwelse vthur Feldtmar-
skalkens Herr Gustaff Horns Hufwud-
Qwarter Vstede den 4. Januarij.

Wij liggia här ännu stilla/ och äre Regimen-
terne fördeelte här om kring/ närmest in til
Malmöö och Christianstadh/til at refrai-
schera sigh något/Effter som ingen Fiende
nu meera är til at spöria på denne sijdan om Sundet.
Lyffzmedel på denne Landzändan äre tämmelige/ och
kunne medh Gudz hielp wäl förslåå/til theß Tijden til-
låter at gåå i någon Action igen. Siukdomen vnder
wårt Folk tagher dageligen meera aff/ ther emoot i
Köpenhamn och annorstädes i Danmarck / taga al-
lahande Siukdomar meera och mera öfwerhanden/
och berättas i Sanning at halffparten aff the Sol-
daterne som hafwa warit på denne sijdan om Sundet
icke skola wara meera widh Lijffwet. Wij hafwe hafft
i theße daghar en Trumslagare i Malmöö til at inkö-
pa här några nödiga Saker för Sal. Her Johan Kru-
ses Lijk/hwilket ock honom tillåtit bleff. Han berättar
elliest at han för denne gången myckit bättre är tracte-
                                                        rat

Above, left The *Ordinari Post* of 1645 reports, in Swedish, from Field Marshal Horn's H.Q. in south Sweden, the closing stages of the war between Sweden and Denmark. 'Sickness among our troops decreaseth daily, tho' in Copenhagen and other parts of Denmark all manner of sickness doth more and more prevail.'

Above, right Théophraste Renaudot.

Europe at the time: Olof Olofzson Enaeo published the first *Hermes Gothicus* in 1624 at the town of Strängnäs as a propaganda instrument to assist Gustavus II Adolphus in the prosecution of the Thirty Years War. In the territories conquered by Gustavus in the 1630s, German-language papers were produced by the Swedish authorities: Leipzig, for example, was provided in 1632 with the *Ordinar Post und Zeitung aus dem schwedischen Posthaus zu Leipzig.* The Swedish upper crust, however, preferred its news in French, and thus Sweden also came to import journalistic influences from Paris, which during the 1630s were to be the most remarkable and, one might say, the most 'professional' of the age.

The flowering of journalistic ingenuity and style in the France of Louis XIII can be largely attributed to one man, the remarkable Théophraste Renaudot, who brought to fruition a series of ideas, partly borrowed from Montaigne, which involved combining advertising with the publication of news. Renaudot was born in 1586 into a Protestant family and qualified as a doctor at the age of nineteen, but before settling down to his practice at Loudun went on a series of journeys through France, Germany, Italy and the Low Countries which presumably brought him into contact with many of the journalistic innovations of the time. In Venice he saw the new single-sheet bulletins of news sold cheaply on the Rialto at the price of one *gazzetta*; in Florence he saw the *fogli avvisi* of Gerolamo Gigli, which combined information on current warfare with items dealing with commerce; at Strasbourg he came into contact with the internal newsletters of the Fugger banking concern, which were then being made available in printed form, and in Holland he had the chance to see the stylish new corantos. Renaudot's fame as a doctor spread rapidly from Loudun to the Louvre, whence a summons arrived in 1612 to take up the post of Physician to the King; he was assigned the special project of enquiring into the causes and cures of poverty, and finally Richelieu persuaded him to give up his practice altogether in order to act exclusively as Commissioner-General for the poor.

It seemed to Renaudot that one of the causes of poverty in the society around him was the fact that those with goods and services to supply often

To Renaudot goes the credit for introducing the Bureau d'Adresses. Sixty years later (this engraving is dated 1697) it was still performing its function as a broker between buyer and seller, forerunner of the modern classified advertisement.

failed to make contact with those who needed them. Montaigne had had the same perception already and had produced a scheme for an institution which would exchange commercial and other useful information. Renaudot moved his headquarters to Paris and set up the first of these institutions, the 'Bureau d'Adresses et de Rencontre', which was conveniently situated near the Palace and provided a universal brokerage between rich and poor. Renaudot's handbills explained that the Bureau provided the means whereby 'anyone may give and receive information on all the necessities and commodities of human life and society'. The aim was to reduce beggary in the streets of Paris by helping the workless to find employment, masters to find apprentices, borrowers to find lenders, the homeless to find shelter, the sick to discover medicaments. From time to time Renaudot made information available in printed form: lands for sale and rent, carpet novelties, new materials for clothes, a young dromedary (very cheap), intending travellers in need of companions for the road. 'It is essential', wrote Renaudot, 'that in a state, the rich help the poor, internal harmony ceasing when one section is inflated beyond measure while another wastes away.' In 1639 it became obligatory for the names of all unemployed persons to be registered at the Bureau d'Adresses.

Montaigne's original plan had been very similar. 'In all cities there should be a certaine appointed place, to which, whosoever should have need of any thing, might come and cause his businesse to be registered by some officer appointed for that purpose.' It was to be a kind of urban barter centre for goods and services, necessary at a time when, in Germany and Italy, to Montaigne's certain knowledge, 'two most excellent men in knowledge have miserably perished for want of food and other necessaries'. It was charity rather than profit which was the ultimate goal of the proposed institution. Renaudot's project, however, was peculiarly suited to the practical problems of the early-seventeenth-century European city, swollen beyond the point at which necessary information could flow reliably by word of mouth alone. Social groupings had grown large enough to be virtually autonomous; large areas of social space separated them, and each saw the other in terms of pre-existing stereotypes, through the medium of information spread by third parties, by politicians, gossips and professional disseminators of news.

Paris was not the only city in which experiments were taking place in the business of communication among the citizens of urgent knowledge of a commercial nature. In London the brilliant turncoat journalist Marchamont Nedham – who changed sides in the Civil War, for professional reasons, three times – supplemented his income from his writings in the 1640s by participating in the ownership of a string of 'Offices of Intelligence' situated around the City; here the applicant received information on goods and services in exchange for cash. It was at this period that the first mass-distributed foodstuffs, coffee and chocolate, were being marketed. Patent medicines flowed from the fervid imaginations of an army of quacks, and toothpaste had been invented: 'most excellent Dentifrices to scour and cleanse the teeth, making them white as Ivory: Preserves from the Touthach, fastens the Teeth, and sweetens the Breath, and preserves the Gums from Cankers and Imposthumes'. People needed rooms to rent, wet-nurses,

language teachers. A rival of Nedham, one Oliver Williams, worked out a scheme for performing the functions of an Office of Intelligence by means of a publication. The client could read a paper which contained the advertisements but withheld the information about where the goods or services described could be obtained; for that intelligence, he must repair to Williams's premises and pay a small sum. Since Nedham was at that time licensed to write a news publication and Williams was not, a long legal feud began between the two men which did not cease until the restoration of Charles II, when Nedham had to take refuge in Holland from his accumulated political infidelities.

Renaudot had no such problems with the Bureau d'Adresses; Richelieu protected his privileges and concessions. Not only did the institution flourish on its own terms, but it attracted to itself an altogether new commodity – news. The Bureau collected useful information of a general kind about events within society, and Renaudot conducted long and elaborate correspondence with many interesting informants. In and around the court of Louis XIII at this time, a war of political pamphlets was breaking out in which the King found himself in need of help. On 30 May 1631 Renaudot obtained in his own name and in the name of his children the sole privilege in France to 'make, print, and to have printed and sold by those appropriate, news, gazettes and accounts of all that has happened and is happening inside and outside the Kingdom'. The first issue of the *Gazette de France* appeared on the same day in a form closely resembling the corantos of Holland and England: that is to say, it used ornamental opening letters and placed sub-titles in the margins of the pages, and the general format was exactly that of a book. The use of the word *gazette* is most significant; it had already appeared, with

Allegorie de la Gazette, an anonymous watercolour showing Renaudot receiving items of news from far and wide.

certain variants, in the titles of several publications earlier in the century, but had not previously been given a precise order of meaning. It derived from the name of the coin used in Venice for the purchase of an *avviso*, but following Renaudot's use it came to be employed to designate a new generation of news periodicals which spread throughout the Continent, specializing in the transmission of items of foreign news which had been collected inside the offices of government. Domestic news appeared towards the end of the four pages of text, which consisted for the most part of single-paragraph résumés of diplomatic dispatches, each bearing its town and date of provenance. The foreign information contained in the issue of 30 May began with news from Rome dated 26 April and ended with an item from Antwerp which had started out only a week before publication. Renaudot penned an essay stating his journalistic aims in the form of an address to the King, whom he reminded of the spread of such publications among the neighbours of France; he explained how the corantos were preventing the dissemination of false rumours which inflamed internal commotion and sedition. Every reader, he said, would be able to benefit from the information provided: the merchant would not find himself sending goods to a town which was besieged or lying in ruins, the soldier would not set out for employment where there was no war. The edition ended with some news of the court, which was taking the waters at St-Germain-en-Laye, and with an appeal to readers to make use of the Bureau d'Adresses.

What Renaudot had achieved was a stabilization of all the previous forms of news publication in a format which was flexible but authoritative; it contained the news which the authorities wished to disseminate. The *Gazette* appeared in the voice of its editor or compiler, but it was not in the same class as the unauthorized Dutch exports slipped into England to the consternation of the English government. 'Everyone knows that the late King did not merely read my Gazettes', Renaudot wrote in 1645, 'and did not suffer any detraction therein, but that he almost regularly sent me memoranda. . . . Was it for me to examine the deeds of the government? My pen was only the grafting-tool.' The *Gazette* was to remain in business as an official paper until the end of the French monarchy in 1789.

Renaudot was constantly dogged, however, by rivals: a group of Parisian booksellers had already, since January 1631, been publishing *Nouvelles ordinaires de divers endroits* ('news from sundry places'), and regarded Renaudot's privilege as an infringement of their own. The King renewed his commitment to the *Gazette* in November, but this was not enough to silence Louis Vendosme and Jean Martin, whose publications were not finally extinguished until a decree of March 1633 which ruled, in some detail, in favour of Renaudot, who was awarded letters patent in 1635 guaranteeing his complete monopoly, together with a substantial state pension.

'In one thing,' wrote Renaudot, 'I yield not to anyone – in the search for truth.' What singles him out among the pioneers of journalistic form is this passion for information and the role he sought to play within the world of politics; the only party he belonged to, even in times of political schism, was that of the King, but within the intellectual life of the city he achieved the kind of position of patronage which has come to be associated with powerful information media. The Bureau d'Adresses would sometimes organize public lectures: one was given in January 1634, for example, in which the doctrines of Galileo were 'authoritatively' refuted, while the *Gazette* simultaneously published an account of the trial and condemnation of Galileo for asserting the centrality of the sun within the universe. Every Monday Renaudot arranged meetings at the Bureau d'Adresses between the brightest minds of the day, as he called them, for the discussion of 'physics, morals, mathematics and other subjects'; the minutes of the meetings were later published. The *Gazette* thus became the centre of a complex intellectual and publishing activity and frequently spilled over into *extraordinaires* and *suppléments*.

With the death of the King, however, France slipped, like its neighbour across the Channel, into a period of internal conflict which rendered the business of publishing news hazardous in the extreme. Renaudot pledged his support to Mazarin and was rewarded with the renewal of his privilege. But during the last dozen years of his life Renaudot was hounded by satirists and malicious pamphleteers; he was attacked for engaging in activities unbecoming to a doctor, for publishing lies and half-truths, for having served as the mouthpiece of a deceased monarch. An *Antigazette* sprang up which competed with him week by week. His sons, both of them doctors, were summoned to Paris to start a new periodical, *Le Courrier français*, which never

The House of Commons during the 'Short Parliament', dissolved by Charles I in 1640 after it had sat for only a month.

31

An Exact and true Relation
of the late Plots which were contrived and hatched in Ireland.

1. A Coppy of a Letter sent from the Lord chiefe Iustices and
Privy Councell in Ireland, to our parliament here in England.
2. Their last Proclamation which they publifhed concerning
those Traytors.
3. The whole Difcourfe of the Plot revealed by Owen Ockquellee
who is now in England.
4. The dangerous and extraordinary deliverance of the party
who narrowly efcaped with his life.
5. The reward the Parliament hath confirmed upon him.
6. The true Relation of the whole Treafon related by the Lord
Keeper, to the Honourable Houfe of Commons the firft of
November. 1641.

London Printed for *Francis Coules*. 1641

Among the many forms of street journalism during the Civil War were 'relations' such as this, revealing the intrigues and plots of one side or another.

acquired the prestige or the skill of the *Gazette* but which sold extremely profitably. The civil war atmosphere of the Fronde encouraged a whirlwind of pamphlets, the government being too weak any longer to control the operations of the press. Thousands of single-sheet *mazarinades* blew about the city, whipping up anger and riposte; not until the return of Louis XIV to Paris in October 1652 did the war of libels subside. Renaudot's death occurred just a year later and his sons took over the management of the ever-growing *Gazette*, which, as the century wore on, became noted for its prose style as much as for its news content; printers in the provinces were given concessions to reproduce it, and both the *Gazette* and the Bureau d'Adresses remained stable and admired institutions well into the following century. The *Gazette* set a style for French news journalism and for a series of semi-governmental publications in other parts of Europe; in his close liaison with Richelieu, Renaudot also defined a role for the gazette as a form which was to set the example for the political content of French journalism until the Revolution.

The Civil War in England had a more drastic effect on journalism than did the Fronde in France: it led to the collapse of the Star Chamber, and with it all effective restraints on licensing and on the publication of domestic news. The historical privileges of the Stationers' Company were swept away. Even before Charles I retired with his troops and his court to Oxford, the printing of speeches and of accounts of the growing fracas within the Long Parliament was becoming more frequent, despite the legal prohibitions. The debates of the Long Parliament made gripping reading, and few printers could resist the temptation. Handwritten copies of speeches circulated in hundreds, occasionally thousands, as the bloody decade of the 1640s opened.

Opposite Many of the Civil War 'mercuries' used a primitive form of news-headlines above the title.

The London Malignants disarmed,
Fifty thousand pounds to be raised,
The Lord Capels Forces dispersed,
The Cavaliers from Glocester repulsed.

Numb. 12

Mercurius Civicus.
LONDONS
INTELLIGENCER:
OR,
Truth impartially related from thence
to the whole Kingdome, to
prevent mis-information.

From *Friday August* 11. to *Thursday August* 17. 1643.

BOth Houses of Parliament and the City of *London,* have
a long time been much indangered through the Plots
and conspiracies of many malignant Inhabitants in that
City, the Suburbs, and parts adjacent; notwithstanding
which, that City, which in many other things of great
consequence to this Nation both in former and latter time, hath af-

M   forded

Archer, Butter and Bourne found that the genre which they had painfully developed, steering it past innumerable legal and political pitfalls, was suddenly outmoded. Printed collections of foreign news, which had been so fascinating twenty years before, seemed extremely dull stuff alongside the heady news being made on one's very doorstep. 'And now by a strange alteration and vicissitude of times we talke of nothing else but what is done in England, and perhaps once in a fortnight we hearken after newes sent out of Scotland,' remarked one of the new domestic journalists. The news pioneers of the 1620s went out of business, though not before being soundly attacked from the other side as well by 'anti-mercurists' and conservative sceptics of the value of public news. The poet Abraham Holland penned a vicious lampoon against Nathaniel Butter and his syndicate, not as playful as Ben Jonson had been in his play *The Staple of News* (1625). The walls, Holland complained, were 'butter'd with Weekly Newes':

> To see such Batter everie weeke besmeare
> Each Publike post, and Church dore, and to heare
> Those shamefull lies, would make a man, in spight
> Of nature, turne Satyrist and write
> Revenging lines, against these shameless men,
> Who thus torment both Paper, Presse, and Pen.

Butter survived the collapse of his business, poor and neglected, until 1664.

While the forms and traditions of French and German journalism were established under conditions of vigorous official control, the great flowering of English journalism took place in a period of political pluralism, indeed at times of total licence. Not for a century was there to be a decade of journalism like that of the 1640s in its rollicking intemperateness and its sheer profusion and variety. In the twenty years between 1640 and the Restoration, thirty thousand news publications and pamphlets emerged in the streets and alleys of London. The street journalism of the Civil War was the real forerunner of popular journalism. All the forms which had been pioneered since the 1580s survived, at least in the catchwords at the beginning of titles: there were relations, corantos, diurnalls, intelligencers and mercuries. The *Marine Mercury* specialized in accounts of amazing sea-beasts ('A True Relation of the Strange Appearance of a Man-Fish about three miles within the River Thames, having a musket in one hand and a Petition in the other, credibly reported by Six Sailors who both saw and talked with the monster, whose names here following are inserted.') Many publications called themselves 'A Continuation of . . .' when in reality they were barefaced piratings of work initiated by other printers. Plagiarism and counterfeiting abounded. Journalists, for all their subservience to one political clique or another, earned little social respect. Samuel Pecke, editor of the *Perfect Diurnall of the Passages in Parliament*, one of the most durable of the Civil War newsbooks, survives in a contemporary physical description as 'a bald-headed buzzard . . . a tall thin-faced fellow, with a Hawks nose, a meagre countenance and long runagate legs, constant in nothing but wenching, lying and drinking'.

The Civil War journalists themselves were more guarded in the presentation of their craft to the public. 'Truth is the daughter of time,'

Opposite 'I am Opinion who the world do swaie' – a mid-seventeenth-century allegory demonstrating the power of printed news.

34

Viator	Who art thou Ladie that aloft art fet	*Viator.*	Cannot OPINION remedie the fame
	In ftate Maieftique this faire fpredding tree	*Opinio*	Ah no then fhould I perifh in the throng
	Vpon thine head a Towre-like Coronet,		Oth giddie Vulgar; without feare or fhame
	The Worldes whole Compaffe refting on thy knee.		Who cenfure all thinges bee they right or wrong
Opinio	I am OPINION who the world do fwaie	*Viator*	But Ladie deare, whence came at firft this fruite
	Wherefore, I beare it, on my head that Towre		Or why doth WISEDOME fuffer it to grow
	Is BABELS: meaning my confufed waie		And whats the reafon its farre reaching roote
	The Tree fo fhaken, my unfetled Bowre		Is water'd by a fillie Foole below
Viator	What meaneth that Chameleon on thy fift	*Opinio*	Becaufe that FOLLIE giveth life to thefe
	That can affume all Cullors faving white.		I but retaile the fruites of idle Aire
Opinio	OPINION thus can everie waie fhee lift		Sith now all Humors utter what they pleafe
	Transforme her felf fave into TRVTH, the right		Toth loathing loading of each Mart and Faire
Viator	And Ladie whats the Fruite, which from thy Tree	*Viator*	And why thofe faplings from the roote that rife
	Is fhaken of with everie little wind		In fuch abundance of OPINIONS tree
	Like Bookes and papers this amufeth mee	*Opinio*	Caufe one Opinion many doth devife
	Befide thou feemest (veiled) to bee blind.		And propagate, till infinite they bee
Opinio	Tis true I cannot as cleare IVDGMENTS fee	*Viator*	Adieu fweete Ladie till againe wee meete
	Through felf CONCEIT and haughtie PRIDE	*Opinio*	But when fhall that againe bee *Viator* Ladie faie
	The fruite thofe idle bookes and libells bee	*Opinio*	Opinions found in everie houfe and ftreete
	In everie ftreete, on everie ftall you find		And going ever never in her waie

VIRO CLA.M D.R FRANCISCO PRVIEANO D: MEDICO, OMNIVM BONARVM AR
tium et Elegantiarum, Fautori et Admiratori summo. D. D. D.   Henricus Peachamus.

explained Sir Henry Waller, editor of the *True Informer* between 1643 and 1646. 'Relations of Battels, fights, skirmishes, and other passages and proceedings of concernment are not alwaies to be taken or credited at the first hand, for that many times they are uncertaine, and the truth doth not so conspicuously appeare till a second or third relation. And hence it is that victories sometimes fall much short of the generall expectation. . . .' Behind the nervousness there lay the factional disputes within the Parliamentary camp. The editor of the *Scottish Dove* complained that he was being persecuted by the authorities, and indeed his paper was once burned by the common hangman and he sentenced by the Lords to apologize to the French Ambassador for slighting references to the Kings of France. Both Lords and Commons kept trying to reassert their control over the presses of London, and appointed censors and licensers of printed books, but faction breeds print, and the powerful controls of Star Chamber and Stationers were not to return until Charles II re-established an effective and legitimized set of statutes. In the meantime, journalists published as much as they dared, and went as far as their political cover permitted. John Dillingham in his *Moderate Intelligencer* explained his predicament very clearly: 'So much exceptions are taken by one or the other that we know not what to narrate. One while the Presbyterians threaten, then the Independents and others. In time of this nature its not good to hold argument, only ask questions. . . .' The tribulations of the journalists during the Civil War provided the infant traumas which shaped the personality of English journalism. The printers, writers and licensers associated with the medium of news were obliged to work out the implications of a professional ideology in which truthfulness, impartiality, loyalty to causes and service to the reader had to be balanced with the need to make profits and to joust constantly with authority. Almost every writer or printer of news active in the period was to spend at least a brief period in prison for overstepping the constantly shifting barriers of permissibility. Between Civil War and Restoration, English journalism was to experience every one of the great dilemmas which baffle the wielders and controllers of media power.

In physical appearance, the newsbooks of this period were scarcely elegant. Their eight to twelve pages were crowded with material, the typeface becoming progressively smaller as efforts were made to cram incoming news into diminishing space, until the final paragraph is often almost illegible. The text was set in a single column, and paragraphing was scanty, with no cross-heads, merely marginal notes to signal each change of subject. Occasionally, above the title, there appeared a kind of 'headline' in doggerel rhyme. Printing was conducted in multiples of 250, and it is unlikely that many editions exceeded 1,000; the potential literate male audience in London could not have been much higher than 60,000. The material was hawked about the streets by women who specialized in the trade and often had to take very great risks when carrying pamphlets or newsbooks which offended one of the powerful factions in Parliament.

Two great talents towered above the crowd of factionalist scribblers: those of Sir John Berkenhead and Marchamont Nedham. The former, a skilful controversialist heavily influenced by the doctrines of Archbishop Laud, was

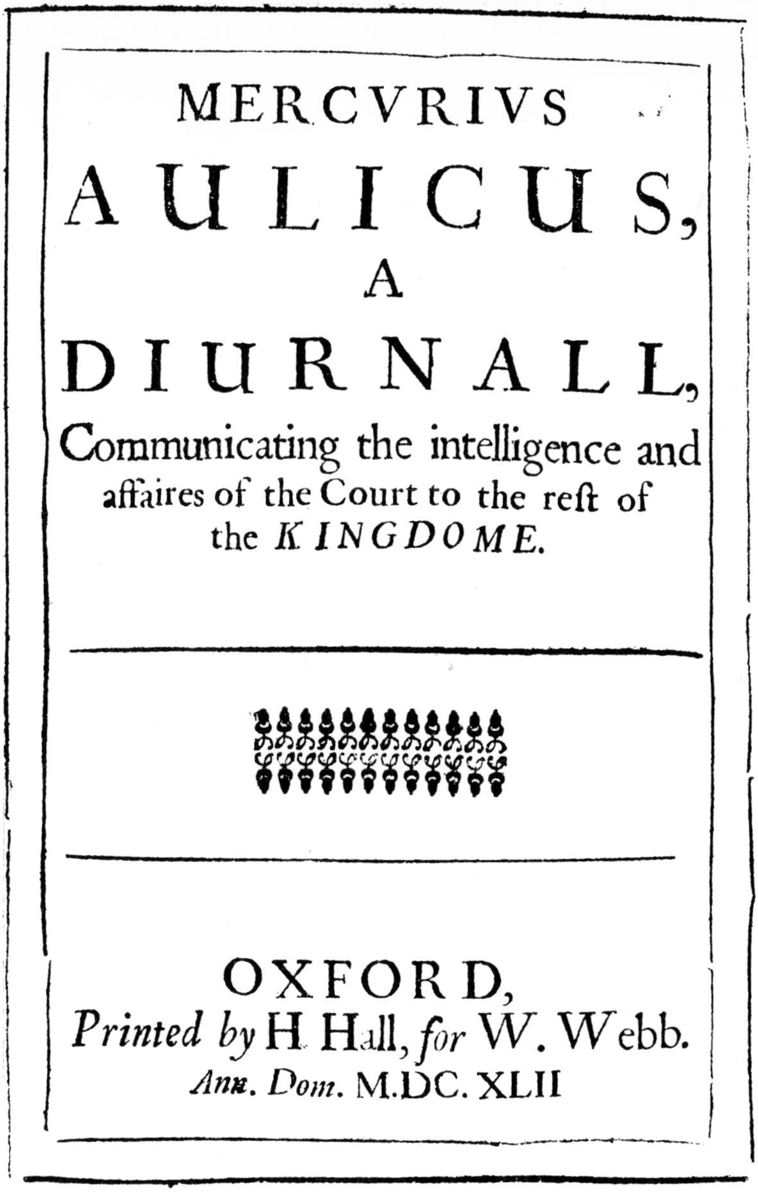

MERCVRIVS AULICUS, A DIURNALL,

Communicating the intelligence and affaires of the Court to the reft of the *KINGDOME*.

OXFORD,

Printed by H. Hall, *for* W. Webb.

Ann. Dom. M.DC.XLII

A 'diurnall' from King Charles's propaganda machine: Sir John Berkenhead's *Mercurius Aulicus* – the Court Mercury.

recruited to help run the King's wartime propaganda machine from Oriel College in Oxford. His journal was called the *Mercurius Aulicus*, and reached 118 editions despite sieges and defeats. It was published with a Sunday dateline to infuriate the Sabbatarian Puritans in London. It hammered at its target week after week with a kind of furious insulting wit which, to judge from the ripostes it brought forth from the Parliamentary presses, reached home. The *Aulicus* was smuggled regularly through the lines to London, sometimes by friendly watermen on the Thames, sometimes by loyalist carriers at Woodstock, by peddlars with licences to cross, by special agents – once even by the French Ambassador, who was caught red-handed with a dozen copies. The biographer John Aubrey described Berkenhead as 'exceedingly bold, confident, not very grateful to his benefactors; would lye damnably. He was of midling stature, great goggli eies, not of a sweet aspect.'

The *Aulicus* was the voice of a régime, produced by propaganda journalists aided by printers; its aim was to raise morale, and it did so by scratching the sores of Parliament, in particular those produced by its internal dissensions. Berkenhead worked vigorously at the task of defaming the rising figure of Cromwell: 'The Cathedral at Lincolne hath lately been prophaned by Cromwell's barbarous crew of Brownists: who have pulled down all the brave carved works there and (for which all Christians will ever abhorre them) have filled each corner of that holy place with their own and horses dung.' As the war dragged on and the King's cause became hopeless, the *Aulicus* tried to blow up stalemates into victories and skirmishes into great battles. With the collapse of the monarchy Berkenhead became a secret agent on the Continent; when the Stuarts eventually returned to the throne he was summoned back into royal service to help set up the new journalistic activities of Charles II's strict régime. He had remained totally loyal to his cause throughout, bestowing upon it all the considerable power of his cynicism.

Nedham could not have been more of a contrast. Born the son of the schoolmaster at Burford, he grew up with the intention of going into the law, but switched first to medicine and then to journalism. He was at Oxford at the same time as Berkenhead and other professional and factional enemies. Nedham's first and most famous newsbook was the *Mercurius Britanicus*, which was immediately noted by Berkenhead: 'All other Newes (I mean Lyes) you must expect from a fine new thing borne this week called Mercurius Britannicus. For Mercuries (like Committees) will beget one another.' Nedham began with a spirited attack on some lords who had defected to Oxford, cast some personal vitriol at the Queen and accused the King of having become a Catholic. Once *Aulicus* was obliged to miss an issue, and Nedham published an obscene obituary on Berkenhead; when Nedham was locked up for two weeks for going too far in his attacks on the King, Berkenhead leapt into sarcastic comment. Nedham, however, grew tired of the stiff-necked pietism of his colleagues, and when the first phase of the Civil War came to an end he observed remorsefully the intimidation widely used against the people by the Independents and the self-righteous doctrinaire hypocrisy to which he had committed himself. 'The way of government in free nations', Nedham had once written, 'is not to be accommodated unto schemes of freedom which lie in melancholy contemplation, but must be suited to that form which lies fairest for practical convenience.'

In the summer of 1647 Nedham defected to the Royalists, taking his skills and inside information with him, and brought out a brilliant new weekly, the *Mercurius Pragmaticus*. He turned against Cromwell, whose real intentions towards Parliament he saw all too clearly: 'For Mr Crumwell hath them in

Opposite Mercurius Rusticus recalled in 1685 'the sad events of the late unparalleled rebellion', which included the fortification of Oxford and Cambridge colleges, and humiliation of the clergy.

Christ Church Coll: Ox:

Canterbury Minster

Trinn: Colledge Camb:

MERCURIUS
RUSTICUS

Countess of Rivers plundered
pag: 11

Sr John Lucas house plundered
pag: 1

THE
COUNTRYS
COMPLAINT
Recovnting
the sad
Events
of the late
unparalleld
REBELLION

Sr Rich Mynshuls hous plundered
pag: 31.

A Bonfire for the voting downe
Episcopacy pag: 26:

Mr Jones a Mini: carried on a
Beare pag: 81.

Warder Castle defended by a
Lady. pag: 41.

Edge hill   Battle

the Mill, and grind they must, seeing they are at his Beck who holds a Whip and a Bell over their guilty heads . . .' *Pragmaticus* was copied and reprinted in the alleyways of London, and lived fugitively, in constant fear of detection by the agents of the new Licenser appointed by Parliament. On the execution of the King, Nedham was unlucky enough to be captured; he escaped, was recaptured and imprisoned for some months, and emerged in an era when desperate attempts were being made to stamp out the remnants of the Royalist press.

Parliament under the Commonwealth now allowed only two publications of news to appear, and one of them was to be edited and written by Nedham at a salary of £100 (slightly less than he had been paid before). He admitted in one issue of his new *Mercurius Politicus* that it was 'a ticklish time to write Intelligence', but threw himself into the new cause, setting up under the supervision of Secretary of State Thurloe one of the best services of information anywhere in the European continent at that time. Cromwell's government was well informed. The Stationers' Company was given a new role in a reorganized licensing system, but with little more independence than a government department. Nedham meanwhile concentrated on straight reporting of all sections of the political world, even recording something of the affairs of the Pretender at 'the little Court lingering at St. Germans building Castles in the air'. Three special commissioners were appointed in 1655 to root out every publication apart from Nedham's *Politicus* and its later sub-edition, the *Publick Intelligencer*, which repeated, at half-weekly intervals, about half of the news and advertisements of its parent paper.

Nedham's pay went up to £500 per year; for this he defended the policies of Cromwell and the activities of the Major-Generals and attacked all other parties, Quakers, Fifth Monarchists, Royalists, Presbyterians and Republicans. He flew political kites to order. One of his growing band of enemies described him as a cat: whichever way you threw him he landed on his feet. But his ability to survive was severely tested by his position as official propagandist during the long-drawn-out collapse of the Commonwealth system. He was thrown out of office by the Commons and then restored to his job after writing a pamphlet re-explaining his position. But he found himself clinging to his job rather than running it, as with obliging tenacity he poured out wholly inaccurate descriptions of the manœuvrings which followed the death of Cromwell. The ageing Milton, who had for a time acted as Licenser of Nedham's publications, now turned to his aid, writing in support of the dying Commonwealth system.

As General Monck made his stately advance towards London, Nedham was attacked in ballads, lampoons, pamphlets. When Charles arrived in London Berkenhead was made Licenser and Henry Muddiman, a schoolmaster, recruited by one of Monck's kinsmen, was invited to bring out a *Mercurius Publicus* to set the tone for the coming Restoration. Nedham packed his things and fled to Holland, returning a year or so later after obtaining a royal pardon. Though he published pamphlets on political and social questions, education in particular, he never returned to news journalism, but lived out the next two decades in constant fear of recognition and apprehension by his many former colleagues (and therefore enemies).

Only one physical description remains of this remarkably talented, 'hawk-nosed' multi-apostate:

> His visage meagre is and long –
> His body slender, but his tongue
> If once you chance to heare,
> Observe it well, it has a grace
> Becoming no such traitor's face . . .

Nedham, together with Berkenhead, added an ingredient to English journalism which was to remain of immense importance, a vein of topical and polemical wit intermingled with reporting. The antiquary Anthony à Wood got him right when he called him 'this seditious, unstable and railing author'.

The Restoration was a bleak period for English journalism. Charles and James ran a very tight media policy, using all the traditional machinery plus refinements of their own, including the supervision by Secretaries of State of all incoming political information and the services of a new Surveyor of the Press with draconian powers of search. None the less, a new professionalism emerged in the collection and arrangement of accurate news; the reader was not left ignorant of important affairs, and the harsh policy was operated chiefly to bring stability to a country wracked by internal dissension, in which Fifth Monarchists continued to haunt the perimeters of London hoping to bring about through propaganda the kind of confusion which was deemed the indispensable herald of the millennium. Clandestine Anabaptists still managed to print and distribute a *Book of Prodigies and Wonders* (a black cloud dripping fire was seen over Whitehall, an ox had burst into speech) designed to spread millenary panic. The Stationers themselves were suspected of harbouring some disloyal printers in their ranks: small wonder, since the new Royal Household was dishing out lavish sinecures and overlapping monopolies for the printing of this and that lucrative class of material to men who were not members of the Company.

Sir Roger L'Estrange published a pamphlet advocating the creation of a really strong central control over publishing and was rewarded with appointment as Surveyor of the Press, together with a series of monopolies which included the printing of 'all Narratives of relacions not exceeding two sheets of paper and all advertisements'. Berkenhead slipped loyally away, leaving his main writer of newsbooks, Henry Muddiman, with the difficulties and embarrassment of having to co-operate with a Surveyor who had been given, exclusively, the very rights which Muddiman had been hired to exercise. L'Estrange was not well suited ideologically to the task of public journalism, having committed himself to the view that news 'makes the multitude too familiar with the actions and counsels of their superiors, too pragmatical, too censorious'. Dryden was to shroud L'Estrange in the character of Sheva in *Absalom and Achitophel:*

> In vain seditious scribes with libels strive
> T'enflame the Crowd, while He with Watchful eye
> Observes, and shoots the Treasons as they fly:
> Their weekly frauds his keen replies detect;
> He undeceives more fast than they infect.

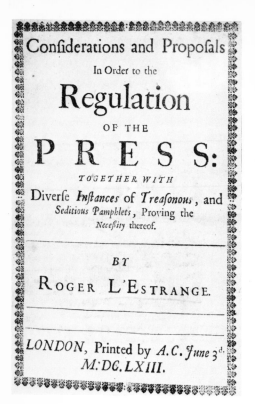

Sir Roger L'Estrange's proposal for a stricter control of the press gained him the lucrative appointment of Surveyor of the Press, to do just that.

The coffee-houses, where newspapers and pamphlets were freely available, were founded to serve political factions, and notorious for unruly argument among the clients.

Opposite The first number of the *Observator*, in 1681, set forth its aims and policies in question and answer form.

Muddiman eked out his living by publishing a handwritten newsletter containing the latest domestic news, sent to subscribers all over the country; his printed publications consisted of neatly summarized versions of similar newsletters from all over Europe with information which had been passed on to him by one of the two Secretaries of State in whose Whitehall offices he worked. Muddiman's basic task was to arrange and maintain his network of contacts, and to do this he used his special privileges of free postage which went with the job of producing the licensed newsbook and also enabled him to operate his private newsletter system at a subscription of £5 per annum. He obtained information from customs officers, local clergy and local postmasters, while through his superiors he had access to the best that state espionage could provide. His privilege provided him with accurate, reliable and on-the-spot news, but the counter-privileges granted to the Postmaster-General and to the Surveyor of the Press meant that his tenure was at times

THE
OBSERVATOR.
In *QUESTION* and *ANSWER*.

Wednesday, April 13. 1681.

Q. *WEll! They are so. But do you think now to bring 'um to their Wits again with a Pamphlet?*

A. Come, Come; 'Tis the *Press* that has made 'um *Mad*, and the *Press* must set 'um *Right* again. The Distemper is *Epidemical*; and there's no way in the world, but by *Printing*, to convey the *Remedy* to the *Disease*.

Q. *But what is it that you call a* Remedy?

A. The *Removing* of the *Cause*. That is to say, the *Undeceiving* of the *People*: for they are well enough Disposed, of themselves, to be Orderly, and Obedient; if they were not misled by *Ill Principles*, and Hair'd and Juggled out of their Senses with so many Frightful *Stories* and *Impostures*.

Q. *Well! to be Plain and Short; You call your self the* Observator: *What is it now that you intend for the Subject of your* Observations?

A. Take it in few words then. My business is, to encounter the *Faction*, and to Vindicate the *Government*; to detect their *Forgeries*; to lay open the Rankness of their *Calumnies*, and *Malice*; to Refute their *Seditious Doctrines*; to expose their *Hypocrisy*, and the *bloudy Design* that is carry'd on, under the Name, and Semblance, of *Religion*; And, in short, to lift up the Cloke of the *True Protestant* (as he Christens himself) and to shew the People, the *Jesuite* that lies skulking under it.

Q. *Shall the* Observator *be a* Weekly Paper, *or How?*

A. No, No; but oftner, or seldomer, as I see Occasion.

Q. *Pray favour me a word; When you speak of a* True Protestant, *don't you mean a* Dissenting Protestant?

A. Yes, I do: For your *Assenting* and *Consenting* Protestant (you must know) is a *Christian*.

Q. *And is not a* Dissenting Protestant *a* Christian too?

A. Peradventure, he *is* one; peradventure, *not*: For a *Dissenter* has his Name from his *Disagreeement*, not from his *Perswasion*.

Q. *What is a* Dissenter *then?*

A. 'Tis Impossible to say either what a *Dissenter IS*, or what he is *NOT*.. For he's a *NOTHING*; that may yet come to be *ANY* thing: He may be a *Christian*; or he may be a *Turk*; But you'l find the best account of him in his *Name. A DISSENTER, is one that thinks OTHERWISE.* That is to say, let the *Magistrate* think what he pleases, the *Dissenter* will be sure to be of *another Opinion.* A Dissenter is not of *This*, or of *That*, or of *Any Religion*; but *A Member Politique of an Incorporate Faction*: or Otherwise; A *Protestant-Fault-Finder* in a *Christian Commonwealth*.

Q. *Well! but tho' a* Dissenter *may be any thing; A* Dissenting Protestant *yet tells ye what he Is.*

A. He does so, he tells ye that he is a *Negative*: an *Anti-Protester*; One that *Protests AGAINST*, but not *FOR* any thing.

Q. *Ay; but so long as he opposes the* Corruptions *of the Church of* Rome.

A. Well: And so he does the *Rites*, and *Constitutions* of the Church of *England* too. As a *Protestant*, he does the *former*; and the *Other* as a *Dissenter.*

Q. *But is there no* Uniting *of These* Dissenters?

A. You shall as soon make the Winds blow the same way, from all the Poynts of the Compass.

Q. *There are Good and Bad, of all* Opinions, *there's no doubt on't: But do you think it fayr, to Condemn a whole Party for some Ill men in't?*

A. No, by no means: The *Party* is neither the *Worse*, for having *Ill* men in it, nor the *Better*, for *Good*. For whatever the *Members* are, the *Party* is a *Confederacy*; as being a *Combination* against the *Law.*

Q. *But a man may* Mean *honestly, and yet perhaps ly under some* Mistake. *Can any man help his Opinion?*

A. A man may *Mean* well, and *Do Ill*; he may shed *Innocent Bloud*, and *think he does God good Service.* 'Tis True: A man cannot help *Thinking*; but he may help *Doing*: He is *Excusable* for a *Private* Mistake, for *That's* an Error only to *himself*; but when it comes once to an *Overt Act*, 'tis an *Usurpation* upon the *Magistrate*, and there's no *Plea* for't.

Q. *You have no kindnesse, I perceive, for a* Dissenting Protestant; *but what do you think of a bare* Protestant *without any Adjunct?*

A. I do look upon *Such* a *Protestant* to be a kind of an *Adjective Noun-Substantive*; It requires something to be joyn'd with it, to shew its *Signification.* By *Protestancy in General* is commonly understood a *Separation* of Christians from the Communion of the Church of *Rome*: But to *Oppose Errors*, on the *One* hand, is not Sufficient, without keeping our selves *Clear* of Corruptions, on the *Other.* Now it was the *Reformation*, not the *Protestation*, that Settled us upon a *true Medium* betwixt the two *Extremes.*

Q. *So that you look upon the* Protestation, *and the* Reformation, *it seems, as two several things.*

A. Very right; But in such a manner only, that the *Former*, by Gods Providence, made way for the *Other.*

Q. *But are not all* Protestants *Members of the* Reformed Religion?

A. Take notice, *First*, that the *Name* came Originally from the *Protestation* in 1529. against the *Decree of Spires*; and that the *Lutheran Protestants* and *Ours* of the Church of *England*, are not of the *Same Communion.* Now *Secondly*, If you take *Protestants* in the *Latitude* with our *Dissenters*, they are not so much a *Religion*, as a *Party*; and whoever takes this Body of *Dissenters* for *Members* of the *Reformed Religion*, sets up a *Reformation* of a *hundred* and *fifty Colours*, and as many *Heresies.* The *Anabaptists, Brownists, Antinomians, Familists, &c.* do all of them set up for *Dissenting Protestants*; but God forbid we should ever enter these *People* upon the Roll of the *Reformation.*

Q. *Well! but what do you think of* Protestant Smith, *and* Protestant Harris?

A. Just as I do of *Protestant Muncer*, and *Prote-*

very weak. Postal officials and Surveyor were constantly trying, through interception of his mail, to steal his lists of contacts and make effective their overlapping rights.

Matters came to a head when, in 1665, the Plague broke out in London and the court shifted to Oxford. L'Estrange remained in London, while Muddiman was summoned to Oxford to edit the *Oxford Gazette*, which was to continue in existence as the *London Gazette* when the court moved back again. The *Gazette* was printed by the university printer in the same format as his Bible, with double columns and a superior typeface. L'Estrange tried to operate his *Publick Intelligencer* alone in London, but made a poor job of it and was compensated with a royal pension, to be paid by Muddiman out of the profits of the *Gazette*, while L'Estrange continued in his job as Surveyor. Muddiman now found himself confronted by another jealous prying official in the office of the Secretary of State; he moved his operations to the office of the second Secretary of State, but failed to maintain the mutually beneficial relationship between the printed and handwritten publications. After the Great Fire of 1666 the *Gazette* emerged from the smoking embers of London under the imprint of Muddiman's rival, though he himself continued working in the Secretary of State's office, producing his handwritten paper for an increasing circle of clients.

Muddiman, as the pioneer of the gazette form in England, helped journalism through one of its most important stages; as the foremost writer of news of his generation he kept high the standards of the basic raw material of journalism, the information collected from a wide variety of sources. He was a linchpin, despite the shakiness with which his authority was wielded, in the media system of an increasingly stable society in which news played a central role. As the King's Journalist, Muddiman exercised part of the brokerage of power within Restoration society.

The *Gazette* itself was an elegant and precise instrument of information. Even today its pages convey to the twentieth-century reader its proud sense of its own modernity as it replaced the chaotic squabblings of the interregnum. It was accompanied by a flurry of advertising papers, such as the *City Mercury* and the *Weekly Advertisements*, which concentrated entirely on their commercial work and were indeed licensed by L'Estrange only for that purpose. The *Gazette* itself managed to collect £6 a week in advertising: there was now land for sale in parcels in the New World, and horses and jewellery lost in the Home Counties. Between the Restoration and the Glorious Revolution, London's exports increased by a half. The city became an entrepôt between the East and the American colonies; one-third of its trade consisted of re-exports, mainly of tea, coffee and tobacco, and several hundred ships plied regularly to and from the various English ports. The scope for the sale of financial information was enormous, and services depending on the accurate supply of simple information multiplied. After 1680 a penny post operated at hourly intervals within London by which printed materials could be quickly transported between suburbs and city.

The most important development of all was the coffee-house, which in the next century was to become the principal means by which newspapers (as they were by then known) were distributed. Charles II detested the coffee trade and frequently tried to stamp it out as a source of sedition, even though it was in the very first London coffee-house, founded in 1657, that his own Restoration had been schemed. The coffee-house became the vehicle and the symbol of political faction; after the Revolution of 1689, faction became the basic unit of political activity. With the arrival of a non-biological succession to the monarchy, supreme power in England rested upon opinion, bringing into being a new media system based upon competitive propaganda rather than upon the fixed centre of a single orthodoxy which could no longer be maintained. The Licensing Act of 1662, upon which Charles had based his vigorous and in the event fairly effective system of control, finally expired when the King deemed it expedient to prorogue Parliament in 1679 to prevent the passage of the anti-Catholic Exclusion Bill. The *Protestant Domestic Intelligence* of Benjamin Harris (who later became the founder of the American press) and the *Paquet of Advise from Rome* sprang up in the period of legal hiatus which ensued, helping to pour oil on the flames. Charles appealed to the courts for support in his attempts to keep licensing going after the expiration of the Act (which no subsequent Parliament succeeded in re-establishing), and obtained legal cover for a proclamation re-enforcing the royal licensing of news. Although several Whig news-writers were hauled before the Privy Council for breaches of the ordinance, a trickle of news pamphlets continued; the opposition imported newspapers from Holland, just as in the days of James I, and the Stationers again imposed their ineffective system of detection and suppression.

Sir Roger L'Estrange, however, now waded into battle with counter-propaganda; his *Observator* rates as the first example of a new Tory journalism, attacking the Whig detractors of James II. Muddiman, too, remained active in the 1680s, printing attacks against His Majesty's enemies and their 'villainous writs'. Beneath the surface, however, an avalanche of propaganda was preparing to descend as soon as James II's régime broke down and the King fled. When it came, no possibility of re-enforcing a licensing system was again practical, though attempts were made even in the days of William and Mary. That power over the press which had seemed to be an indispensable element in the system of divine right ('. . . intire and inherent in Your Majestie's Person and inseparable from Your Crown', as L'Estrange had put it in his pamphlet pleading for total control) had declined in a quarter of a century of increasing political stability into a veritable intrusion upon good government, an 'Embargo upon Science', as one pamphleteer expressed it. 'Yet we do in a manner Libel our own Truth, when by Licensing and Prohibiting, fearing each Book, and the shaking of each Leaf, we distrust her own strength: Let her and Falsehood grapple; who ever knew Truth put to the worst in a free and open Encounter?' With such Miltonic echoes the old licensing system, which had prevailed in various forms throughout the news-publishing activity of Europe for a century and a half, came to an end in England. By 1695 licensing was finished for ever, and new forms of newspaper were to spring up, exploiting the skills which had accumulated in the seventeenth century but applying them to wholly new tasks. The newspaper of the Revolution had reached a kind of maturity; it now had to begin again with a new infancy.

3

'Serious, Sarcastic, Ludicrous or Otherwise Amusing'
1695–1776

Writers and statesmen throughout Europe observed the development of England's unlicensed newspaper system with a combination of envy and horror. A swarm of new writers had emerged in London to fill a whole new generation of publications; printers and their apprentices fanned out from London into the provinces in the early years of the eighteenth century, setting up newly legalized printing establishments and local news-sheets in a growing number of towns. Looked at from Paris, Milan or Frankfurt, the English authorities appeared to be playing with fire. The press which was growing in London was wholly unreliable in its information; it found its basic support in political factionalism and thus made the task of steady government doubly difficult. It also made it expensive, since government, too, had to wade into newspaper battle, incurring the enormous inconvenience and expense of large-scale bribery of printers and writers. The sovereigns of Europe watched with distaste and saw to it that their own newspaper industry grew within the system of absolutist authority. Nowhere was the centralized model more sophisticatedly practised than in Paris, where political and intellectual information was being raised to a very high level of perfection, with no concession to the idea of liberty of publication.

In France there existed a great diversity of forms, but all of them emerged under official supervision. There was still, in the eighteenth century, a steady stream of *occasionnels* and *canards* offering single narrations on single sheets, sometimes with woodcut illustrations. As in England, handwritten newsletters competed expertly with the printed publications. In times of political tension *lardons* ('jibes') full of scurrilous attacks on the King and his Ministers would appear from Holland, smuggled inside other, innocent-looking publications; these *lardons* were produced by exiled Huguenots driven from France when Louis XIV revoked the Edict of Nantes. Some of the exiles had started in the 1690s to turn out regular periodicals in the French language in Amsterdam and to have them smuggled into Paris: Gabriel d'Artis ran a successful *Journal sur toutes sortes de sujets* ('journal on all kinds of subjects'), and the philosopher Pierre Bayle, during his exile in the United Provinces, started planning a publication which 'would speak neither of peace nor of war – that is good only for the gazettes or other news publications' and which, in the event, became the major intellectual publication of Europe.

In Paris the illiterate could repair to one of several public reading places and, for 6 sous, listen to the latest news being read aloud. So well organized was every aspect of the business of news dissemination that the Paris authorities insisted that all the *colporteurs* who hawked news about the streets

Opposite A Parisian *colporteur* or hawker of news – by law, he had to be licensed and literate.

should be registered and able to read for themselves. The provinces, too, were carefully organized, and local censors existed in 120 towns by 1760 – vitally important when the death penalty could be imposed for the illegal printing of any material which 'tended to attack religion, arouse feelings against or pronounce attacks upon the authority of the Government, or undermine due order and tranquillity'. (Even Diderot was to spend a hundred days in the dungeon at Vincennes, and one erring printer at Mont-St-Michel was placed in an iron cage until he died.) Local police lieutenants could give permission for a broadsheet to be issued, but larger works required permission from the government in Paris. Malesherbes supervised the French licensing system for many years, and saw it as an opportunity to help and enlighten rather than to repress; he became extremely angry when one periodical produced a 'ridiculous article praising the English nation', but frequently reproved local censors who had overstepped the mark.

Perhaps the most interesting element of the French information system was the semi-official *nouvellistes*, organized gossips who kept their regular seats in the Tuileries or the Luxembourg at which they regaled listeners with information from embassies, ministries, the court itself; they gradually turned to supplying their material in written, though never in printed, form, and could ply their trade without molestation if their work was submitted first to the police. In the middle of the century it was discovered that there existed a 'chief' among the *nouvellistes* who employed fifty copyists and had hundreds of regular subscribers. From time to time the authorities tried to stamp out the system, but much of the time it was merely subjected to careful inspection.

Higher in the social hierarchy there existed the private salons of Paris, some of which specialized in the dissemination of written news. One Madame Doublet, widow of a court official, held a salon every day for thirty-six years at which news was collected on the theatre and literature; people brought notices of new books, reports of interesting trials, information on clandestine publications, satirical songs and sketches, epigrams and gossip from the court, and these were written up into Madame Doublet's regular *Mémoires secrètes*. The entire collection derived from her salon was published in many volumes in 1787, but even her works were scrutinized by an official, as were other salon bulletins.

At the hub of the Parisian news arrangements were three officially printed periodicals licensed to perform different functions. First there was the *Gazette de France*, highly profitable and produced by Eusèbe Renaudot, the son of its founder Théophraste. Its purpose was to reproduce official documents and collect information from the *intendants* throughout the provinces, some of whom produced local variants of it. The *intendants* were enjoined to send in material 'to fulfil public curiosity, particularly all that pertains to physical and natural history, to commercial projects, manufacturing establishments, new agricultural schemes, singular and extraordinary occurrences'. It was essential that the information should be reliable and prompt. The *Gazette* carried the royal arms in its title to emphasize its formal and official nature. In 1761 its monopoly was re-established and a new method of supervision devised within the Ministry of Foreign Affairs, through whose good offices most of its material arrived. It was particularly well informed on distant

Opposite Listening to the news in France – for a small fee.

49

Mᵐᵉ Doublet et Mᵗ Son frère l'abbé Le Gendre, conseiller de Grand'chambre. 1754.

Madame Doublet with her brother, the Abbé Legendre, a frequent source of titbits for her *Mémoires secrètes*.

countries, all French Consuls in the Levant, the East and Turkey being instructed to supply news. The historical nature of the *Gazette* was constantly stressed; it was to be the great well from which posterity would draw the material for the future history of France. During certain periods it was farmed out to editors who paid an indemnity to the Ministry out of which the pensions of their predecessors were paid; at other periods the editors were employed directly and all revenue returned to the Exchequer. The paper would appear on Mondays and Thursdays, having passed through a complex censoring process in which any Ministry could compel cuts, alterations or additions. In the 1780s it reached a total of 12,000 regular subscribers, each paying 15 livres per annum. During the last years before the Revolution the *Gazette* was sorely vexed as a result of a series of concessions granted to rival publications which undermined its circulation. The most serious of these (legal) infringements of its prerogatives was occasioned by the *Journal politique*, which developed into a direct rival.

The second publication was the *Journal des Scavants*, which became a monthly after 1724 and concentrated on scientific information; it produced notices of works and reports of scientific developments. One of its detractors described it as 'a means for satisfying the curiosity . . . invented to console those who are too busy or too idle to read whole books'. Its charter confined it to 'geography, chemistry, botany, astronomy, architecture, painting, sculpture, numismatics and epigraphy'. In addition it was permitted to report the meetings of the Parlement de Paris and publish university proclamations and academic discourses, as well as news of the arts culled from foreign publications. Apart from its immensely important role in the creation of an authoritative source of topical information on modern science, the *Journal des Scavants* was also involved in the working out of the controversy between Jansenists and Jesuits. Voltaire contributed two memoranda to its columns in 1738 on the elements of Newton's philosophy, but Rousseau turned down the invitation of Malesherbes to write for it: 'They think I could write to order, commercially like all the other writers, but really I know how to write only out of passion.'

As the years passed, additional publications were permitted so long as the editor of the *Journal des Scavants* agreed and was paid an indemnity. Within a system of organized licensing, the payment of indemnities by new publications to the primary holder of a privilege was essential. The *Journal des Scavants* became a periodical of European stature and contributed greatly to the intellectual prestige of France. In London the Royal Society's *Philosophical Transactions* were partly modelled on it, and in Leipzig the *Acta Eruditorum* borrowed extensively from it.

The *Mercure de France* was the third publication, concentrating on social and literary news, with the addition of odes and sermons. 'The *Mercure* must always be neutral and never enter into cabals . . . impartiality is the first of our Duties,' explained one of its editors. It too appeared monthly and was farmed out to its editors, who found that half their annual turnover of 60,000 livres (derived from 1,600 subscriptions in the 1760s) was used for the payment of pensions to distinguished men of letters.

The importance of the *Mercure* grew with time, and in 1778 a wholly new contract was awarded to Charles Panckoucke and thence to his brother-in-law Jean-Baptiste Suard as editor; under this new régime a political supplement was permitted and a 25-year agreement was concluded with the licensing authority, the Ministry of Foreign Affairs, which contributed 28,000 livres a year to the latter's revenue. Each subscriber had to pay 30 livres a year in Paris and 32 in the provinces. By the time of the Revolution, no fewer than 15,000 subscribers existed for this 'oldest and most varied of all newspapers', as it described itself. Although packed with information to fascinate its readers, it tended to avoid all the burning topics of the day; it steered clear of materialism and deism and preached tolerance.

The nomenclature of these licensed publications is of crucial importance. A *gazette* of political news implied a publication which drew its material from multiple sources; a *journal* dealt with a pre-stated zone of social information. When, in 1771, inspired by the *London Evening Post*, a new daily *Journal de Paris ou la Poste du soir* was licensed, its readers all understood that it was not a political publication. This paper in fact dealt with social, artistic and theatrical news; it covered the Bourse, objects lost and found, *faits divers* and weather information. It was not a success, since with daily publication it ran quickly up against the great difficulty of licensing: it was impossible to collect enough material, of a sufficiently varied nature, without straying into the privileges of other licensed publications. Voltaire, however, had welcomed the *Journal de Paris* and had contributed a letter to its first edition: 'The plan of your *journal* seems to me to be as intelligent as it is interesting and curious. . . . If I had one request to make it would be to undeceive the public on all the small paragraphs which are constantly ascribed to me.' It was the form known as the *journal* which gradually, in more successful hands, became the standard daily publication, and the term therefore triumphed over *gazette* and, indeed, *mercure* to become the modern French word for a newspaper. The admixture of political information came with the social upheaval of the Revolution, which in any case swept away the post-feudal system of privileges and concessions.

Alongside the major publications there were other, smaller efforts which eventually merged into the central current of the newspaper. Among the larger of these was a series of religious publications, notably the *Mémoires de Trévoux*, which also depended for much of its material on reports of newly published books. Critical reviews were different from 'notices' (the mainstay of the journal), and a different journalistic ethic pertained. In choosing extracts from new works and in setting out their contents, a journalist was to ignore all works whose authors had requested attention. 'It is a duty we owe the public which is our judge, not to mix criticism with the extracts . . . that would be to betray our readers who take us for a guide to the knowledge of books.' The *Mémoires de Trévoux* played an important part in guiding the French reader through the religious controversies and doubts created by the works of Newton and the reconsiderations of Descartes.

The *Gazette* and the Bureau d'Adresses attempted to start up a rival to the *Journal de Paris* called the *Journal général de France*, and drew for their material on another local form which had existed since 1716 in several parts of France, the *affiches*: these were reports on the commercial and trading affairs of a region, carrying advertising for tutors and medicines, the promulgation of by-laws, shipping news and so on. In 1777 the *Journal général de France* emerged as a daily version of the *affiches*, its editor, the Abbé Aubert, being granted a 40-year concession to produce the paper for an annual subscription of 30 livres. On the very eve of the Revolution, therefore, the licensed press system of France achieved its first sustained daily news publication.

London, however, had seen its first regular daily paper established in 1702, to exploit the increasing flow of news from France. Samuel Buckley, a shrewd and opportunistic entrepreneur, took note of the enormous public interest in the conflict with France over the Spanish Succession and of the

de Pieces. On admire dans toutes ce charme piquant, ces tournures heureuses qui le caractérisent & lui assurent le sceptre des Poésies légeres. la principale est *Séfostris*; Allégorie ingénieuse, dont tout Français perce aisément le voile, & qui ne pouvoit être mieux placée qu'à la tête de ce Recueil.

Après M. de Voltaire, M. Dorat est un des Auteurs qui l'enrichissent le plus. On verra avec plaisir treize ou quatorze petites Pieces de ce Poéte aimable, qui sont presque toutes de différens tons. Celle qui a pour titre, *Regrets de l'Amitié*, est un tribut payé aux mânes de M. Colardeau. On croit, en la lisant, que l'amitié a emprunté les pinceaux doux & suaves de ce Poéte mélodieux, pour célébrer sa mémoire. Deux *Epitres*, l'une adressée *à Délie*, & l'autre intitulée, *l'Amitié en défaut*, doivent être comptées parmi les badinages les plus agréables échappés à la plume de M. Dorat.

Quatre Femmes déjà célebres par la délicatesse & les graces de leur esprit, Mde. la Marquise d'Antremont, à présent Mde. de Bourdic, Mde. la Comtesse de Beauharnois, Mde. Verdier, Mde. la Comtesse de Bussy paroissent toutes avec avantage dans cette lice poétique. Nous invitons les amateurs d'Homere à lire les *Adieux d'Hector & d'Andromaque*, Piece de Mde. la Comtesse de Bussy, qui a concouru cette année pour le Prix de Poésie de l'Académie Française: ils verront un style soutenu, & un grand nombre de très-beaux vers.

On distingue aussi cinq ou six des meilleures Pieces fugitives de feu M. Piron, des vers de M. Imbert; entr'autres une Epitre pleine de sensibilité & de philosophie. *Le Ruisseau de la Malmaison*, par M. l'Abbé Delisle, où l'on retrouve la maniere de cet excellent Poéte; de très-jolis morceaux de MM. de B***, le Chevalier de B., Berquin, Bertin, de Cubieres, G*** de M***, Grouvelle, le Mierre, l'Abbé le Monnier, le Marquis de Pezai, Sélis, &c. mériteroient chacun une annonce particuliere; mais les bornes de cette Feuille nous réduisent à une simple Indication. Nous ne pouvons cependant nous refuser à ranger encore, parmi les Poésies qui nous ont fait le plus de plaisir, une *Imitation de Strada* de M. Bérenger, une *Epitre* de M. Maisonneuve, & ce qui plaira peut-être à un plus grand nombre de Lecteurs, deux Contes fort plaisans, l'un qui a pour titre: *La Superstition*, ou *le Saint Antoine Portugais*, par M. de Fumars; l'autre, *la Consultation épineuse*, par M. François de Neufchâteau.

Nos citations ne pouvant être que très-courtes, nous nous bornerons à rapporter la Piece suivante, c'est un Couplet charmant de M. le Chevalier de B***.

Faisons l'amour, faisons la guerre:
Ces deux métiers sont pleins d'attraits.
La guerre au monde est un peu chere,
L'amour en rembourse les frais.
Que l'ennemi, que la Bergere
Soient tour-à tour serrés de près!
Quand on a dépeuplé la terre,
Il faut la repeupler après.

Ce volume est terminé par une Notice curieuse de toutes les Pieces qui ont paru pendant l'année.

On trouve chez le même Libraire des Collections complettes de l'Almanach des Muses, formant en tout 13 vol. qui se vendent 16 liv. 16 sous.

EXTRAIT d'une Lettre de M. de Voltaire, datée de Ferney le 22 Décembre 1776, aux Auteurs de ce Journal.

Le Plan de votre Journal, M., me paroît aussi sage que curieux & intéressant. Mon grand âge, & les maladies dont je suis accablé, ne me laissent pas l'espérance de pouvoir produire quelque Ouvrage qui mérite d'être annoncé par vous.

Si j'avois une priere à vous faire, ce seroit de détromper le Public sur tous les petits Ecrits qu'on m'impute continuellement. Il est parvenu dans ma retraite des volumes entiers, imprimés sous mon nom, dans lesquels il n'y a pas une ligne que je voulusse avoir composée. Je vous supplierais aussi, M. de vouloir bien, par un mot d'Avertissement, me délivrer de la foule de Lettres anonymes qu'on m'adresse. Je suis obligé de renvoyer toutes les Lettres dont les cachets me sont inconnus. Cet Avertissement inséré dans votre Journal, m'excuserait auprès des personnes qui se plaignent que je ne leur ait pas répondu; je vous aurais beaucoup d'obligation.

Je ne doute pas que votre Journal n'ait beaucoup de succès. Je me compte déjà au nombre de vos Souscripteurs.

Le premier volume du Journal d'Education de cette année (1777) par M. le Roux, Maître de Pension, au Collège Royal de Boncourt, parut hier, chez

Dawks's News-Letter.

Sr London *October 15. 1698.*

Lyons, September 30. On the 26th instant the Intendant of Languedoc pronounced a very severe Sentence against the new Converts that were taken Prisoners in their return from Orange; 150 of them from 17 to 70 years of Age, are condemned to the Gallies, and their Estate confiscated, among them Messieurs Tonque and Ribes, the latter of which is reckoned to be worth 50000 Crowns, who though they made it appear that they were Merchants, and were going from Nimes to Avignon and Orange, about driving their Trade, they were forthwith sent away with the rest of those that were condemned to the Gallies, for Marseilles, to be chained to their Oars. All those that were under 17 and above 70 years of Age, were spared from the Gallies, but have so high a Fine upon them to purchase their Liberty, that most of them being unable to pay the same, must Live and Dye in Prison. Most of them were Burghers of Nimes, Uzez, and Montpellier, and other Neighbouring Places. Besides the Men, there were also many Women and Maidens, who were Sentenced to have their Heads Shaved, and to be confined close Prisoners to the Castle of Sommieres.

Madrid, Sept. 25. Our Letters from Ceuta say, that the Moors who Besiege that place, have lately received a Reinforcement of 800 Men and 50 Bombs; but the Alcaid who commands them, is so Ill that his Life is despaired of.

Stockholm, Sept. 30. The Count de Bond, who was our chief Plenipotentiary at the Treaty of Reswick, and Ambassador Extraordinary to his Majesty of Great Britain, has given the King of Sweden a Satisfactory Account of his Negotiations. The Baron de Lelienroot, who was another of the Plenipotentiaries, hath received his Instructions to go Ambassador to the States of Holland.

Geneva, Sept. 30. Some days ago 230 of the Poor Refugees, banished from Piedmont by the Duke of Savoy, arrived here in a forlorn Condition: Our Magistrates relieved them with Money, and sent them to Swisserland, where the Governors of Bern, Schaffheusen and Zurich divided them amongst themselves, and took care of 'em. The Canton of Bern hath at least taken two thirds of 'em to provide for.

Naples, Octob. 1. It was thought that the French Gallies would have gon as far as Messina and Malta, but of a sudden they returned hence to Marseilles. Our Politicians are at a loss, to conjecture what might have been the motive of their Voyage, except it was to have secured the Possession of the Spanish Dominions in Italy, in case of his Catholick Majesties death; but however it was, our Government here thought fit to treat their Officers with the greatest Civility imaginable.

Mastricht, Octob. 30. Four Scots Companies, who were paid off here, march'd hence yesterday, in order to embark for their own Country. Our Magistrates have taken a particular Account of all the Corn in this City, in order to regulate the spending of the same according as they shall see occasion. We continue to send Ammunition hence to Namure; and divers Vessels are sent by the Rhine and the Mosselle to Luxemburg. The Magistrates of Liege have regulated the Price of Corn there, and forbid the distilling of Spirits from it, to prevent the Dearth of Bread. The Elector of Bavaria hath done the like in the Spanish Netherlands.

Amsterdam,

Dawks's News-Letter printed in elegant italic script to resemble the handwritten newsletter, dying out early in the eighteenth century.

need of the government to ensure that the public understood its policy towards the war. Buckley announced in his first edition that his intention was 'to give news, give it daily and impartially', and he added a list of all the foreign publications from which he intended to derive his information. His paper, the *Daily Courant*, was fundamentally a gazette and contained little of the kind of material met with in the journal. It continued for over 6,000 editions; by mid-century it had given way to five London dailies, each with an average circulation of 1,500.

Pegasus,

With *News,* an *Observator,* and a *Jacobite Courant.*

From Munday July 6. to Wednesday July 8. 1696.

Dunton's *Pegasus:* news first, then an 'Observator' or political essay – ancestor of the leading article.

With the collapse of licensing in 1695 there had been an immediate flurry of new publications, starting that same year with the *Intelligence Foreign and Domestic* of Benjamin Harris, followed by Edward Lloyd's *Weekly News* a year later and by an attempt by one Ichabod Dawks to produce, in printed form but in italic type, a public version of the private handwritten newsletter. *Dunton's Pegasus* and Harris's *London Post,* foreshadowing future developments, had begun to include a political essay in each edition, and Abel Boyer, a French immigrant, had started one of two London papers carrying the title *Post Boy* which offered their readers a blank last page on which to inscribe their own news for onward transmission to friends in the country. Provincial papers were springing up, consisting almost entirely of extracts of the numerous new London papers delivered outside the capital by the rapidly expanding stage-coach and postal services. Ralph Allen's six-day post in the 1740s, with its cross-road services, increased the whole sphere of influence of the newspaper industry. The provincial printers promised their readers nothing but the best of the London papers, 'the quintessence of every print'; not until the middle of the century did they manage to get circulations sufficiently large and geographically concentrated to support their own gathering of local news.

Only the Dutch outstripped the English in the freedom with which they could print and dispatch news material. Licensing, however, continued to have its supporters in Britain, and occasionally fresh plans were drawn up for adopting a system similar to that of France. When theatre licensing began in 1737 a similar statute for the press was talked about, but gradually the view came to prevail that within certain limits differences of published opinion were not a threat to constitutional authority. Furthermore, the press could be controlled by manipulation, and its power limited through harassment, bribery and taxation.

In the first decade of the eighteenth century the press increased in variety and in specialism: women's papers, entertainment papers, social and political papers proliferated, each innovation breeding hangers-on, spoofs and plagiarists. The *Tatler* and the *Spectator*, for example, which after 1709 popularized the genre of the weekly essay concentrating on moral and social improvement, were followed rapidly by the *Female Tatler*, the *Tory Tatler*, the *North Tatler*, the *Hermit*, the *Rhapsody*, *Titt for Tatt*, the *Gazette à la Mode*, the *Tatling Harlot*, the *Whisperer*, the *Rambler*, *Miscellany* and *Serious Thoughts*, all in the space of a few years, though few survived more than an issue or two. The *Post Boy* innovation had several direct contemporary imitators. Nothing but the common law stood between the market and the scores of potential suppliers: by 1715 there were seventy printers in London, each with two or more presses and a group of apprentices; by 1755 the number had doubled, and some of the larger firms had acquired the capacity to produce several regular publications simultaneously. Samuel Richardson, for instance, the novelist and bookseller, employed no fewer than twenty professional compositors and turned out, at the height of his activity, two weekly papers and two or possibly three dailies, each in the standard four-page, three-column format. By mid-century, however, an important shift was visible in the pattern of news publication: as circulations grew, titles became more constant, a few important newspapers and journals clearly began to dominate, and all of them attempted to incorporate more of the different strands of material with which the multitudinous publications of the post-1695 era had experimented. The periodical had discovered that a wider variety of subject-matter gave it a better chance of survival in the market.

By 1750 London had five daily papers, six thrice-weeklies, five weeklies and, on a far less official level, several cut-price thrice-weeklies, with a total circulation between them of 100,000 copies (up to one million readers) a

The HAWKER

In times of War tho Lyes prevail;
All Ears are open to the Tale;
Impossibilities believ'd;
And Man by Man is still deceiv'd.
The lowest Vulgar, knowing this, —
Can bawl aloud, A new Exprefs!

A Sharp, or Bloody, cruel Fight!
In which the French were put to flight.
A new Gazette!—is bawl'd aloud,
Attentive are this list'ning Croud;
—tte!—Gazette!—here,here come, — here!—
When read, — no Battle any where.

The hawker of news-sheets, often prosecuted for the sins of the papers they sold, sometimes over-cried their wares as this doggerel verse complains.

week. The average weekly wage, at ten shillings, was higher in London than in the provinces, and brought the purchase of an occasional newspaper well within the reach of all but the poorest workers.

Inside London, distribution was in the hands of networks of hawkers which grew with the development of unlimited publication into highly organized businesses. Two major dealers, Mrs Nutt and Mrs Dodd, controlled a total weekly circulation of many thousands in and around London; these ladies themselves bore the brunt of prosecutions against the papers they circulated, and even after reaching their seventies continued to be arrested and held for days in gaol. Many printers had their own agents. Within the City, however, the most important means of circulation were the coffee-houses, which existed by the score and organized themselves into a loose federation for mutual protection against the publishers and printers. The coffee-men desired to limit the number of papers published daily in order to keep their costs down, and normally supported government measures which tended to control the tally of titles; sometimes they threatened to start their own newspapers if proprietors made things difficult for them. Some proprietors, notably those of the major advertisers, gave their papers gratis to the coffee-men. By 1743 the latter had their way and a major crackdown on illicit (i.e. untaxed) papers took place, resulting in dozens of prosecutions and the complete disappearance of a group of very cheap (farthing) papers which had for years evaded, often through their obscurity, the King's Messengers.

Newspapers were conveyed out of London by professional news-carriers and by the agents of the six Clerks of the Road, sinecurists within the Post Office who held a special privilege covering free franking of newspapers. The Clerks occasionally took a direct pecuniary interest in a paper themselves – Edward Cave, owner of the *Gentleman's Magazine*, abused his place in the Post Office by openly touting for custom for his own journal at the expense of rivals – and simultaneously acted as part of the governmental machinery of press manipulation. A committee of inquiry in the 1760s calculated that the Clerks, between them, drew £3,000–4,000 a year in special dues paid by newspaper proprietors to obtain free distribution. Officials at the War Office and the Admiralty enjoyed comparable privileges, and so did the Secretary of State, who was traditionally at the centre of official control of the press.

The final price of a newspaper at the point of reception varied considerably, therefore, depending on the method by which the reader came by it, and depending, too, on whether he took the trouble to collect it himself from a local postmaster or had it delivered. In country districts a paper could cost up to five or six pence, though it had started out at twopence.

All official efforts to control the press centred upon special taxes which began with the Stamp Act of 1712, designed to curb production and confine circulations while providing revenue for further government activity in the press. A newspaper proprietor had to pay one penny per sheet printed plus one shilling for every advertisement inserted. The amounts increased under successive Acts until 1836, when they were reduced. During most of this period a fixed sum was payable on every advertisement printed, irrespective of length. There were several ways of evading the 1712 Act, however, the most notable being that of printing on one and a half printer's sheets and claiming the status of a 'pamphlet': this was taxed according to the number of sheets used in a single copy, whatever the final circulation, and the charge was a mere two shillings a sheet. However, enlarging the paper meant finding additional copy and paying for the extra paper used, and this tended to reduce the advantages of the strategem. Enforced price increases probably lowered circulations, increasing the proportion of readers who hired a newspaper rather than bought it. In any case, much reading was done at coffee- and ale-houses.

The hawker as well as the printer had to carry the can when illegal unstamped publication was detected: the hawker could be sent to gaol for three months, the printer fined or imprisoned. Government controls did not stop with the stamp, however. The Secretaries of State kept small squads of agents throughout England and Scotland reporting on the contents of the newspaper press. From 1722 onwards Nicholas Paxton, as assistant to the Treasury Solicitor, was paid £200 per annum to check the contents of all papers and act as a quasi-licenser; he eventually became Treasury Solicitor himself and held the post until his death in 1745, when the system was changed. The Ministry of the day thus obtained early warning of impending attacks, and the Secretary of State could decide whether to initiate proceedings for seditious libel, for profanation, or on some other charge; his most powerful weapon was the general warrant, the dubious legality of which was finally exposed in the famous struggle of John Wilkes over No. 45 of his *North Briton*, in which he was considered to have insulted the King. A general warrant enabled arrests and seizures of unnamed persons to be made almost indiscriminately until the actual perpetrator of an alleged press offence was detected and apprehended. The King's Messengers had enormous freedom in the conduct of their searches; they were, in effect, a semi-official group of hired thugs, with power to arrest, seize property, break up type, hold printers and their employees in unlimited confinement and take bail, sometimes of hundreds of pounds. Trials could be delayed for months or even years and on conviction the printer could be pilloried, fined exemplarily and re-imprisoned. It was hardly surprising that convictions were exceedingly difficult to obtain from juries, but this only tended to encourage the employment of deterrent violence by the Messengers.

In law the printer was responsible for the contents of his paper, even though his 'editing' function consisted in little more than checking for obvious libels. The hawkers, too, were aware of their responsibilities, and would negotiate with proprietors over the terms for distributing particularly risky papers. When summoned before the court the printer could use many devices to conceal or evade responsibility: he could deny knowledge of the contents, or blame the compositors, who might not even be able to read. It was considered to be the printer's duty to keep secret the identity of an offending writer, even though he would automatically escape liability if he passed on this information to the court; printers would always guarantee the concealment of an important journalist or proprietor, but would frequently provide the identity of a writer directly employed by them. The system was universal and lasted throughout the century. In 1719, one John Mathews was found guilty of high treason in a publication on the evidence of two of his apprentices; when one of the apprentices happened to die a few weeks later, a vast crowd of printers gathered at the cemetery to insult the corpse. The printers had a direct pecuniary interest in maintaining their honour code, since the market for the newspaper was largely a political one, which responded favourably to the more sensational reporting. As one popular dramatist, James Branston, put it in 1733 in *The Man of Taste*:

> Can statutes keep the British press in awe,
> When that sells best, that's most against the Law?

THE

NORTH BRITON.

NUMBER XLV.

To be continued every *Saturday*. Price Two pence Halfpenny.

SATURDAY, APRIL the 23, 1763.

The following advertisement appeared in all the papers on the 13th of April.

THE NORTH BRITON makes his appeal to the good sense, and to the candour of the ENGLISH nation. In the present unsettled and fluctuating state of the *administration,* he is really fearful of falling into involuntary errors, and he does not wish to mislead. All his reasonings have been built on the strong foundation of *facts;* and he is not yet informed of the whole interiour state of government with such *minute precision,* as now to venture the submitting his crude ideas of the present political crisis to the discerning and impartial public. The SCOTTISH minister has indeed *retired.* Is HIS influence at an end? or does HE still govern by the *three* wretched tools of his power, who, to their indelible infamy, have supported the most odious of his measures, the late ignominious *Peace,* and the wicked extension of the arbitrary mode of *Excise?* The NORTH BRITON has been steady
in

No. 45 of John Wilkes's *North Briton*. Its publication led to Wilkes's arrest under a 'general warrant', which the Lord Chief Justice later declared to be illegal.

Prosecution was, therefore, a day to day risk for the proprietors and printers of opposition papers. One of the critics of the *Craftsman* claimed in 1730 that the authors of this paper were obliged 'to write something every now and then for which they hope to be sent for by a Messenger, otherwise the Paper is supposed to have lost its poignancy'. In 1765 the courts ruled that it was illegal to arrest a person unnamed in a warrant, but this was in practice interpreted as rendering general warrants legal provided they resulted in the arrest of the actual author, printer or publisher of offending material. Even when, a year later, the Commons declared general warrants altogether illegal, the judges continued to admit cases brought as a result of them. A typical case was that of Robert Nixon, charged in 1737 with having ridiculed five Acts of Parliament: he was found guilty, sentenced to make a tour of the law courts bearing a paper on his head declaring the offence (a common treatment of convicted printers), fined 200 marks, imprisoned for five years, obliged to provide two sureties of £250 plus his own surety of £500, and placed on good behaviour for life. Nixon, like other printers in similar plight, was probably permitted to continue his business from the gaolhouse. Less fortunate perhaps was the celebrated Nathaniel Mist, whose *Weekly Journal* was one of the foremost papers of the period; in 1729 it fell foul of the authorities, changed its title to *Fog's Weekly Journal* and was continued by Mist by remote control from Boulogne, where he was obliged to reside for several years, fearing the consequences of suspected Jacobinism. The Duke of Wharton, who controlled the *True Briton*, once complained that he had to have a total of £3,000 paid into court as bail for its printers, held on multiple charges.

Despite the institutionalized harassment of the press, newspapers and journalism were steadily gaining acceptance as indispensable parts of the constitutional life of society. They became important, though not respectable, in politics, and came to play a new role within economic life as the nature of their ownership changed; after the 1730s, most London newspaper activity passed gradually into the hands of the city's main booksellers, leaving the printers as small shareholders or simply contractors. The *London Gazetteer*, for example, a paper founded by a printer in 1715, was refounded in 1748 and divided into twenty shares, most of them in the hands of booksellers. This new form of group ownership came about gradually, partly to distribute the higher costs of producing papers with larger circulations, partly to provide the booksellers with a cheap means of advertising their principal wares, and partly as a means of mutual self-protection in a period when copyright had become highly problematical. An Act of 1710 had created a 28-year system of copyright, but bookseller-publishers still felt they needed the protection against pirating which could come only through combination. The bookseller-owned newspaper could also block the advertising of books sold or published by non-participants. Some papers refused to take advertisements for the circulating libraries, which tended to reduce the sales of books. Many newspapers, of course, remained in non-professional hands for political reasons, and some continued to be owned by the printers or occasionally by groups of political writers. None the less, the general trend was for papers to belong to co-operatives of

Nicholas Amhurst of the *Craftsman*, one of the foremost of the eighteenth century's political journalists.

booksellers, and the fixed capital which they comprised increased. The printers now tended to have a smaller part in the management of papers, and therefore found the constant threat of prosecution even more inconvenient; in groups, however, booksellers were able to offer printers large indemnities and compensation in the event of prosecution. Although a paper could cover its basic paper and printing costs with a sale of 600, the tendency was for papers with full coverage of events to aspire to circulations of two or three thousand; the major political papers, such as the *London Journal*, Mist's *Weekly Journal* and the *Craftsman*, all reached well over 10,000 before the middle of the century. At this point, advertising became a really important element in total revenue: in 1731, with a huge and expensive circulation of some 12,000, the *Craftsman* claimed that half of its paper and printing costs were covered by advertising.

Another reason for the switch towards stability was the consolidation of the Hanoverian monarchy and the role of journalism within it. The development of the political essay, as the defining content of the weekly journal, was a phenomenon of supreme importance. It brought writers like Fielding, Defoe, Swift and Amhurst into news publication. They established journalism as a direct form of political power: the prose employed by Swift in his pamphleteering (which gradually gave way to newspaper journalism) struck like an arrow against his political foes. It became a basic tool of politics. Nicholas Amhurst's *Craftsman*, Daniel Defoe's *Review* and Jonathan Swift's *Examiner* transformed the political scene and paved the way for the existence of the full-time paid journalist in the 1740s. The *Craftsman* began in 1726 and survived in one form or another, albeit faded, until the last part of the century. It was the first journal to be operated by a group of politicians, in this case Lord Bolingbroke and the Pulteneys, and functioned as a political catalyst and as a Tory weapon against the prevailing Ministry. Although opposed to the government, it was fundamentally loyal to the Crown, and as it grew it played as important a part in economic life as it did in political. It was profuse with advertisements, greatly in demand when the economy settled down again after the shock of the South Sea Bubble.

The appetite for news grew apace. Papers started to boast to their readers of the extensiveness of their contacts in town and country. The *London Evening News* was at pains quite often to emphasize its local network of contacts to impress out-of-town purchasers. Mist was said to have had 'an agent scraping the Jails in Middlesex and Surrey of their Commitments; another has a warrant for scouring the Ale-houses and Gin-shops for such as dye of excessive Drinking; a Person is posted at the Savoy to take up Deserters and another in the Park to watch the Motions of the Guards'. It was charged that the demand was such that coffee-men would 'haunt and loiter about the Publick Offices like House-breakers, waiting for an interview with some little Clerk, or a Conference with a Door-keeper, in order to come at a little News'. Such were the sources of the new forms of content required to widen the readership of papers and secure the custom of women and of semi-literates. The *Universal Spectator* in 1728, seeing the needs of this new audience, proclaimed its concern with 'the Progress of Wit and Humour, Free from Politicks and Raillery, Religious Controversy, or Dulness'. Defoe had stood at the foot of the scaffold to collect the dying words of convicts. With the maturity of miscellaneous newspapers, trials and executions became not a rarity but a regular stock-in-trade. Every morbid interest was captured by the papers, all bizarre occurrences, sexual outrage and romantic adventure. The *Penny London Post* in March 1745 ran a series on hurricanes, earthquakes and volcanoes. The newspapers went out to meet their readers.

The one area of major news interest closed to the press was Parliament: although the political essay papers included explanations of pending parliamentary business, the actual reporting of debates constituted a breach of privilege. In order to deal with the events of the moment, newspapers resorted to pseudo-historical accounts, to allegory, to all sorts of tricks of evasion or euphemism. The *Gloucester Journal* was severely dealt with in 1728 and 1729 for giving too open an account of the debates. It was an early martyrdom in an important cause which gathered in determination as the era of reform drew near. When the eighteenth-century English press reached its maturity, it initiated a series of struggles against harassment, against the privilege of judges rather than juries to decide the fact of a libel, and, most fervently of all, against the prohibition on the reporting of Parliament. Against great opposition, and after a series of deliberately contrived crises, the galleries of Lords and Commons were prised open by an eager group of London proprietors and editors in the last decades of the century.

Throughout the European continent, censorship was all the more carefully enforced as a result of the spectacle of English journalistic chaos. It was the age of absolutism. An edict issued throughout the Holy Roman Empire in July 1715 commanded all who had any connection with the press to observe keenly and to the letter all the laws against slander previously enacted but fallen into disregard. Thirty years later the Emperor made it clear that the controls applied to newspapers and pamphlets as much as to ordinary books; in 1795 Francis II, terrified by the spread of revolutionary ideas from France, strengthened the controls against the importation and copying of foreign printed matter which advocated the overthrow of the existing constitution or the disturbance of public peace. Not all the tiny

The Penny London Post,

OR, THE MORNING ADVERTISER.

From FRIDAY March 22, to MONDAY March 25, 1745.

Printed and Sold by J. NICHOLSON, at the Printing Office near *Black-and-white-Court*, in the *Old Bailey.*

To the AUTHOR, &c.

SIR,

THE late Genuine Account of the Hurricane at Jamaica publish'd in your Paper of Wednesday last exciting a Curiosity to enquire into the Cause of such furious Agitations, (which with their frequent Earthquakes must make that part of the World not very delectable) I have been induced to look into the Historical Accounts of that Island, and find they are so frequent with them, they have particular Signs to discover the Approach of these first Calamities by, and prepare for them accordingly.

One of their principal, is, that all Hurricanes come either on the Day of the Full, Change, or Quarter of the Moon; A turbulent Sky, the Sun red, an universal Calm, the Stars appearing red, Noises in Hollows or Cavities of the Earth, a strong Smell of the Sea and a settled Westerly Wind, are certain Prognosticks.

It is the Custom for the French and English Inhabitants in the Caribbee Islands, to send every Year about June to the native Caribbees of St. Domingo and St. Vincent, to know whether there will be any Hurricanes that Year, and about ten or twelve Days before any Hurricane comes, they constantly send them Word.

They begin in the North, some say, the West, but turn round, and in a little Time veer thro' all Points of the Compass. They appear so dreadful that all Ships are afraid to put to Sea, while they last, but chuse rather to perish at Anchor in the Roads, yet with good Management a Vessel may lie out at Sea in these, as safely as other Storms by taking Care the Ports be well barr'd and calk'd, the Top-masts and Tops taken down, the Yards a-port lasht, and the Doors and Windows secured. With these Precautions that experienced Navigator Capt. Langford preserved his Vessel in two great Hurricanes and taught others to do the same by putting out from Port where they would infallibly have perish'd.

From the above Prognosticks, the Knowledge of which Capt. Langford obtain'd by being extraordinary civil to a Barbarian of the Caribbees, he foretold several Hurricanes at Land; He adds, that all Hurricanes begin from the North and turn to the Westward, till arriving at the South East their Force is spent.

The Case the Captain suggests to the Sun's leaving the Zenith of those Places and going back towards the South, and the repelling or bounding back of the Wind occasioned by the calming of the general Trade Wind.

As to Earthquakes, one of which Sir Hans Sloan informs us, they expect every Year; I shall give you an Extract of that most remarkable one which happened in the Year 1694; probably many of your Readers may never have met with it —— 'Tis not indeed quite concordant with the Subject of a Hurricane, but as we are looking towards Jamaica, and considering the Inconveniencies of that Latitude by a Chain of thinking, (or as Mr. Lock calls it, a Concatenation of Ideas) I hope it is not a very unnatural Succession; however give me Leave to proceed with my Extract.

'In two Minutes time it shook down and drowned nine tenths of the Town of Port-Royal. The Houses sunk out-right 30 or 40 Fathoms deep. The Earth opening, swallowed up People; and they rose in other streets; some in the middle of the Harbour, and yet was saved; though, there were 2000 People lost, and 1000 Acres of Land sunk. All the Houses were thrown down throughout the Island. One Hopkins had his Plantation re-

moved half a Mile from its Place. Of all Wells, from one Fathom to six or seven, the Water flew out at the top with a vehement motion. While the Houses, on one Side of the Street were swallowed up, on the other they were thrown on Heaps; and the Sand in the Street rose like Waves in the Sea, lifting up every body that stood on it, and immediately dropping down into Pits; at the same Instant, a Flood of Water breaking in, rolled them over and over; some catching hold of Beams and Rafters, &c. Ships and Sloops in the Harbour were overset and lost; the Swan Frigate particularly, by the Motion of the Sea, and sinking of the Wharf, was driven over the Tops of many Houses, It was attended with a hollow rumbling Noise like that of Thunder. In less than a Minute, three Quarters of the Houses, and the Ground they stood on, with the Inhabitants, were all sunk quite under Water; and the little Part, left behind, was no better than a Heap of Rubbish. The Shake was so violent, that it threw People down on their Knees, or their Faces, as they were running about for shelter. The Ground heaved and swelled like a rolling Sea; and several Houses, still standing, were shuffled and moved some Yards out of their Places. A whole Street is said to be twice as broad now as before; and in many Places, the Earth would crack and open, and shut quick and fast. Of which openings, two or three Hundred might be seen at a time; in some whereof, the People were swallowed up; others, the closing Earth caught by the middle, and pressed to Death; in others, the Heads only appeared. The larger Openings swallowed up Houses; and out of some would issue whole Rivers of Waters, spouting up a great Height into the Air, and threatening a Deluge to that Part the Earthquake spared.

(To be continued.)

FOREIGN NEWS.

PETERSBURGH, February 24. The Day before Yesterday we celebrated, with prodigious Eclat, the Anniversary of the Birth-Day of the Grand Duke. The Empress dined on her Throne, with the Grand Dutchess by her Side, in the great Hall of the Place. The Clergy of the highest Rank, and other Persons of Distinction, to the Number of 200 dined at several Tables in the same Hall: The Grand Duke sate alone in his own Apartment with his Mother-in-Law, to avoid the Fatigue of a long Entertainment. All the Foreign Ministers were entertained by C. Bestuchett in the Noble Palace which lately belong'd to Count Osterman, who died a little while ago at the Place of his Exile. Prince Augustus of Holstein, who arrived here about a Fortnight ago, could not be present at this Feast, by reason of an unlucky Accident; Part of his Nose being frozen in his Journey.

GENOA, March 6. The Senate continue to take all the necessary Precautions for the Safety of this City, in Case the English Fleet should appear again upon our Coasts. The Batteries on our Ramparts are almost finished.

The Spanish Troops in the Neighbourhood of Oneglia are preparing to attempt again the Conquest of the Marquisate of Maro; for which Purpose they will march in three Columns, and take different Routes: So that we expect an Action on that Side, the King of Sardinia having sent thither a Reinforcement of regular Troops to sustain the independent Companies and the Peasants.

MADRID, March 1. The King and the Court, continue to enjoy, at the Pardo, as good Health as can be desired; the Princes and Princesses dined together the Six last Days of the Carnival, and there was a Ball every Evening at the Apartment of Madame de France, Infanta of Spain. On the 25th the Count de Thoring presented a Letter from the Elector of Bavaria, containing an Account of the Death of his late Imperial Majesty, his Father. It was observed, that this Letter was sign'd simply Maximilian, without any Title whatever. The

Marquis de Villarias has since been with the Count de Thoring, in the Name of the King his Master, to inform him, that his Catholick Majesty persists in his Resolution of fulfilling punctually whatever has been on his Part stipulated in the Treaties of Nymphenbourg and Francfort, for the Support of the just Pretensions of the House of Bavaria, and for obtaining a settled and lasting Peace. The Duke de Montemar is in greater Credit than ever, and is said to have convinc'd their Majesties, that M. Campillo, who procur'd his Disgrace for not prosecuting the War in Italy, actually put it out of his Power; and we hope very soon to see that, and the rest of this Minister's Intrigues made publick; which however the Marquis de Ensenada opposes as a Thing capable of giving great Lights into the Mysteries of the Spanish Government to Strangers.

BERLIN, March 16. Before the King set out for Silesia, he sent Orders thither for getting every Thing in Readiness to open the Campaign immediately after his Arrival. It was thought that his Majesty would confine himself to remain on the Defensive, in hopes of an Accommodation; but we are now assur'd that he has resolv'd to act offensively in the Upper Silesia, and even penetrate into Moravia before the Austrians are able to oppose him, and to make a powerful Diversion in favour of his Allies.

FRANCFORT, March 21. The French Cavalry that was in the Neighbourhood of Hanau, began their March Yesterday, in order to join the main Body of Marshal Maillebois's Army: The other Troops that are dispers'd in divers Places, have so receiv'd Orders to join that General, and the French, give out that the whole Army will march this Day, or To-morrow, in order to draw near the Laline and give the Allies Battle. They have actually 5000 Men at Witbaden, and have likewise thrown some Troops into Iditein. This last Place was occupied before by five Dutch Companies and 60 Dragoons, but they evacuated it in Order the 15th Instant, upon Advice of the French Army's having passed the Mayn. The French Independent Companies make Incursions all over Wetteravia, but commit no Excesses, only obliging the Peasants to furnish them with Provisions, and Forrage for their Horses.

BRUSSELS, March 22. We hear from the Frontiers, that a Detachment of French Troops have taken Post at Bossu, between Mons and St. Guislain; and they write from Courtray that Marshal Count Saxe arrived at Lisle the 18th Instant.

HAGUE March 25. The Veldt Marshal Count Konigsegg will set out To-morrow for Brussels. All the Letters we received from the Lower Rhine confirm, that the Duke of Aremberg only waits for the Junction of the Troops of Munster, in order to execute a Design which he has had in his Head since his being obliged to retreat from the Mayn.

DAILY ADVERTISER POLITICS.

An Extract of a Letter from BERLIN, to a Foreign Minister at the HAGUE, March 10.

'The Marquis de Valori has sustained a great deal of Raillery since his Return from Dresden, he indeed seems highly dissatisfied with having gather'd so little Fruit from his Negotiation: He is however greatly puffed up with future Hopes, and with the Honours which he pretends to have received from his Polish Majesty. But what he is willing to continue Honours, fall very short of being so. M. Valori was on the contrary a Burthen to the Ministers of the Court of Dresden, and exceedingly troublesome to them, by continually representing to them the Lustre of the Imperial Dignity. He told them, amongst other Things, of the Advantages which the preceding King had drawn from that Dignity, would not be turned to those which it would procure for his ...... provided he would enter into the ...... and act in Concert with that Court ...... Christian Majesty, as well as the King of Prussia, countries within the jurisdiction of the Emperor observed the same restrictive statutes, however, and things were made more complicated when Denmark in 1776 abolished censorship in all its dependent territories, including the German states of Schleswig and Holstein.

In Prussia the controls on the press were less comprehensive. The King forbade the importation of foreign newspapers, being especially vigilant in regard to papers coming from Holland, and instituted a censor in the Department of Foreign Affairs. Domestic productions, however, enjoyed considerable freedom, though even these were supervised by the legal authorities of the land. In time of war Frederick the Great, keenly aware of the economic importance of the press, virtually made himself editor-in-chief of the Berlin papers. During the Seven Years War (1756–63) no criticism whatsoever of Frederick's conduct of affairs was permitted, while he himself used descriptions of the war as a tool for manipulating public opinion.

Austria presents the strictest example of censorship in eighteenth-century Europe. Until 1715 only the Jesuits administering the University of Vienna had power of censorship, but with the establishment of secular media in the early eighteenth century the function was divided between the university and state authorities, although Maria Theresa tried without success to return the administration to the university. In the middle of the century a special Censorship Commission was set up whose powers, after a brief liberalization under Joseph II, were progressively strengthened until prohibitions and caution moneys were imposed upon all publications, including purely literary ones. So total was the Austrian repression of the press – at one point the police banned 2,500 publications in two years – that it amounted to an attempt to stamp out all contact between Austria and the intellectual movements of the Continent. One or two papers had succeeded very well in Vienna in the previous century; the *Extraordinari Mittwochs Post Zeitung* ('Wednesday post') survived for half a century until 1698, with competitors springing up towards the end. After 1703, however, only the *Wienerisches Diarium* (which changed its name to *Wiener Zeitung* in 1780) remained, with a solitary monopoly of news until 1848. During the brief reign of Joseph II several dailies sprang up in Vienna, but these were soon crippled by further decrees and by police surveillance. A few papers in the provinces struggled on, but the main content consisted in reprints of the *Wiener Zeitung* and later of the *Oesterreichischer Beobachter* ('Austrian observer'). Not until Metternich tried to start up a patriotic newspaper press did any sign appear that Vienna was one day to become one of the great newspaper cities of the world.

Throughout the German-speaking world in the early eighteenth century there was a rapid development in the communication of commercial information, built round a number of enterprises established on the model of the Montaigne/Renaudot Bureau d'Adresses. The information collected through these agencies came to be printed in the form of the *Intelligenzblatt*, the earliest known example of which was the *Wienerisches Diarium* of 1703. Frederick William I of Prussia was among the first enthusiasts for this form, and allowed *Intelligenzblätter* to start up throughout his realm as official publications supporting the state monopoly of advertising. The normal *Zeitung* was not permitted to print advertisements. The scope for these

Opposite The *Penny London Post* made much play with hurricanes and earthquakes in the Caribbean, which 'must make that part of the World not very delectable'. It carries its stamp at the foot of the page.

The 'Brunswick Advertiser': advertisements and commercial information rather than news.

publications was enormous, and the *Intelligenzblatt* form created virtually a sub-industry in news publishing which is still in evidence today. The *Braunschweigische Anzeigen* ('Brunswick advertiser'), founded in 1746, promised to provide regular information on, for example, things for sale or hire, property lost, stolen or found, details of trials, legal decisions, auctions and concessions, arriving and departing visitors from abroad, persons seeking work or seeking employees, births, marriages and deaths, currency exchange rates, the prices of gold, silver, grain, hops, tobacco, wool, yarn, wood and other materials, and of salt, meat, bread, beer and other foodstuffs – an enormously wide array of commercial information which provided the mainstay of a news publication similar to the London advertisers. In time, the *Intelligenzblatt* came to offer a certain amount of political information in places where state authorities took over direct editorial control. These papers tended to have much lower circulations than their quasi-counterparts in London, Dublin and elsewhere, seldom achieving more than 200 copies per issue, with a peak of 2,000 by 1800.

In German-speaking territory the strict division between official and commercial papers in the eighteenth century meant that journalism as a profession simply did not exist. There were, of course, academics, scientists, literati and state officials writing for innumerable specialist journals, but throughout the century no daily news publication provided an opportunity for a voice to be raised throughout the press on a political topic. Many towns had family-owned papers which have survived from the early eighteenth century until the twentieth, the oldest extant being the *Hildesheimer Relations-*

санктъпітербурхъ.

СЕНТЯБРЯ 20 ДНЯ ПОЛУЧЕНЫ
изъ ЛАГАРЯ отъ ТАРКОВЪ.
ВѢДОМОСТИ.

1

Ихъ Велічествы со всѣмъ Флотомъ
прібыли Моремъ. до Агроханского
залігу, Іюля протівъ 28 числа.
благополучно. И здѣлавъ лагарь.
былі

2

былі съ недѣлю, для выгрузки
правіанту, а наіпаче для Транжа-
менту, которои дѣлали вновь.

2

Получена вѣдомость въ лагарь отъ
брегадіра Вітеронія, что онъ съ 2000
драгунъ и съ 400 Казаковъ Андрееву
деревню, гдѣ здѣлана была крѣпость
нарочітая, въ которои отъ 5, до
6000 Кумыковъ взялъ шпюрмсмъ,
и многіхъ ихъ порубілъ, а достальные
розбѣжалісь, и по томъ оную крѣпость разорілъ и жіліща ихъ зжегъ.

3

Августа въ 5 чіслѣ, оставя у того
Транжамента всѣ суды, такожъ и
правіантъ, и болныхъ салдатъ и при
ніхъ въ Гварнізонѣ 300 человѣкъ
съ Подполковнікомъ Масловымъ
салдатъ

Courier, founded in 1705 by the printer Johann Christian Hermitz.

Side by side with the *Intelligenz* network of papers, which spread rapidly after the 1720s from town to town, there arrived the prototypes of the cultural publication or feuilleton: in 1729 the Chancellor of the University of Halle, Johann Peter von Ludewig, started the *Wochentliche Hallische Prage- und Anzeigungs-Nachrichten* ('Halle weekly press and advertiser'), which concentrated on appropriately learned articles and announcements of books. The establishment of publications based on universities was common by the mid-century. Even the new Moscow University produced its *Moskovskiye vedomosti* ('Moscow journal') in 1755, building on the example of the *St Peterburgskiye vedomosti* ('St Petersburg journal'), a twice-weekly government paper published after 1720 which contained a special academic supplement the *Primechanie* ('comments'), to which Michael Lomonossov was an early contributor. Peter the Great had inaugurated Russian news journalism with his own handwritten publication at the start of the century. The Tsarina Catherine also had her own periodical, *Vsyakaya vsyachina* ('a cornucopia for all') which provoked Nikolai I. Novikov to issue a series of spirited satirical replies supporting the peasants and pillorying the landowners; this unfortunate journalistic pioneer was condemned to death, imprisoned for fifteen years and eventually released by Paul I, without ever again publishing a word of political commentary. Thus a pattern was established very early in the history of the Russian press which is recognizable even today: on the one hand, official publications, and on the other academic material without political or critical comment, both with high circulations and great

First page of the *Sankt Peterburgskiye vedomosti* of 29 September 1722.

longevity; alongside them a host of short-lived private papers, mainly literary in content, staggered on.

The German system of having two parallel kinds of news periodical was adopted in Switzerland, and in Scandinavia and other countries on the fringes of the Continent. An interesting exception was Hungary, where an anti-Austrian press, in Latin, existed during the course of the struggle led by Count Francis II Rákoczi: the *Mercurius Hungaricus* was edited by the Commander-in-Chief, Count von Esterházy, to counteract the *Wienerisches Diarium*, the main propaganda tool of the Vienna régime. The paper was used, however, only outside Hungary – hence the Latin language – to gain the support of the influential in Poland, Russia, Sweden and France. With the victory of Austria, the German system of control was imported, and the *Nova Posoniensia* ('news from Poznan'), started in 1721, was published in the form of an *Intelligenzblatt*. Not until 1780 did a paper appear in Hungarian.

Influences from Germany and France entered the small states of Italy through Venice, which alone among the city states had power over a very large territory through which its flourishing printing industry could distribute its products. Ludovico Antonio Muratori founded the *Primi disegni della repubblica letteraria* ('first outlines of the republic of letters') in a period when Venice presented itself as neutral in a firmly divided Europe; while elsewhere in Italy the Counter-Reformation brought about a shutdown in the intellectual and literary worlds, Venice succeeded in acting as the entrepôt for European influences and information. Many of the Italian towns started to develop ecclesiastical papers in the eighteenth century, and a few had journals dedicated mainly to literature and the arts. In one or two places, notably in Lombardy, a flow of political information reached the press, but for the most part European information reached Italians only in direct translations of the corantos and newspapers from Holland. However, the later traditions of Italian intellectual journalism were established by three important figures who were active in the first half of the century, the Venetian Apostolo Zeno, the Veronan Scipio Maffei, and Antonio Vallisnieri, an academician at Padua. These drew upon the earlier 'relation' form to build up a periodical system within the university life of the country. Apart from such activities, news publication remained scanty and local in Italy, and grander efforts of a more national scope awaited the foundation in Venice in 1770 of the *Gazetta*, which tried to copy and develop many of the achievements of the great Parisian publications.

The American colonies in the early eighteenth century presented all the classic preconditions for the rapid growth of a newspaper industry. They consisted of communities of craftsmen and tradesmen serving rapidly rising populations settling in new communities connected by new roads and postal services. The seaboard population rose from 300,000 to one and a quarter million in the half-century after 1700, and in a further half-century had doubled again. The town of Boston, which was the birthplace of the American press, grew from 7,000 inhabitants in 1700 to 20,000 by mid-century, and was connected by regular posts after the 1690s with a growing series of towns. It was often, in fact, the postmasters who effected the transition between the hand-copied letters of news which they composed and

APOSTOLOS ZENOS.

Apostolo Zeno, one of the
founders of Italian journalism.

set out as one of their informal duties and the first printed newspapers. The
fact that postmasters were state-appointed contributed to the early tensions
between British authorities and American postmaster-printer-editors. The
printing-press, imported in parts from England until the first Isaac Doolittle
machines were made in America after 1769, represented the technology of
independence through its function of linking the colonies, and the cause of
press freedom became one of the founding principles of the republic.

PUBLICK
OCCURRENCES

Both *FORREIGN* and *DOMESTICK*.

Boſton, Thurſday Sept. 25th. 1690.

It is deſigned, that the Country ſhall be furniſhed once a moneth (or if any Glut of Occurrences happen, oftener,) with an Account of ſuch conſiderable things as have arrived unto our Notice.

In order hereunto, the Publiſher will take what pains he can to obtain a Faithful Relation of all ſuch things ; and will particularly make himſelf beholden to ſuch Perſons in Boſton whom he knows to have been for their own uſe the diligent Obſervers of ſuch matters.

That which is herein propoſed, is, Firſt, That Memorable Occurrents of Divine Providence may not be neglected or forgotten, as they too often are. Secondly, That people every where may better underſtand the Circumſtances of Publique Affairs, both abroad and at home ; which may not only direct their Thoughts at all times, but at ſome times alſo to aſſiſt their Buſineſſes and Negotiations.

Thirdly, That ſome thing may be done towards the Curing, or at leaſt the Charming of that Spirit of Lying, which prevails amongſt us, wherefore nothing ſhall be entered, but what we have reaſon to believe is true, repairing to the beſt fountains for our Information. And when there appears any material miſtake in any thing that is collected, it ſhall be corrected in the next.

Moreover, the Publiſher of theſe Occurrences is willing to engage, that whereas, there are many Falſe Reports, maliciouſly made, and ſpread among us, if any well-minded perſon will be at the pains to trace any ſuch falſe Report ſo far as to find out and Convict the Firſt Raiſer of it, he will in this Paper (unleſs juſt Advice be given to the contrary) expoſe the Name of ſuch perſon, as A malicious Raiſer of a falſe Report. It is ſuppos'd that none will diſlike this Propoſal, but ſuch as intend to be guilty of ſo villanous a Crime.

THE Chriſtianized *Indians* in ſome parts of *Plimouth*, have newly appointed a day of Thanksgiving to God for his Mercy in ſupplying their extream and pinching Neceſſities under their late want of Corn, & for His giving them now a proſpect of a very *Comfortable Harveſt*. Their Example may be worth Mentioning.

'Tis obſerved by the Huſbandmen, that altho' the With-draw of ſo great a ſtrength from them, as what is in the Forces lately gone for *Canada*, made them think it almoſt impoſſible for them to get well through the Affairs of their Huſbandry at this time of the year, yet the ſeaſon has been ſo unuſually favourable that they ſcarce find any want of the many hundreds of hands, that are gone from them ; which is looked upon as a Merciful Providence.

While the barbarous *Indians* were lurking about *Chelmsford*, there were miſſing about the beginning of this month a couple of Children belonging to a man of that Town, one of them aged about eleven, the other aged about nine years, both of them ſuppoſed to be fallen into the hands of the *Indians*.

A very *Tragical Accident* Happened at *Water-Town*, the beginning of this Month, an *Old man*, that was of ſomewhat a ſilent and Moroſe Temper, but one that had long Enjoyed the reputation of a ſober and a pious Man, having newly buried his Wife, The Devil took advantage of the Melancholly which he thereupon fell into, his Wives diſcretion and induſtry had long been the ſupport of his Family, and he ſeemed hurried with an impertinent fear that he ſhould now come to want before he dyed, though he had very careful friends to look after him who kept a ſtrict eye upon him, leaſt he ſhould do himſelf any harm. But one evening eſcaping from them into the Cow-houſe, they there quickly followed him found him hanging by a Rope, which they had uſed to tye their Calves withal, he was dead with his feet near touching the Ground.

Epidemical *Fevers* and *Agues* grow very common, in ſome parts of the Country, whereof, tho' many dye not, yet they are ſorely unfitted for their imployments ; but in ſome parts a more *malignant Fever* ſeems to prevail in ſuch ſort that it uſually goes thro' a Family where it comes, and proves *Mortal* unto many.

The *Small-pox* which has been raging in *Boſton*, after a manner very Extraordinary is now very much abated. It is thought that far more have been ſick of it then were viſited with it, when it raged ſo much twelve years ago, nevertheleſs it has not been ſo Mortal, The number of them that have

Benjamin Harris, an ally of Titus Oates and one of the anti-Catholic conspirators against Charles II, had taken refuge across the Atlantic and hastened to start a newspaper, *Publick Occurrences*, as early as 1690. This and Increase Mather's *Present State of the New-English Affairs* of 1689 were single-issue failures, and the first important newspaper foundings were those of the Boston postmaster John Campbell (the *Boston News-Letter* of 1704), of the Franklin brothers (starting with James Franklin's *New England Courant* of 1721) and of Andrew Bradford and his family (starting with the *American Weekly Mercury* of 1719). All the early papers were precise models of the London press of the time and included a great deal of London political information. Benjamin Franklin was to import into America the new *Spectator*-type weekly essay, and in the character of 'Silence Doogood' he contributed to the genre himself. The *Courant* and the other papers started or influenced by the Franklins throughout New England introduced the American reader to information about his own society. James Franklin's papers, like most others of the time, invited unpaid contributions from the readers and turned the newspaper into the intellectual forum of a community. Franklin's contributors were mainly Episcopalians, opposed to the Puritans and more secular in their interests. He called for contributions in his paper which were 'Serious, Sarcastic, Ludicrous or otherwise Amusing'. The newspaper of the early decades of the century created the sense of common interest among the settlers, and linked the rather different cultures on which the various colonies had been founded. The carefully drafted four-page

Above, left Increase Mather, one of the most powerful men in the American colonies and one of the founders of the American newspaper.

Above, right Benjamin Franklin, alias 'Silence Doogood', the most influential journalist in early America.

Opposite America's first newspaper: the first and last issue. It was promptly suppressed by the colonial government of Massachusetts.

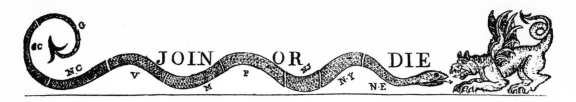

The snake in nine sections, scoffed at by Tory wits as a snake in the grass.

reports which circulated among this generation of Americans provided the basic iconography of freedom, and Franklin's first cartoon (published originally in the *Pennsylvania Gazette*), which depicted a snake divided into nine parts to represent the colonies, with the slogan 'Join or Die', was repeated again and again in all the papers of America at the beginning of the fight for independence. The collapse of licensing in England led to its collapse in America also, although the authorities clung still to the hope that, either constitutionally or through the postmasterships, the American press would be controlled.

The trial of the German immigrant printer John Peter Zenger, imprisoned on a charge of criminal libel in 1735 for presuming to attack in the columns of his *New York Weekly Journal* the administration of Governor William Cosby of New York, was one of the classic fights for press freedom of the eighteenth century. His attorney, the ageing Andrew Hamilton, made the case for juries rather than judges deciding whether offending words constituted libel, and thus ensured his client's acquittal, although English law waited until Fox's Libel Act was passed half a century later before liberalizing the laws of libel in this way. Zenger first raised the voice of libertarian truculence in American journalism, and he and his wife Anna, who continued bringing out the *Journal* during his months in gaol, became two of the earliest members of the American pantheon. As Hamilton had plainly told the court, theirs was 'not just the cause of the poor printer.... It is the best cause; it is the cause of Liberty.'

Zenger's struggle, of course, and that of other early editors such as James Franklin, was part of a British struggle for press freedom. The American colonists were experiencing, in a form sharpened by their separation from the social structures which made it meaningful in England, the same tension between editors and authorities as suffered by the Whig journalists of London. The American Revolution was the product of a more clearly felt need to change those central structures of power which subjected the prosperous mercantilism of New England to the crabbed procedures of an aristocratic method of government. The imposition of the Stamp Act in 1765, which imposed a severe tax on all newspapers as well as on a wide variety of other goods, provided a cause much more specifically American, and one which led directly to the demand for separation from the Crown.

England was trying to raise, through her colonies, the revenue to pay for the expensive wars against the French in North America. Among the colonists there were, on the one hand, men like James Rivington who took a straight Tory line and opposed all forms of insurrection against London rule. There were others who agreed with John Dickinson, author of the 'Letters from a Farmer in Pennsylvania' of 1767, which were reprinted in the

Opposite Governor Cosby's proclamation offering a reward for the conviction of John Peter Zenger.

By his Excellency

William Cosby, Captain General and Governour in Chief of the Provinces of *New-York*, *New-Jersey*, and Territories thereon depending, in America, Vice-Admiral of the same, and Colonel in His Majesty's Army.

A PROCLAMATION.

WHereas by the Contrivance of some evil Disposed and Disaffected Persons, divers Journals or Printed News Papers, (entitled, *The New - York Weekly Journal, containing the freshest Advices, Foreign and Domestick*) have been caused to be Printed and Published by *John Peter Zenger*, in many of which Journals or Printed News-Papers (but more particularly those Numbred 7, 47, 48, 49) are contained divers Scandalous, Virulent, False and Seditious Reflections, not only upon the whole Legislature, in general, and upon the most considerable Persons in the most distinguish'd Stations in this Province, but also upon His Majesty's lawful and rightful Government, and just Prerogative. Which said Reflections seem contrived by the wicked Authors of them, not only to create Jealousies, Discontents and Animosities in the Minds of his Majesty's Leige People of this Province, to the Subversion of the Peace & Tranquility thereof, but to alienate their Affections from the best of Kings, and raise *Factions, Tumults* and *Sedition* among them. *Wherefore* I have thought fit, by and with the Advice of His Majesty's Council, to issue this Proclamation, hereby Promising a Reward of *Fifty Pounds* to such Person or Persons who shall discover the Author or Authors of the said *Scandalous, Virulent* and *Seditious Reflections* contained in the said *Journals* or *Printed News-Papers*, to be paid to the Person or Persons discovering the same, as soon as such Author or Authors shall be Convicted of having been the Author or Authors thereof.

GIVEN under My Hand and Seal at Fort-George in New-York this Sixth Day of November, in the Eighth year of the Reign of Our Sovereign Lord GEORGE the Second, by the Grace of GOD, of Great-Britain, France and Ireland, KING Defender of the Faith, &c. and in the Year of Our LORD 1734

By his Excellency's Command,   **W. COSBY.**
   Fred. Morris, D. Cl. Conc.

GOD Save the KING.

Pennsylvania Chronicle and other papers and laid down the basis for the demand for home rule but spoke with the voice of mild Quaker conservatism, unwilling to undermine the property-holding basis of society. It was the more radical style of journalism created by Isaiah Thomas and Samuel Adams, however, which caught the mood of the rank-and-file colonists and worked up the spirit of rebellion of the 1770s.

In the *Boston Gazette and Country Journal* Adams created a revolutionary weapon which used the power of vituperative uncompromise to work for the intended change in the organization of power. Adams was perhaps the first professional agitator to see the real possibilities of the press as a direct tool of social and political change. He had been introduced to the world of radical politics as a young man through the Caucus Club, and its paper, the *Independent Advertiser*, had revealed to him the latent power of journalism. He organized groups of agents to cover important political meetings and record the speeches; he moved restlessly round the colonies 'assassinating reputations', as his opponent Governor Hutchinson put it, stirring the resentment of the colonists to the highest pitch.

Thomas spoke more easily to the working man. He had begun as an apprentice printer at the age of six, but became a great scholar, a historian of the American press and an important popular educator, publishing the first American dictionary and hundreds of other contemporary classic works at his seven-press business in Worcester, Massachusetts, which at its height employed 150 printers and apprentices.

During the War of Independence, as in the English Civil War, home news became so immediate and fascinating as to blot out all interest in imported news. The idea that domestic events could provide the major topics for a newspaper first dawned when a blockade was preventing the collection of news from Europe. Several dozen new papers sprang up in the course of the war; so acute did the paper shortage become that General Washington found it necessary to appeal to all patriot women to save their rags for paper-making. A paper like the *Connecticut Journal*, for instance, which manufactured its own paper, succeeded in finding the means to print 8,000 copies of each edition; this represented an enormous circulation for the 1780s, greater than that of any London journal.

The newspaper pioneers of the American colonies fanned out northwards into Canada, where the first printing-press was imported in 1751 by Bartholomew Green of Boston; his *Halifax Gazette* emerged soon afterwards, but was banned in 1766 because of his criticism of the Stamp Act. Several of the provinces originated their first papers during the period of the American struggle for independence: the *Quebec Gazette* appeared in 1763, the *Halifax Journal* in 1781 and the *Weekly Chronicle* in 1786, all on the classic model of the English-language papers of the Enlightenment, in the tradition of Franklin and Paine.

The language of agitation is a language of emotion, of overstatement and, necessarily, of frequent inaccuracy. The ethic of the revolutionary press was different from that of the press which preceded it: Thomas Paine, whose writings were actually read out to the troops before battle, succeeded in representing to the average non-reading revolutionary soldier the meaning of

Isaiah Thomas, radical
American journalist of the
1770s.

the cause for which he was about to fight. Paine had arrived in America with
the intention of running a girls' seminary, but found his true calling as the
great journalistic agitator-advocate of the cause of freedom in both France
and America. 'Tyranny, like hell, is not easily conquered; yet we have this
consolation with us, that the harder the conflict the more glorious the
triumph. What we obtain too cheap, we esteem too lightly.' These words
from the first of his 'Crisis' papers of December 1776 were the model for
popular agitational journalism, perhaps the greatest enduring product of the
press of the eighteenth century; with this style came a newspaper which
combined information on day-to-day events with the constant advocacy of a
cause dear to its readers. Each paper found its own circle of readers, and their
loyalty became its financial and moral life-blood.

By the time the colonists had drawn up their Declaration of Independence
from England, the demand for freedom of the press was sweeping across

Europe, linked to demands for individual liberty which were to reach their crisis in the French Revolution and eventually to collapse in the Napoleonic Wars. Voltaire, Rousseau and above all Diderot had all demanded press freedom from the 1750s on. The *Encyclopédie* had declared that 'any country in which a man may not think and write his thoughts must necessarily fall into stupidity, superstition and barbarism'. In country after country, the spirit of liberty was being kindled in a generation of newspaper-writers who had been born after the carnage of the Counter-Reformation and had grown up under the influence of the Enlightenment in a period when absolutist monarchs were attempting to govern increasingly urban societies on the basis of information entirely controlled by themselves. The struggle for press freedom fought out in England over the publication in the *Daily Advertiser* of the anonymous 'Letters of Junius' attacking the government, over the admission of reporters to the galleries of Parliament, over the right of juries to decide the law as well as the fact of libel, was a struggle basically for freedom of information. The struggle for the freedom of comment was really the cause of a later period which began with the pull-back of Napoleon's defeated armies in the second decade of the nineteenth century and climaxed with the Revolution of 1848. For the moment, the new readers of newspapers wanted merely to know what was happening in their law courts and parliaments, in all the council chambers of the mighty; they did not yet think of themselves as complete citizens wishing to use their press as part of the apparatus of self-government.

Without the free public reporting of Parliament, literary talents – the ability in particular to write pamphlets – were more helpful to a rising man than the ability to speak. Joseph Addison, for instance, had become Under-Secretary of State, Chief Secretary for Ireland and Secretary of State without any oratorical talent and with only nine years of parliamentary experience. The newspaper of the eighteenth century slotted into a society of factions in which political capital was acquired by marshalling the support of small groups. After the era of the great journalist-essayists – Addison, Swift, Richard Steele – journalism steadily sank in social esteem. Montesquieu in 1730 condemned the scurrility of the London papers. Dr Johnson, in his prospectus for the new *London Chronicle* of 1757, attacked those who gave or sold their abilities 'to one or other of the parties that divide us . . . without a Wish for Truth or Thought of Decency, without Care of any other Reputation than that of a stubborn Adherence to their Abettors'. The low reputation of journalism took a long time to evaporate: as late as 1810 the Benchers of Lincoln's Inn tried to forbid membership to anyone who had ever written for hire in newspapers. In 1777, during the trial for forgery of the Reverend William Dodd, it was said, almost as confirmation of the case against him, that 'he had sunk so low as to have become the editor of a newspaper'. Sir Walter Scott was to write in his *Journal* that 'nothing but a thorough-going blackguard ought to attempt the daily Press unless it is some quiet country diurnal'. None the less, the day was drawing near when editors would dine with dukes and printers stand for Parliament; but before that could happen a new journalism would have to be forged on the anvil of revolution and beneath the hammer of military occupation.

Opposite Tom Paine: 'Tyranny, like hell, is not easily conquered.'

AREOPAGITICA;

A

SPEECH

OF

Mr. JOHN MILTON

For the Liberty of Vnlicenc'd
PRINTING,

To the Parlament of ENGLAND.

Τὰλήθερον δ' ἐκεῖνο, εἴ τις θέλﻼ πόλ
Χρησόν τι βἐλﻼμ' εἰς μέσον φέρειν, ἔχﻼν.
Καὶ ﻼαῦθ' ὁ χρﻼζων, λαμπρὸς ἐσθ', ὁ μὴ θέλων,
Σιγﻼ, τί τὲτων ἐϛιν ἰσαί περον πόλﻼ;

Euripid, Hicetid.

Ex Dono Authoris

This is true Liberty when free born men
Having to advise the public may speak free,
Which he who can, and will, deserv's high praise,
Who neither can nor will, may hold his peace;
What can be juster in a State then this?

Euripid. Hicetid.

noumb. 24. LONDON,
Printed in the Yeare, 1644.

4
'Tocsin of Nations'
1776–1815

When the colony of Virginia proposed the Declaration of Independence in 1776, no country in the world gave its citizens the right of free publication. Sweden had passed a new law in the same year which guaranteed press freedom, but its absolutist sovereign ignored the statute for all practical purposes. In the United Provinces newspapers still needed an official privilege and even then they were forbidden, in the very birthplace of the periodical press, to discuss local politics; the great freedom of the Dutch press was in fact restricted to the coverage of the internal affairs of other countries. After the brief interregnum of the patriotic revolution (1783–7) the Dutch were again placed under severe censorship. Christian VII had abolished censorship in 1771 in Denmark, but made important exceptions which included all periodical publications. In Germany the severity of the restrictions varied from state to state, but many of the 1,200 newspapers were free to discuss the internal affairs of all the neighbouring states, and a similar vicarious freedom existed in the states of Italy, in Switzerland and the Austrian Netherlands (Belgium). Britain was something of a paradox: it had been the first country to abolish licensing of newspapers, and Milton's *Areopagitica* (1644) was the universal text in the struggle for the freedom of newspapers from licensing, caution money, stamp duties, libel laws and governmental censorship, yet Britain's press still laboured under a series of frustrating restrictions which rendered newspapers, though legal, inaccessible to all but the well-to-do, and made every editor and writer live in permanent fear of fines, imprisonment and the humiliation of the pillory.

In the age of revolution, new freedoms were to be achieved temporarily in the new libertarian régimes, only to be brutally extinguished when the night of absolutism fell again. By 1819, England was subjected to the repressions of the Six Acts. In Germany, the Carlsbad decrees of 1819 left the press under lock and key. American newspapers were still recovering from the shock of the vindictive Alien and Sedition Acts, and the press of all the countries from which Napoleon's troops had retreated was watching restored *anciens régimes* unravelling the hopes of freedom which had been aroused at the ending of the French Imperial censorship.

None the less, during this period newspapers underwent a transformation. For one thing, they became much more valuable enterprises than ever before. The *Morning Chronicle*, which James Perry had acquired in 1789 with a circulation of 350, was by 1819 making an annual profit from advertisements and sales of £12,400. Newspapers which had been hard put to it to fill their four closely printed sides were now having to make judgments of Solomon between the desire to print advertisements and the need to find space for two

Opposite Areopagitica, Milton's classic call 'for the liberty of unlicenc'd printing', which became the basic text of the struggle for press freedom in the eighteenth and nineteenth centuries.

The Stanhope press,
'cumbersome but
manageable'.

or three hours of parliamentary debating. In the United States a technical revolution had quickly spread throughout the printing industry in the developed areas of the country, and circulations which had seldom topped 800 or 1,000 in 1800 were regularly reaching 4,000 in the larger cities by 1830. The relationship between the newspaper and the events of the revolutionary era had been such as to give the press a completely new 'image' in the minds of governments, whether liberal or oppressive. Its technical and financial organization enabled it to become part of the machinery of the new politics of the post-Napoleonic era. In America the linkages of a new society without the class structures of Europe were being partly created by this rising medium of information.

The Stanhope cast-iron press, which was the same in principle as the presses of the seventeenth century, except that it was no longer made of wood, was popular with printers. It was cumbersome but manageable, and reduced considerably the sheer effort entailed in every manœuvre, since its metal parts swung easily from stage to stage. It started to spread from England to America in the year 1789. Only in 1816 was a method developed for replacing the central screw, which still resembled that of Caxton's converted wine-press, with a set of levers; in this device George Clymer offered the world the first specifically American development in printing. His Columbian press, as it was called, also brought in a larger page size.

In America, each new community acquired its printer. There were towns with three hundred inhabitants and a weekly newspaper. To attract the printers, inducements were available in the form of contracts for official printing and occasional postmasterships. In 1798 the town of Michigan refused to wait and started a spoken newspaper, declaimed daily by an appointed crier and later written down by hand by the local priest; the institution continued until the first printer arrived in 1809. By 1786 Pittsburgh, despite its few inhabitants, had become the first town on the far side of the Allegheny range to enter the newspaper age; it was the starting-point for the journey by sail down the Ohio River and on to the Mississippi and so down to New Orleans, so its importance for the circulation of news throughout the Midwest and the South was considerable. After 1792 Congress officially allowed all papers cheap access to the postal services, and publishers were allowed to exchange material by post free of all charges. Jefferson had described the newspaper as 'the only tocsin of a nation': the opening up of the country to the press was considered to be crucial in the creation of the political infrastructure of the new American nation.

It was still a novel experience for the separate colonies to think and act as a cohesive national unit. The press had been active in explaining the case for the new Constitution and discussing the need for a Bill of Rights which was to embody the First Amendment, right of press freedom, demanded everywhere by the colonists. The men who actually drew up the Constitution, however, were not so enthusiastic in support of a specifically constitutional basis for a free press, partly because they thought this would be better enshrined in common law and in State constitutions, partly because they foresaw endless quarrels over the creation of appropriate limits to such freedom, and partly because, as the new governors of a nation which had now achieved its revolution, they were beginning to look at the press in a rather different light. It was the breaking out of dissension in the first government of the United States between the aristocratic Alexander Hamilton and the democratic Thomas Jefferson, between Federalists and Republicans (as the anti-Federalists were temporarily labelled), which provided the newspaper with what was, in America, an entirely new function – the fixing of the lines of party warfare. The *Gazette of the United States* was founded in 1789 by John Fenno in the nation's first capital, New York, as a specifically Federalist organ directed at voters (mainly merchants, shippers and large farmers). The lawyer and lexicographer Noah Webster founded the *American Minerva* (later the *Commercial Advertiser*) to defend Federalism against the increasingly venomous attacks of its opponents, which were being administered in the *National Gazette*. His main rival was William Coleman's *New York Evening Post*, the first paper to fight for the classic 'consumer' causes: street lighting and cleaning, the removal of slaughterhouses from central New York, the prohibition of hogs in the streets, municipal control of the water supply. Its leading articles – the strong right arm of Federalism – were still in the eighteenth-century mould and wandered from subject to subject, providing a sort of running commentary on everything happening at the moment rather than pinpointing specific topics or causes; many of them were written by Alexander Hamilton himself.

Gazette of the United States.

NUMBER I.   WEDNESDAY, APRIL 15, 1789.   PRICE SIX-PENCE.

PLAN OF THE GAZETTE of the UNITED STATES.
A NATIONAL PAPER.

To be published at the SEAT of the FEDERAL GOVERNMENT, and to comprise, as fully as possible, the following Objects, viz.

I. EARLY and authentick Accounts of the PROCEEDINGS of CONGRESS—its LAWS, ACTS, and RESOLUTIONS, communicated to as to form an *HISTORY of the TRANSACTIONS of the FEDERAL LEGISLATURE, under the NEW CONSTITUTION.*

II. Impartial Sketches of the Debates of Congress.

III. ESSAYS upon the great subjects of Government in general; and the *Federal Legislature in particular*; also upon the *national* and *local Rights* of the AMERICAN CITIZENS, as founded upon the Federal or State Constitutions; also upon every other Subject, which may appear suitable for newspaper discussion.

IV. A SERIES of PARAGRAPHS, calculated to catch the "LIVING MANNERS AS THEY RISE," and to point the publick attention to Objects that have an important reference to *domestick, social,* and *publick happiness.*

V. The Interests of the United States as connected with their literary Institutions—religious and moral Objects—Improvements in Science, Arts, EDUCATION and HUMANITY—their foreign Treaties, Alliances, Connections, &c.

VI. Every species of INTELLIGENCE, which may affect the *commercial, agricultural, manufacturing,* or *political INTERESTS* of the AMERICAN REPUBLIC.

VII. A CHAIN of DOMESTICK OCCURRENCES, collected through the Medium of an extensive Correspondence with the respective States.

VIII. A SERIES of FOREIGN ARTICLES of INTELLIGENCE, so connected, as to form a general Idea of publick Affairs in the eastern Hemisphere.

IX. The STATE of the NATIONAL FUNDS; also of the INDIVIDUAL GOVERNMENTS—Courses of Exchange—Prices Current, &c.

CONDITIONS.

I.
THE GAZETTE of the UNITED STATES *shall be printed with the same Letter, and on the same Paper as this publication.*

II.
It shall be published every WEDNESDAY *and* SATURDAY, *and delivered, as may be directed, to every Subscriber in the city, on those days.*

III.
The price to Subscribers (exclusive of postage) will be THREE DOLLARS *pr. annum.*

IV.
The first semi-annual payment to be made in three months from the appearance of the first number.

SUBSCRIPTIONS

Will be received in all the capital towns upon the Continent; also at the City-Coffee-House, and at No. 85, William-Street, until the 1st of May, from which time at No. 9, Maiden-Lane, near the Oswego-Market, New-York.

N. B. By a new Arrangement made in the Stages, Subscribers at a distance will be duly furnished with papers.

POSTSCRIPT.—*A large impression of every number will be struck off so that Subscribers may always be accommodated with complete Sets.*

To the PUBLICK.

AT this important Crisis, the ideas that fill the mind, are pregnant with Events of the greatest magnitude—to strengthen and complete the UNION of the States—to extend and protect their COMMERCE, under *equal* Treaties yet to be formed—to explore and arrange the NATIONAL FUNDS—to restore and establish the PUBLICK CREDIT—and ALL under the auspices of an untried System of Government, will require the ENERGIES of the Patriots and Sages of our Country—*Hence the propriety of increasing the Mediums of Knowledge and Information.*

AMERICA, from this period, begins a new Era in her national existence—" THE WORLD IS ALL BEFORE HER "—The wisdom and folly—the misery and prosperity of the EMPIRES, STATES, and KINGDOMS, which have had their day upon the great Theatre of Time, and are now no more, suggest the most important Mementos—These, with the rapid series of Events, in which our own Country has been so deeply interested, have taught the

EPITOME OF THE PRESENT STATE OF THE UNION.

NEW-HAMPSHIRE,

WHICH is 180 miles in length, and 60 in breadth, contained, according to an enumeration in 1787, 102,000 inhabitants—is attached to the federal Government—engaged in organizing her militia, already the best disciplined of any in the Union—encouraging the domestick arts—and looking forward to the benefits which will result from the operations of the New Constitution. New-Hampshire, from her local advantages, and the hardihood of her sons, may anticipate essential benefits from the operation of equal commercial regulations.

MASSACHUSETTS,

450 miles in length, and 160 in breadth, contained, according to an enumeration in 1787, 360,000 inhabitants—Since the tranquility of the late insurrection, the whole body of the people appears solicitous for the blessings of peace and good government. If any conclusion can be drawn from elections for the Federal Legislature, this State has a decided majority in favour of the New Constitution. The great objects of Commerce, Agriculture, Manufactures, and the Fisheries, appear greatly to engage the attention of Massachusetts. Fabrication of Cotton, coarse Woolens, Linens, DUCK, IRON, Wood, &c. are prosecuting with success—and by diminishing her imports, and increasing her exports, she is advancing to that rank and importance in the Union which her extent of territory—her resources—and the genius and enterprise of her citizens entitle her to—and although the collision of parties, at the moment of Election, strikes out a few sparks of animosity, yet the decision once made, the " *Calumet of Peace* " is smoked in love and friendship—" *and like true Republicans they acquiesce in the choice of the Majority.*"

CONNECTICUT,

81 miles in length, and 57 in breadth, contained, agreeably to a Census in 1782, 209,150 inhabitants, enjoying a fertile soil, this truly republican State is pursuing her interest in the promotion of Manufactures, Commerce, Agriculture, and the Sciences—She appears to bid fair, from the peaceable, loyal, and federal Character of the great body of her citizens—from the Enterprise of her men of wealth, and other favourable circumstances, to attain to a great degree of opulence, power, and respectability in the Union.

NEW-YORK,

350 miles in length, and 300 in breadth, contained, agreeably to a Census in 1786, 238,897 inhabitants, This State appears to be convulsed by parties—but the CRISIS is at hand, when it is hoped, that the " *Hatchet* " will be buried. Exertions on one side are making for the re-election of Gov. CLINTON, and on the other for the introduction of the Hon. Judge YATES to the chair—both parties appear sanguine as to their success. It is ardently to be wished, that *temper* and *moderation* may preside at the Elections; and there can be no doubt of it, as that Freedom, for which we fought and triumphed, depends so essentially upon a FREE CHOICE.— It is greatly regretted, that this respectable and important member of the federal Republick, should not be represented in the Most Honourable Senate of the United States. New-York, however, is rising in her federal character, and in manufacturing, agricultural, and commercial consequence: Evidenced in her federal elections—her plans for promoting Manufactures, and the increase of her Exports.

NEW-JERSEY,

160 miles in length, and 52 in breadth, contained, by a Census in 1784, 149,435 inhabitants. This

tions are now permitted by law—and the city has been incorporated: Experience will determine the eligibility of the two latter transactions.

DELAWARE,

92 miles in length, and 16 in breadth, by a Census in 1787, contained 37,000 inhabitants. This State, though circumscribed in its limits, derives great importance from its rank in the Union—attached to the New Constitution, and having the honour to take the lead in its adoption, there is no doubt of its giving efficacy to its righteous administration.

MARYLAND,

134 miles in length, and 110 in breadth, by a Census taken in 1782, contained 253,630 inhabitants. From its favourable situation in the Union, this State bids fair for prosperity, wealth, and eminence. Warmly attached to the New Constitution, and enjoying a central situation, the publications there have teemed with tempting inducements to Congress, to make Baltimore the Seat of the Federal Legislature.

VIRGINIA,

758 miles in length, and 224 in breadth—by a census taken in 1782, contains 567,614 inhabitants. From the natural ardour of her sons in the cause of freedom, is frequently convulsed in her elections, and has been torn by factions—Possessing an extensive territory and a vast income, her funds are placed on a respectable footing; but as her representation in the federal legislature is decidedly attached to the union and the new constitution—there is now no doubt but that she will see her interest and glory finally connected with a few temporary sacrifices upon the principles of mutual concession.

SOUTH-CAROLINA,

200 miles in length, and 125 in breadth—and contains, by a census in 1787, 180,000 inhabitants, an important member of the union, has appeared lately to vibrate between opposing sentiments—Her attachment to *national* measures we doubt not will evidentally discover itself when all *tender Laws* and *pine barrens* shall be done away. The prohibition of the importation of slaves, and the provision lately made for the reduction of her foreign debt are federal traits—add to these that their electors have given an unanimous vote for his Excellency GENERAL WASHINGTON, as President of the United States—by which the memorable circumstance is authenticated, that the voice of the WHOLE CONTINENT has *once more* called our FABIUS MAXIMUS to rescue our country from impending ruin.

GEORGIA,

600 miles in length, and 250 in breath,—by a Census in 1787, contained 98,000 inhabitants. This state is compleating her federal character by conforming her state constitution to that of the union —and being the youngest branch of the family— and a frontier—she will doubtless experience the supporting and protecting arm of the federal government.

FOREIGN STATES.

RHODE-ISLAND,

Is 68 miles in length, and 40 in breath, and by a Census taken in 1783, contained 51,896 inhabitants. This state has again refused to accede to a union with her sister states, and is now wholly estranged from them; and from appearances, will long continue so, unless the measure of the iniquity of her "KNOW YE" gentry should be speedily filled up—or the delusion which has so long infatuated a majority of her citizens, should be removed.—Anxious of enjoying the protection of the union, the inhabitants of Newport, Providence and other places, are determined to sue for its protection, and to be annexed to Massachusetts

First number of the *Gazette of the United States*. It led off with an 'Epitome of the present state of the Union'; Rhode Island is treated as (technically) a foreign state.

Opposite In an early issue of the *New York Evening Post*, more than two columns of the front page are taken up by shipping notices, the rest by notices of goods for sale.

Among the most vigorous supporters of the Federalist cause was William Cobbett, who had first visited North America as a sergeant-major posted to Nova Scotia in the English army. He had returned to England to expose corruption and maltreatment of soldiers in the army and had then had to flee the country, taking with him his mastery of literary device and his biting humour to place them at the service of the American cause most nearly corresponding to English Toryism. His *Porcupine's Gazette and United States Advertiser*, started in 1797, continued until he lost all his capital in a libel action and was forced, after briefly attempting a further publishing adventure in New York, to return to London, where he played a major role in the political education of a new generation of working men with his *Political Register*.

Attacking the Federalists was a group of virulently scurrilous and argumentative journals, among them John Holt's *Independent Gazette or New York Journal Revived* (1783). Holt was one of the editors who returned from the revolutionary wars to re-found pre-existing papers; on his death the paper

Long after his satirical *Porcupine's Gazette* had failed and he had returned to England, William Cobbett could still be caricatured as the prickly porcupine.

was left in the hands of his wife, who continued to run it alone, as did a good number of printers' widows in the eighteenth century in all parts of Europe and America. The leading journal of the Republicans was the twice-weekly *National Gazette* edited by Philip Freneau, a Huguenot poet from Princeton (one of the main centres of anti-British sentiment) chosen by Jefferson, the Secretary of State, to work up political sentiment with the most powerful weapon available. Jefferson had to make two attempts to recruit Freneau, and after failing the first time wrote to a colleague explaining how he had meant to employ the writer: 'I should have given him the perusal of all my letters of foreign intelligence & all foreign newspapers; the publications of all proclamations & other public notices within my department & the printing of all laws. . . .' In the event he insisted that Freneau be left free to edit the *National Gazette* as he wished, even though Washington denounced the editor frequently at Cabinet meetings. Jefferson was laying the foundation-stone of an American newspaper system in which the purveyors of information functioned, as it were, *of* the government, often with the aid of

The Independent Gazette – virulently anti-Federalist.

SATURDAY, JANUARY 17, 1784.

THE
INDEPENDENT GA
OR THE
NEW-YORK JOURNAL

Published every THURSDAY and SATURDAY, at the PRINTING-OFFICE of JOHN
YORK, No. 47, Opposite the Upper Corner of the OLD-SLIP MARKET, HANOVER-SQU

To the PUBLIC.

ON the advice and request of many friends and customers, it is concluded to publish *The New-York Independent Gazette, or Journal revived*, twice a week, viz. every *Thursday* and *Saturday* morning, at 24s. a year.

Due care will be taken, to make the paper as useful and entertaining as circumstances will allow ; of which, it is hoped our readers will be assured, on recollection of the manner and principles on which, *The New-York Gazette*, formerly, and afterwards, *The New-York Journal*, were from the year 1763, many years conducted in this city, under the superintendency of the same Printer, who upon all occasions, and in the most dangerous times, asserted, and to the utmost of his ability, endeavoured to maintain the rights and freedom of his country :—And he had the satisfaction to find that his publications obtained general approbation, and had some considerable effect in kindling that noble flame that has glowed in the breast of his countrymen, raised them above their enemies and established their freedom on a permanent foundation.

The *public good*, was then the principal object of the Printer's pursuit—and it is still the same, tho' in different respects.

On the approach of the British invaders, he was obliged to retire into the country, leaving a considerable part of his effects a prey to the enemy, who likewise destroyed or plundered him (of most of the property he had saved from New-York) at Danbury, Kingston and Philadelphia.

He is lately returned to this city, in an exhausted state, from a more than seven years exile—and, though perhaps, not with equal abilities, yet with an unaltered disposition to the same object, the PUBLIC GOOD.

And as his own private interest is involved in that of the public, he hopes for that assistance from his former customers, and countrymen, that will enable him to do them service.

The gentlemen in the neighbouring States, and in this city, who will be so kind as to take in subscriptions for this paper, according to the terms proposed, shall for every dozen receive one paper gratis, with thanks, from their humble servant,
JOHN HOLT.
New-York, January 15, 1784.

NOTICE.

Peter Cantine, jun. } BY Order of the
Versus   } Honorable Rich-
Peter Van Alstyne. } ard Morris, Esquire,
Chief Justice of the Supreme Court of Ju-
dicature for the State of New-York; Notice

Samuel Franklin and Co.

*Have just imported in the Edward, Capt. Cou-
par, from London, an assortment of Goods,
consisting of the following articles ; which
they will sell on reasonable terms, for cash,
at No. 183, in Queen-street, viz.*

MOREENS—black, dark, and Saxon-blues, dark and Saxon-greens, pinks, crimson, London brown, claret, &c.
Callimancoes, 15 inches and half ell wide, all colours,
Durants, black, blue, green, white, pink, brown, and cloth, and drab colours,
Tammies, ditto, ditto, ditto,
Shalloons,
Everlastings, black,
Saminet Lastings, ditto,
Tabberets, black, blue, green, crimson, pink, brown, claret, &c.
Camblets, best boiled, dark brown and blue,
Corduret, Florentines, and Prunellas,
Wildboars, black, brown and mulberry,
Bed-Ticks, Flanders and British,
Dowlas, 3-4 and 7-8,
Buckrams, and brown Hollands,
Brown Quadruple Silesias,
Brown and white Russia Sheetings,
Ravens Duck,
Linen Handkerchiefs, printed, blue, red and white, plain and bordered,
Purple Callicoes,
Copperplate Furniture Callicoes, blue, red, and purple,
Printed Cottons,
India Callicoes, 3-4, yard and ell wide,
Muslins of various sorts and prices,
Cambricks and Lawns,
Cotton Romals,
Black Barcelona Handkerchiefs of all prices,
Cloth, and Changeable ditto,
Black Mode Squares,
Ditto half ell Modes,
Black Taffaties,
Sewing Silks of all colours.
Silk Twist, ditto.
Death Head and Basket Buttons,
Mens Worsted Hose, white, black, marbled, and grey, plain and ribb'd,
Womens ditto, white, black, and blue,
Womens Silk Mitts, black,
Ditto Worsted, ditto ditto,
Quality and Shoe Binding,
Garterings,
Writing Paper,
Blank Books, ruled, bound in Calf and Parchment,
Dilworth's Spelling Books,
Sealing Wax and Wafers,
Slates for school boys,
Tapes Bobbins, Threads, &c.

Lands for sa

ONE FARM, co
130 acres of land, situate
cinct of New-Marlborough, cou
ster, and State of New-York,
miles above Newburgh, two mile
Jugs-Creek landing, and one mi
meeting-houses ; and four mills
miles. The house is situated at
of four public roads, a most bea
for a trader or tradesman ; the
orchard of 100 trees, and is wel
and timbered, with a good frame
four rooms, three fire-places, an
a large frame barn, neatly finishe
out buildings, &c.

One other small farr
acres, on which is a snug frame
barn, and a good proportion cle
is about two miles west from the
scribed place, with fruit trees, an
on a public road.

One other farm, cor
300 acres, which has a log-house,
frame barn on it, with some m
plough land cleared ; the rest ne
a large quantity of swamp land to
is situate about 5 miles from Hud
on a very public road, and an exce
for business, 6 miles from the
places.

Two other farms, of
cres each, both joining each ot
some improvements, about two
the last mentioned place. Posses
be given, of this place, next Apr

One other lot of most
sent new land, containing 30
same precinct.

One other lot of 23
with some improvement, a fine s
subject to a certain lease ; there
saw-mill now on the stream in the
cinct, about 8 miles from Hudson

Another farm of 300
lying at the foot of Shawongunk
in the precinct of Mamacoting,
miles from Newburgh landing,
houses, and other buildings ; a co
quantity of cleared land, excellen
ing wheat.

Hard cash, good bills and bond
depreciation notes, Morris & Hill
Pickering's notes, or any other p
rities, as may be agreed on, will b
payment for said lands ; or will be
for one or two good sloops, or fo

public officials, but not *in* the government. Freneau's problem was to marshal political support from a group of voters who were scattered and unorganized, farmers and frontiersmen as well as small townspeople spread all over the country. In the custom of the time, he was furnished with a government job to eke out his salary and provided with much of his political news by Jefferson himself; the printing of congressional debates was the mainstay of the paper, which also opened its columns to its readers for contributions in verse or prose. The dogfight which ensued between Freneau and Fenno was one in which low accusation was mingled with histrionics. Freneau's desire was that the United States should respond to the call of Citizen Genet, representative of revolutionary France, to provide direct support to the government in Paris by damaging the interests of its enemy Britain. Supporting Freneau was the *General Advertiser* of Benjamin Franklin Bache (grandson of Franklin), which managed to publish a draft of the peace treaty between England and America, purloined from the locked desk of General Washington, as a way of opposing compromise with the hated British.

The Federalists, stung by the unrestrained nature of the attacks in the press, passed the Alien and Sedition Laws in 1798 with the scarcely concealed aim of curbing the Republicans, whose unceasing abuse had become a powerful force, even helping to drive Washington into early retirement. Under a thin pretence of restraining the activities of foreign interlopers and other deliberate attempts to subvert the new government, these laws brought about a situation which was compared by its victims to the Reign of Terror in Paris. Seven editors were convicted, fined and imprisoned, all of them anti-Federalists. Secretary of State Timothy Pickering personally read each Republican paper searching for possible grounds for indictment under the new laws. Within two years, however, the Alien and Sedition Acts had caused a backlash of opinion and a complete reversal of politics, with Jefferson himself elected President. It still took some years, however, for the United States to acquire the full range of journalistic freedoms; in 1805, for example, juries were first made responsible for deciding whether offending words constituted libel. Jefferson's policy was to make selective attacks on opposition newspapers through the use of State libel laws rather than attempt again the wholesale crippling of an opposition press.

When the American capital moved to Washington in 1800 a new set of papers sprang up, each tied to one of the main political factions in a pattern reminiscent of the London press. The new party conflict brought about a new journalistic professionalism. It was no longer sufficient for political essays to be written by articulate amateurs; instead a new type of editor, separate from the entrepreneur-printer, emerged to marshal political sentiment nationally. The parties contributed subsidies and when in government distributed postmasterships and other inducements.

The country had a population of three million at the time of the Revolution, and by 1830 it had grown fourfold, with a parallel flowering of advertising and vigorous competition between papers. American papers now had four or five columns to the page, and smaller type helped more material to be crowded in. Before the end of the war with Britain in 1815, daily and weekly excitements had brought the use of headlines ('Detroit is taken!').

The first Sunday paper appeared in 1809, modelled on the London *Observer*, which had started in 1791. Editors fought hard to be first with the foreign news, and special newsboats were constructed to sail up to a hundred miles out to sea to greet approaching ships and bear away their cargo of European newspapers. At the end of the war, the running time to England was reduced to three weeks, though it still took another six or seven before the news was disseminated, paper by paper, along track and river, throughout the United States.

What had happened throughout the European world and its overseas sphere of influence in the late eighteenth century was that the cause of press freedom had, for the first time, started to become a popular cause, especially among the newly urbanized groups of factory workers. When Louis XVI decided to recall the Estates-General he first took a series of soundings throughout his realm (the *cahiers de doléances* or bills of grievances) to ascertain the feelings of the various sectors of the country. The country districts turned out on the whole to be indifferent to the idea of press freedom conceived as a basic right; the towns were universally in support, as were the aristocracy and the third estate. When the Revolution came it was clear that the traditional restrictions were going to be lifted, and Article XI of the Declaration of the Rights of Man spoke of the free communication of thoughts and opinions as the most precious of human rights: everyone was to be able to speak, write and print freely, limited only by legal curbs on the abuse of such freedoms. But what were these controls to be? Under the old system of licensing an author had been safe once the censor had permitted him to publish; with a so-called 'free' press, an author could live in fear of reprisal from offended parties. Malesherbes, who had been the most efficient and understanding of the censors of the *ancien régime*, had proposed a mixed system, halfway to the English: an author could choose either to be censored and then enjoy legal immunity, or he could undergo, uncensored, the risks of prosecution. Others now thought that a sort of tribunal of writers should sit in judgment on all intended publications. A few thought that the English system of stamping the press would bring down circulations and constitute an adequate safeguard against material of an insurrectionary intention. Not until August 1792 did the Paris Commune succeed in agreeing a formula by which the concepts of sedition and libel were defined (ambiguously, as it turned out) and a system of control instituted. Complete press freedom, then, had existed in France for three years only, the duration of the debate.

The newspaper was the medium by which the revolutionary experience spread in the period following American independence. One can see a useful illustration in the example of the young French writer Jacques-Pierre Brissot, who was visiting America when he heard the news of the recalling of the Estates-General in 1789; he set off for home immediately and founded the *Patriote français*, which bore at its masthead the motto: 'A free newspaper is the forward sentinel of the people.' In 1780 Brissot had been in England and seen the agitational power of the press in the hands of the angry Irish; two years later, in Geneva, he had watched and reported as the brief independence of this tiny republic was crushed by the combined forces of its neighbours. After a brief spell in the Bastille for debt, he had gone to Holland and witnessed the patriotic uprising of 1785. In each case it was the press which had been the guardian of the revolutionaries, and a free press was among the things for which they had clamoured. The press was fused with the idea of revolutionary liberty for forty years.

Brissot's *Patriote français* was among the first of an extraordinary torrent of papers which circulated throughout France in the years of press freedom; up to one thousand publications are known to have existed, incorporating all the political tendencies which were to crop up in French politics for a century to come. The pamphlet also was an important form, and sometimes appeared in series, to the point at which it too became a kind of periodical publication. Mirabeau, who had translated Milton's *Areopagitica* into French, started his *Etats généraux* shortly before the fall of the Bastille, Louis Prudhomme started the extremely successful *Révolutions de France* and Jean-Paul Marat his *Ami du Peuple*. But royalist papers too were very active, including Antoine Rivarol's *Actes des Apôtres* (started by a group of twelve monarchists) and the Abbé Royou's *Ami du roi*, the organ of ultra-royalism.

This copy of Marat's *Ami du Peuple* is stained with his own blood, shed by the knife of Charlotte Corday.

(8)

la pétition de la gendarmerie nationale, (1)

Ces feuilles teintes du sang de Marat se trouvoient sur la tablette de sa baignoire lorsqu'il fut poignardé par Charlotte Corday. Mes yeux ont recueilli et conservées par sa sœur Albertine Marat qui a bien voulu me faire le sacrifice pour accroître ma collection de souvenirs patriotiques de l'époque.

Paris a 26 mai 1837.

No. 678.

L'AMI DU PEUPLE,

JOURNAL POLITIQUE ET IMPARTIAL,

Par J.-P. MARAT, auteur de l'Offrande à la patrie, du Moniteur, du Plan de Constitution, et de plusieurs autres ouvrages patriotiques.

Vitam impendere vero.

Du Mardi 13 Août 1792.

Le Peuple abusé par ses Représentans, ou les nouvelles trahisons des pères conscrits depuis la prise du château des Tuilleries.

Meanwhile the *Gazette de France* and the *Journal de Paris* continued in existence as official publications, chronicling the discussions of the assemblies while attacking revolutionary measures. The *Mercure de France* welcomed the declaration of freedom of the press but opposed the Revolution; its policy was to oppose all forms of excess. Another group of papers came into existence which concentrated simply on professionally compiled information: Panckoucke, in November 1789, started the *Moniteur universel*, which became the most important of these, accepting the *status quo* but opposing further dramatic social or political change while faithfully recording everything which was happening around it.

In Paris and the provinces newspapers modelled on these main groupings spread, multiplying monthly and weekly until Article 7 of the new Constitution of 1793 made clear that the right of free expression of thoughts and ideas no longer held. Press liberty was not compatible with external or internal warfare, and France was now subjected to both. The journalists of the previous three years were among the early victims of the Terror, Marat the first among them, assassinated by Charlotte Corday. With the fall of Robespierre a half-liberty returned briefly to the French press, but on 19 Fructidor in the Year V (6 September 1797), the day after an attempted royalist *coup d'état*, the whole of the French press was put under police control. Forty-four Paris papers were proscribed and their publishers, editors and writers deported, some to America. Thereafter the police received copies of all papers together with the names of all subscribers. A stamp tax, *à l'anglaise*, was imposed at the rate of 5 centimes per page, which effectively increased the price of many papers by two-thirds and drastically reduced the total print orders of all. The regulation was to last one year only but was extended, virtually illegally, beyond that date by the deportation of another large batch of journalists and the banning of a further dozen papers on the pretext of an intended *putsch*.

By the time of Napoleon's *coup* on 18 Brumaire (9 November), French press liberty was utterly destroyed. The Constitutions which created the Consulate and later the Empire both omitted to define a status for the newspaper, a task which was left to a series of ordinances concerned not so much to censor the press as to transform it into an instrument of direct propaganda. The Press Bureau was set up to supervise the nominations of all editors and publishers; Napoleon took direct control of the administrative apparatus. 'Tell the journalists', he wrote to the head of the Press Bureau, 'that I will not judge them for the wrong which they have done, but for the lack of good which they have done.' Month by month the freedoms of the French newspapers were sliced away; they were obliged finally to take their foreign news only from the official *Moniteur*. By 1810 only one newspaper was allowed in each *département*, and that only under the supervision of the prefect. In Paris four papers only were permitted, the *Moniteur*, the *Journal de l'Empire*, the *Gazette de France* and the *Journal de Paris*. The press had returned to the position of 1788, except that the head of state was not in possession of the property of all newspapers. Although the Paris Chief of Police kept a special censor for each remaining Paris paper, four *hommes surs*, Napoleon was still discontented with the results, constantly complaining to the police that the

A revolutionary committee under the Terror; freedom of the press rested in such hands as these.

press was lifeless, that it did not 'seek to do good'. In the whole of France the total number of newspaper subscriptions fell to 60,000 under the Empire. In all the constitutional discussions which followed the defeat of Napoleon, the crucial question which bedevilled and complicated the planning of the Restoration (and which was to be one of the reasons for the setting up of barricades again in 1830) was how to provide press freedom within the political conditions of France. The thought of the unbridled liberty which the press of France had seized in 1789 struck terror into the hearts of all who intended to govern her.

In October 1814, after much discussion which paralleled the debates of the Estates-General, a new law was passed which established preliminary censorship before a panel of distinguished literary and political men; it applied to all publications of less than twenty pages. Newspapers also required a form of prior authorization supervised by the Director-General of Police in Paris and by the prefects in the provinces. In Paris each newspaper had its own *commissaire*, who visited several times daily and could withdraw any article over the heads of editors; after a few months the *commissaires* were reassigned, in case they had started to fraternize too closely with their papers. None the less, within a brief time every major political group had at least one publication loyal to it, including the Bonapartists with their *Nain jaune*

('yellow dwarf'): the paper mocked the newly returned aristocrats, but some people believed that Louis XVIII himself contributed anonymous articles to it, just for fun.

Napoleon did more than stifle the press of France; he virtually extinguished journalism in a large number of conquered, client and simply frightened countries. In the conquered German provinces one paper was permitted in each region; all its important news had to be copied from the *Moniteur*, to which Napoleon himself contributed many of the major political articles. The states of the Rhineland, which after 1806 were in theory an independent federation, had no press freedom in practice. Their position, however, was better than that of their directly occupied neighbours, at least to the extent that they could use their own language. The occupied German states had papers only in French and English, including the titles: the *Hamburger Nachrichten* ('Hamburg news') was made to appear also under the title *Affiches, annonces et avis divers de Hambourg* ('notices and information from Hamburg'). Prussia and Austria remained unoccupied, and although the Viennese police were instructed to watch over all newspapers a certain amount of polemic and satire survived, even when Metternich became Chancellor in 1809. The *Wiener Zeitung* was virtually edited by the Chancellor himself, and all the provincial papers of Austria took their

When Napoleon stifled the French press, Gillray's cartoon made a characteristic comment on the tyrant's inability to extend his influence across the Channel.

91

political news from it. The *Oesterreichischer Beobachter*, the second paper of Vienna, functioning as a semi-official organ, was edited by Friedrich Schlegel, who tried to create through its agency some kind of public opinion.

In Prussia an English-style stamp tax was imposed, and after 1813 the censorship was loosened to allow for expression of long-pent-up anti-French hatred. The *Berliner Abendblatt* ('Berlin evening news'), edited by Heinrich von Kleist, who had already sailed close to the wind with satirical observations on the Napoleonic censorship, deliberately tried to court a popular readership with local reports drawn from the Berlin police headquarters. For a time it became fairly lively, but as the authorities closed in on it again Kleist tired of his charge and ceased publication.

The convulsions of France were echoed, imitated and reacted to throughout Europe. Commercial development in the eighteenth century had led to the creation in various countries of newspapers using English, French and German models, but the impetus behind the new wave of journalism was political and most of it was condemned to be blotted out at the moment of the Restoration. In Italy, for example, a clutch of daily papers came into being after the invasion in 1796, all under the influence of the *Moniteur*. The *Monitore Napolitano*, edited by the Countess Eleonore Fonseca Pimentel, benefited briefly from the atmosphere of new freedom, but in 1799 a fresh censorship arrived and in 1806 a Press Law created an 'Office of Press Freedom' which simply took over the old apparatus of censorship; gradually stamp taxes and licensing were added, and each Italian state was left with a single newspaper until the Risorgimento movement started up in mid-century, when 'literary' periodicals were circulated and political journals were edited in exile. In Spain José Napoleón took over an existing paper, renaming it the *Gaceta de Gobierno* ('government gazette') and making it into a daily. (There was already a commercial and information daily in existence, the *Diario de Madrid* of Manuel Ruiz de Urive y Compañia.) In southern Spain, unoccupied by the French, there developed a royalist opposition press, in particular the *Semanario Patriotice* ('patriotic weekly') of Isidor de Antillón which came out in Madrid, Seville, Cadiz and elsewhere. The Cortes in Cadiz in 1812 proclaimed a Constitution which provided a complete set of intellectual freedoms, only to have them abrogated with the return of Ferdinand VII from his French prison: a royal decree of April 1815 brought an end to all newspapers apart from the *Gaceta* and the *Diario*. Five years later an insurrection brought the Constitution back again; an enormous journalistic upsurge took place which lasted until the revolution was put down by the King in 1823 with the aid of French troops.

Further to the east the political upheavals had their reverberations in the press. Hungary had produced its first Hungarian-language paper in 1780, the *Magyar Hirnondo* ('Hungarian herald'), which produced a wave of patriotic imitations to compete with the older Latin papers, the only previous periodical publications. Vienna, determined to put down these anti-Habsburg strivings, imposed censorship, licensing and the closing down of reading-rooms, with subsidies to helpful papers and death penalties for offenders. In Poland the period between 1795 and 1814 was one of incessant political interference with the newspapers, which withered under pressure.

With the creation of the Congress of Poland in 1815 the press revived; in Vilna the *Kurjer Wilenski* ('Vilna courier') and the *Dziennik Wilenski* ('Vilna journal') were born, in addition to many literary papers which flourished for over a decade until the collapse of the rebellion of 1830–31, when the Polish press disappeared into exile all over Europe. In Belgium and Holland the press, which had been growing in the late eighteenth century, had been subjected to the Napoleonic press system based on the *Moniteur*. The creation in 1815 of the Kingdom of the United Netherlands brought an end to foreign domination of the press but gave little internal freedom.

Far away in Greece, a native press was struggling to be born. George Vendotis had started a paper in 1784, which had been quickly put out of business after Turkish objections; his brother Poulios had then attempted to continue publication from Vienna, but Metternich received representations from the Sublime Porte against the revolutionary tendencies of this publication and stopped it. However, a group of local internal papers started up in the second decade of the century: the *Ellinikos Telegraphos* ('Greek telegraph'), of 1811, the *Logios Hermes* ('intellectual messenger') of the same year and later the *Kalliope*, which established a Greek-language journalistic tradition, although the papers were, under Metternich's supervision, totally co-operative with the Turkish authorities. A Greek press was simultaneously emerging in exile; the *Athena* began in Paris in 1815, then the *Melissa* ('the bee'), while in London the *Mouseion* ('temple of the Muses') started in 1809 and the *Iris* in 1820. They prepared the way for the Philhellenic movement which sprang up later in the century.

Across the Mediterranean, Napoleon's expeditions had introduced the first newspapers to Egypt – the *Courrier de l'Egypte*, for instance, was founded originally by and for French soldiers – but when the French finally departed they took their printing-press with them and Egyptian journalism remained merely a memory, although plans were made from time to time to start an Arabic paper. In 1822 the Viceroy Muhammad Ali himself became the founder and editor of the *Journal du Khédive*, which appeared in French and Arabic with a circulation of 100 copies in each language; it offered its readers official bulletins plus extracts from *The Thousand and One Nights*, and it soon acquired a counterpart in Turkish and helped to spur the movements for language reform and Europeanization.

One of the few countries where the press acquired any lasting advantage from Napoleon's activities was Switzerland, where an inter-cantonal censorship system had been in operation since 1767: each canton tried to repress criticism of the authorities elsewhere in exchange for similar services. With the Helvetic Republic in 1798 came the granting of press freedoms, and the character of the existing newspapers changed rapidly from commercial to political. Many of the earlier creations, including the *Neue Zuerche Zeitung* (1780), the *Feuille d'Avis de Lausanne* (1762) and the *Thurgauer Zeitung* (1798) still exist today, as do many of the papers founded in the era of freedom. There was a period between 1803 and 1813 when the new press activity seemed to have been extinguished under the impact of Napoleon's taxation and censorship, but after 1813 a troubled freedom returned which was progressively strengthened throughout the rest of the century.

'Mealtime of politicians, or the newspaper-eater', an anonymous French cartoon of 1815. By that time, reading-rooms were proliferating, and inns and coffee-houses offered their customers a wide selection of newspapers.

It remains for us to look back at the development of the press in the country whose newspapers attracted the most admiration and puzzlement in the pre-1815 period. England had become the most powerful country in the world, despite the loss of America, but suffered difficult domestic and social problems. Political power was passing finally away from the aristocratic territorial oligarchy which had dominated since the Revolution of 1688, and a new press came into being to serve the interests of the growing class drawing its income from manufacture. The newspaper entered the same phase of technical development as the other mechanical industries for whose owners and managers it provided information. Friedrich Koenig came over from Saxony to settle in England because he saw it as a country which would more quickly adopt his ideas for transforming the techniques of printing. He made a number of models of a press which dispensed with the platen and used cylinders to pick up the paper and ink; before the Napoleonic Wars were over *The Times* – in all its eight pages – was being printed on one of his machines, to which a steam-engine had been added.

In 1783 there had been one newspaper for every 300 inhabitants of the British Isles. By 1820 the country was thick with newspaper reading-rooms taking up to four score papers each. John Doherty, the radical reformer, ran a 'Coffee and Newsroom' in Manchester which opened at six in the morning and remained open until late at night, with 'the most able and popular publications of the day, whether political, literary or scientific, in a comfortable and genteel apartment, in the evening brilliantly lit with gas'. The ale-houses took in newspapers to attract customers where an eighteenth-century inn would have charged for the right to read them. The reductions in the newspaper taxes in the late 1830s brought prices down and increased potential circulations considerably; until then paper, advertisements and newspapers themselves were all heavily taxed, the paper itself at threepence halfpenny per sheet (i.e. four pages). The number of readers, therefore, far exceeded the number of purchasers: in 1798 the *Anti-Jacobin* had 2,500 subscribers but claimed a readership of between 17,500 and 50,000.

The press was a more active instrument of propaganda than the platform until the Corn Law agitation of the 1840s, but much of the agitational literature had to circulate illegally and unstamped. William Cobbett was among the first to exploit the medium of print to build up a radical mass public opinion dedicated to dismantling the oligarchic political apparatus surviving from the previous century; he attacked the administration's sinecurists and pensioners until the very words seem to rot in the air. The government made tremendous efforts to counter Cobbett's propaganda, especially in the period after 1816 when an attempt at revolution was thought to be imminent and the *Political Register*, at twopence, was selling 40,000–50,000 copies a week – much more than all the rest of the normal newspapers put together – even though it was banned from the postal services. It was sold for the most part by its readers, who could acquire a hundred copies for twelve shillings and sixpence, or eleven shillings if taken regularly. (When in 1827 Cobbett succumbed to the stamp and became legal at sixpence a copy, his circulation dropped to 400 a week.)

The French Revolution had had the effect of magnifying the cause of liberty, supported by much of the middle class in the days of John Wilkes, into a struggle from which this class was separated. There was in the early nineteenth century a common defence by the propertied against attacks by the unpropertied classes, and this caused an apparent break in the radical tradition and in the evolution of the radical press. Lord Grenville was among those who thought that the press was creating a revolutionary frenzy among the lower orders: 'The seditious writers of the present day, who deluge the country . . . with their wicked and blasphemous productions, do not make it a question of by whom the government is to be administered, but whether government should exist at all.' As long as the stamp taxes remained, the newspapers of the working class tended to be illegal affairs, surreptitiously printed by sympathetic pseudonymous printers and clandestinely circulated. This section of the press was, therefore, almost totally cut off from the libertarian parliamentary tradition. It was none the less a professional press containing news and entertainment material; it still had to balance its budget through its circulation. It struggled against middle-class material designed to

THE MAN WOTS GOT THE WHIP HAND OF
'EM ALL

reach the same working-class readership, in particular the influential *Penny Magazine*. The unstamped press had to find its own army of street vendors and arm them morally as well as financially for the difficult lives they had to lead. The bulk of the prosecutions were brought not by government, however, but by a group of voluntary prosecuting societies which the radical press hoped to wear down by sheer persistence.

Yet these papers provided good service. Richard Carlile reported the Peterloo massacre for the radical *Sherwin's Political Register* (its title later changed to *The Republican*), and his account of the good discipline of the meeting served to alarm the Home Office even further and to land the reporter in prison. After Peterloo a large crop of new twopenny papers appeared, and the radical *Manchester Observer* could rival five other Manchester weekly papers, though it was later crushed by competition from the new *Manchester Guardian* (started by a group of cotton-manufacturers) and worn down by prosecutions and official harassment. The most important of the unstamped radical papers of the period up to 1835, Hetherington's *Poor Man's Guardian*, the *Destructive* and the *Gauntlet*, all served as instruments of education, repeating the arguments for the great new radical causes in a didactic style: the working-class reader was instructed in his own political economy and his own constitutional arguments, systematically trained to reject the ideas emanating from the prevailing social order. Political radicalism, trade unionism, co-operation and administrative reform were grouped together into a cohesive set of causes under which the illegal press survived its harassments, including the fourth of the Six Acts of 1819 which had redefined the term 'newspaper' and imposed a new tax of fourpence on all publications sold at less than sixpence.

The eighteenth-century newspaper had been synonymous with political bribery and journalistic scurrility. It had become normal for editors to charge 'insertion and contradiction fees', a polite euphemism for a system by which anyone could print attacks on his enemies at the price of an advertisement, and his enemy then pay the editor for the chance to return them in kind. Even John Walter I, the founder in 1785 of the *Daily Universal Register* (later *The Times*), made money by this means. Samuel Foote, in his farce *The Knight* (1793), which centres on the affairs of a newspaper-obsessed country politician, Sir Gregory Gazette, has a character say: 'Oh, if you are inclin'd to blacken, by a couple of lines, the reputations of a neighbour whose character neither your nor his whole life can possibly restore; you may do it for two shillings in one paper: or if you are displaced or disappointed of a place, a triplet against the ministry will be always well received at the head of another.'

Despite the unsavoury milieu in which the late-eighteenth-century press was conducted, important advances were made in the techniques of journalism and in the production of newspapers. Until this time there had been no system of reporting speeches and debates apart from private systems of shorthand which were not transferable from person to person. William Woodfall, owner and editor of the *Morning Chronicle*, became one of the most famous figures in Parliament because of his much-publicized facility for remembering debates and recording them in his paper; he started operating in

Opposite A somewhat euphoric symbolization (1829) of the power of a free press. Even the great Duke of Wellington can be sent flying (top right). The machine represented is clearly a 'Stanhope'.

A FREE BORN ENGLISHMAN!
THE ADMIRATION of the WORLD!!!
AND THE ENVY of SURROUNDING NATIONS!!!!!!

The passing of the Six Acts in 1819 inspired this sardonic view of the free-born Englishman. There were to be heavier penalties for seditious libel, and increased taxes on newspapers.

the days before it was legal even to take notes in the Commons, and he would sit for twelve hours at a time, pausing only to crack a hard-boiled egg into his hat to supply himself with surreptitious refreshment, and then return to his office at midnight to transcribe the entire proceedings. To his contemporaries it seemed a miraculous feat, although in practice his reports were little more than rough summaries of arguments advanced by Members. He gave up his paper in 1789 when James Perry succeeded in reorganizing the *Gazetteer* into an effective and profitable rival journal and undermined Woodfall's great gift by bringing in a new system of reporting debates: he employed young barristers to take notes in relays, half an hour at a time. Woodfall's paper

John Walter I, founding father of the *Great Universal Register* which later became
The Times.

collapsed and Perry took it over, turning the *Morning Chronicle* into an important instrument of impartial political reporting which survived until a bad investment in 1882; indeed, it rivalled *The Times* itself in quality of reporting until the 1820s. Perry refused to take insertion and correction fees; he refused to accept free theatre tickets in exchange for printing puffs. ('It will be essentially better', he wrote to one theatre manager, 'for both of us to put an end to this pitiful arrangement, and resolve in future to pay for admission to each other's premises.') Lord Derby defended Perry in 1798 against a charge of breach of privilege and argued a powerful case for the superiority of Perry's methods; the *Morning Chronicle*, he said, was 'distinguished by its regard to the decencies of private life, by its disdain of all scandal on individuals and those licentious personalities by which the peace of families was disturbed'. Perry helped to make journalism respectable among politicians as well as necessary to them; he even once invited the Duke of Sussex to dine with him. William Jerdan, the editor of the *Sun*, a government organ, was another journalist frequently summoned to dine with members of the Cabinet. Editors were still far from enjoying the status they were to achieve in the mid-century when, for example, Peter Borthwick of the *Morning Post* could boast of being known to every single member of the government. None the less, the general social level of journalists was rising steadily: of the twenty-three reporters working in Parliament in 1810, no fewer than eighteen had university degrees. The *Edinburgh Review* in 1816 spoke of the 'superior talents, judgment and character of the proprietors, and the improved advantages and better condition in every respect, of the gentlemen employed under them'.

John Walter II succeeded to the management of *The Times* in 1803 as 'joint proprietor and exclusive manager'. He was saddled with the results of a curious and complicated will made by his father which distributed the ownership around various branches of the family, producing problems which lasted for a century. John Walter I had disapproved of the way in which his son wanted to make *The Times* rather than the printing business the main activity of the firm; he also disliked his son's increasing resistance to official pressure. In both respects the younger man seemed to be indulging in risky and wayward self-indulgence. The son, however, produced a better written and better informed paper, and battled successfully against the Post Office's expensive monopoly of the right to translate foreign newspapers during the passage across from the Continent to England, for which service the English newspapers had to pay one hundred guineas a year. He successfully outwitted the government's efforts to intercept mail from his network of foreign correspondents and contacts. In 1807 the Post Office boarded ships arriving at Gravesend and seized all mail addressed to *The Times*: Walter published a detailed account of the marauding practices of these officials, and no further interference took place. The new manager took every opportunity which offered in news coverage, advertisement practice and technical improvement until *The Times* acquired a circulation larger than that of all its competitors combined, an advantage which it retained until the *Daily Telegraph* arrived as the first penny paper in the 1850s.

Walter's father had started the paper to demonstrate a new system of

Yours ever

W Jerdan

THE EDITOR OF THE LITERARY GAZETTE.

William Jerdan, editor of the *Sun* and confidant of cabinet ministers.

printing called logography, in which familiar groups of letters and whole words were soldered together in order to speed up the process of composition. The new paper saw its way ahead – despite the imprisonment of its sole owner for two years for seditious libel on two of the royal dukes – as an organ of the new middle and commercial classes.

It would seem that every Newspaper published in London is calculated for a particular set of readers only. . . . A News-Paper, conducted on the true and natural principles of such a publication, ought to be the Register of the times, and faithful recorder of every species of intelligence . . . the great object . . . will be to facilitate the *commercial* intercourse between the different parts of the community, through the channel of *Advertisements*; to record the principal occurrences of the times; and to abridge the account of debates during the sitting of Parliament.

The 'Thunderer', marshal of the middle classes.

Opposite One cartoonist's view of the supposed power of *The Times* over its readers.

Under John Walter II *The Times* helped journalism for the first time to rely upon itself; no longer did any Ministry hope to manipulate its material, no longer did the Treasury dole out cash, and all continuing attempts by the Post Office to control incoming news were defeated by ingenious and often expensive counter-measures. By 1823 William Hazlitt, an ex-employee of the paper, could write in the *Edinburgh Review* that *The Times* was

the greatest engine of temporary opinion in the world. . . . It is the witness of the British metropolis; the mouthpiece, oracle and echo of the Stock Exchange, the origin of the mercantile interest. . . . It takes up no falling causes; fights no uphill battle; advocates no great principle. . . . It is 'ever strong upon the stronger side'.

Hazlitt identified accurately, but disliked, the one great innovation which *The Times* brought into the relationship between newspapers and readers: its leadership of a clearly delineated demographic block. *The Times* took its position just behind the front line of the middle class, and this became the customary seat from which the political engine of the nineteenth-century paper was driven. It tried to marshal its readers, not goad them. The newspaper during the era of revolution had ceased to be the simple handmaiden of parliamentary faction and taken on the more mature role of independent actor in the political world. The solid pressure of radical public opinion which brought about the great Reform of 1832 was trained over decades by the press to pit itself against the will of a reluctant legislature.

JOHN BULL,

or

THE MAN WOT IS EASILY LED BY THE NOSE.

Published by Tho.ˢ Mᶜ Lean 26 Haymarket 10ᵗʰ Sep 1830.

5

'La Presse est Libre...'
1815–1880

In 1815 press freedom in Europe was an idea, a dream, an experiment, a fearful dread; by 1881 it had become an enduring institution, its most admired text enshrined in the French Press Law passed in July of that year. In 1881 also Britain abolished the obligatory depositing of cash by newspaper publishers which had survived from the hated Six Acts of 1819, and passed a new Libel Act which freed publishers from the fear of prosecution for criminal libel. In the 1820s it was exceptional for newspaper publishers in any country to behave like ordinary industrial entrepreneurs; everywhere they were crippled by police inspection, perversely extensive libel laws, complicated catch-all clauses listing endless 'press offences'. By the 1880s it was exceptional for such systems to survive. The newspaper had been brought inside the industrial framework; the editor had become the linchpin of all party political activity; and the readers had been drawn into the vastly expanded role of the newspaper, which aroused them to political action, helped them in their businesses, taught them the arts of urban life or just entertained them.

It was also in the course of these six decades that many countries established the basic pattern of the press which has survived into the late twentieth century. One may take the example of a small country like Norway. In 1814 its new Constitution proclaimed the freedom of the press, rather reduced in practice because of administrative interference and a low level of literacy, but by 1870 there were eighty newspapers, largely built round the political rivalries of the liberal Venstre Party, with papers like the *Norske Intelligenz-Seddeler*, and the conservative Høyre Party, with its *Constitutionelle*. Town by town these parties had set up their presses, the latter dominating in the capital and the east and the former in the south and the west. In the 1880s a series of socialist papers arrived, and a generation later the Centre Party added the final journalistic stratum. The country became divided into a hundred or so separate 'markets' for newspapers, and to this day the typical Norwegian town has three competing papers, each making its play for a fundamentally political audience. Newspaper founders like Christian Schibsted, whose *Aftenposten* ('evening post') was started in 1860, were mainly in the business of politics. Circulations were not large enough to be the main motive of a publisher: an annual subscription cost as much as a workman earned in a week, and advertising was in its infancy.

One may also look at a less unified country like Italy, where regional, political, commercial and religious papers built themselves up round small client groups until, towards the end of the century, publishers tried to synthesize these specialist publications into larger papers catering for a range

Opposite Eight-feeder vertical machine by Applegath and Cowper, used for printing *The Times*. It could turn out 5,000 copies an hour.

of tastes with a broader spectrum of material. In the press repression which followed the Napoleonic era, each of the Italian states had had one paper only, and the case for unification was put in the freer, 'literary' papers such as *Il Conciliatore*, started by Silvio Pellico in Milan in 1818. Giuseppe Mazzini edited the *Indicatore Genovese* a decade later and then, in exile, started his *Giovine Italia* ('Young Italy') which, with other exile papers, was distributed illegally inside Italy. However, in the climactic year of 1848 a number of Italian states passed liberal press laws and a new generation of political papers sprang up, encouraged by Cavour (who had started *Il Risorgimento* in Turin in 1847) as part of his campaign for unification under the House of Savoy. The new Constitution of 1848 established a typical new-style set of press regulations: first a 'guarantee' of freedom, second police registration by newspaper publishers, third the promulgation of a set of 'press offences' for which the latter could be prosecuted, and finally an apparatus for preventive censorship through official scrutiny. Side by side with the propaganda papers supporting Cavour there grew up a Catholic press of a political nature, including the *Unità Cattolica* of Turin, founded in 1863, and *L'Osservatore Cattolica* of Milan, started a year later. Each new political group laid down a new stratum of papers: the democrats' most important journal was *Il Secolo* ('the century') of Milan (1866), while the left democrats founded *Il Popolo Romano* in the 1870s and the liberals started *La Stampa* – foremost among many liberal papers – in Turin in 1886 under the original title of *Gazzetta Piemontese*. The socialists too were active from the 1860s, with *Il Giornale degli Operai* ('workers' journal') in Genoa, *Libertà e Giustizia* in Naples and, nearer the end of the century, *Avanti!*, which appeared as a Rome paper and was edited for a time in 1914 by Mussolini himself.

Everywhere in Europe and America the mechanical and organizational basis was being laid for the popular newspaper of the twentieth century. A much greater range of forms was developing than had ever been known before – Sundays, evenings, regional and local editions, financial papers, women's papers – aided by a proliferation of experiments with new techniques and new methods of organizing the flow of material through private telegraphs, news agencies, syndication, serialization of fiction. The French Revolution, though its journalistic freedoms had been virtually obliterated by 1820, had provided a lasting comprehension of the *point* of a free press, showing that the newspaper could behave as an instrument of power, not of a faction but of a party, and attempt to mobolize a segment of society.

There were other changes outside politics which had a direct effect on the development of newspapers. Millions of new consumers were being brought inside a manufacturing economy. By 1850 three million American children were attending primary schools, creating a vast new potential audience for cheap newspapers. And, the newspapers could now reach them. Post offices were multiplying, and an American law of 1852 allowed postage to be prepaid on newspapers, at one cent within the State. Property restrictions on the right to vote were being gradually reduced or eliminated in many countries, increasing the demand for political material. In 1830 the kerosene lamp was invented – perhaps the most potent new influence of all – which meant that the reader had access to printed material during the hours of

Opposite First issue of Cavour's daily, *Il Risorgimento* (Resurgence).

Anno I.   **Torino, 15 Dicembre 1847.**   **N° 1.**

IL
RISORGIMENTO

GIORNALE QUOTIDIANO
POLITICO, ECONOMICO, SCIENTIFICO E LETTERARIO

PATTI DELL'ASSOCIAZIONE
DA PAGARSI ANTICIPATAMENTE

	Annata	Sem.	Trim.	Mese
Torino . . . . . . Franchi.	40	22	12	6
Stati Sardi, franco al luogo. .	44	24	13	6 50
Altri Stati Italiani ed estero franco ai confini. .	50	27	14 50	—
Un sol numero, cent. 40

Mercoledì

LE ASSOCIAZIONI SI RICEVONO

dagli Editori Cotta e Pateno, dalla Minerva Subalpina, ed in Provincia agli uffizi postali. La distribuzione nella Capitale avrà luogo a domicilio per gli Associati che ne facciano la domanda alla Tip. Editrice. Le lettere saranno inviate franche alla Direzione del Giornale IL RISORGIMENTO. L'Ufizio del Giornale starà aperto dalle 10 antimerid. alle 2 pomerid.

Prezzo delle inserzioni: — Centesimi 15 per riga.

PROGRAMMA

Molte volte tra i lunghi secoli delle nostre miserie, si sognò di risorgimenti d'Italia. Il menomo raggio par gran luce tra le tenebre. Talora una nuova combinazione politica, o una guerra, o una pace, o un trattato avvenuti in Italia od anche fuori; talora il salir al trono d'un buon principe, o il nascer d'un fanciullo che si profetava buono; talora, che fu il più vergognoso, l'entrare di nuovi stranieri nella patria nostra; e talor anche, il buon gusto o il vigore rinascente nelle nostre lettere, tutto servì, tutto bastò a sperare ed annunziare risorgimenti all'Italia. La quale non volle, nè poteva, risorger così.

Ora poi, novissimamente, dall'Alpi al mar d'Africa, pur si spera, si grida, RISORGIMENTO D'ITALIA! Sarà egli un inganno anche questo? Vediamone i fatti duci, i caratteri principali.

Il primo fatto politico, a cui si possa far risalire il RISORGIMENTO presente non è antico che di 18 mesi; è quello del re nostro, di Carlo Alberto, nel maggio 1846. Fu, doveva essere necessariamente un fatto d'indipendenza. E i risultati immediati furono due: 1° instaurar l'INDIPENDENZA, dimostrando che si poteva essere indipendenti, dando anima a diventar tali tutti: — 2° instaurar ne' fatti quell'UNIONE tra principi e popoli, tra governanti e governati, che non era guari allora instaurata se non in alcuni scritti, dal Primato di Gioberti in qua.

Il fatto più grande poi, il più fecondo, il più meraviglioso, e quasi miracoloso o soprannaturale, seguì dappresso in giugno del medesimo anno. Fu l'elezione di Pio IX, seguita fra un altro mese dall'amnistia; e quindi via via rapidamente ed uniformemente, dalle concessioni d'un governo consultativo, di una larghezza o poco men che libertà giusta di stampa, di una guardia civica, e di altre riforme minori. E i risultati furono immensi: furono portar in pochi mesi i Pontificii dal fondo alla cima de' popoli italiani; stabilir a un tratto indissolubile cola l'unione tra principe e popolo; instaurar la sola via a ciò, la sola buona a tutto, la sola di fuggic la cattiva via delle rivoluzioni, la via che è diventata via italiana, LA VIA DELLE RIFORME. — E, venuta in breve l'occasione di rivendicar l'indipendenza propria e d'Italia in quella via, Pio IX ve la rivendicò; e vi si tien forte, grande e progrediente, e così applaudito da tutta Europa, da tutto il mondo civile.

Il Gran Duca ebbe in sul principio del 1847 il merito, l'onore, la gloria d'acceder primo alla via delle riforme di Pio IX; ed esso e Carlo Alberto accedettero, dieder forza alla difesa fattane da Pio IX.

E pochi giorni fa, addì 29 ottobre, Carlo Alberto accedè premeditatamente, d'un tratto, grandemente, alla nuova via, v'oltrepassò in alcuni punti i predecessori; e donò così definitivamente al Risorgimento Italiano la propria spada, un esercito di 100 mila Italiani, e un popolo di quattro milioni e più.

E i tre principii hanno, al 3 novembre, sancita l'indipendenza, sancita l'unione tra principi e principi riformatori, tra principi riformatori e popoli riformati; sancita la via delle riforme, sancito in tutto il Risorgimento, con una LEGA alla quale invitano gli altri principi italiani. Evidentemente il Risorgimento così condotto e sancito, non somiglia a nessun altro sperato od annunziato in Italia, dalla fine del secolo XII in qua.

E i popoli? o piuttosto (perchè uno apparisce l'impulso, una la volontà, uno l'animo) il popolo italiano che fece a tal risorgimento? Il popolo italiano s'è alzato come un uomo; ma non a rivoluzioni, anzi a riforme; non ad ostilità, anzi ad unione co' principi suoi; non ad eccessive pretese popolari, non a gare provinciali, a fazioni, a violenze; anzi ad una FORTE ED ORDINATA MODERAZIONE ne' fatti, nelle parole e nelle opinioni; la quale se non è senza eccezioni perfetta (come niuna cosa quaggiù), è tale almeno che non se ne trova esempio, nè nei secoli oscuri nostri od altrui, che è naturale; nè in questo stesso secolo progredito, che fur forse inaspettato. Oh! diciamolo arditi, e sicuri di non piaggiare nemmeno il popolo: anche nell'opera del popolo italiano, il Risorgimento presente non somiglia a nessun altro sperato da sei secoli e mezzo in qua.

Dunque, e ne' fatti de' principii, e ne' fatti del popolo, il Risorgimento italiano è certo, è grande, è santo, è sancito oramai. — Dio lo vuole, Dio lo vuole; Dio ce lo diede, guai a chi lo tocchi.

Dunque ancora: I. Indipendenza; II. Unione tra principi e popoli; III. Progresso nella via delle riforme; IV. Lega de' principi italiani tra sè; V. Forte ed ordinata moderazione: questi sono i fatti duci, i caratteri innegabili, e innegabilmente buoni del nuovo Risorgimento italiano. Manteniamoli e svolgiamoli: ecco il dovere di tutti oramai.

Ed a mantenerli, e svolgerli per la parte loro, i sottoscritti, uniti con alcuni amici, hanno fondato il presente giornale: ecco tutto il loro programma.

Del quale sono conseguenze minori e naturali: non far nè a principi, nè a popoli quelle adulazioni che guastano, che sviano, che impediscono gli uni e gli altri, più assai che non faccia qualunque opposizione; — non far nè a principi, nè a popoli niuna opposizione sistematica, niuna, se ci regga Iddio, appassionata, nè ingiusta; non lasciarci imporre, nemmeno in nome dell' unione, nè il silenzio, nè anche meno niuna cessione delle opinioni nostre; chè l'unione non è identità, ma cooperazione; — e quindi, dar mano senza invidia a' consenzienti,

spiegarci senza puntigli ed amor proprii co' dissenzienti men discosti; combattere i più lontani senza ire, senza rancori, senza ingiurie, colla speranza di ricondurli a noi un dì o l'altro, colla promessa qui anticipata, di accoglierli fra noi, sempre, a qualunque dì. — Fu già nella vecchia e stretta politica il principio: di partarsi sempre con gli amici, prevedendo il dì che si diventerebbe nemici. Noi prendiamo il principio diametralmente opposto: di portarci con gli avversari ed anche nemici, prevedendo, desiderando ed affrettando il dì di diventar amici.

CESARE BALBO.

SARDEGNA E SICILIA

Il moto politico che vivifica a poco a poco tutta l'Italia continentale, è passato nelle nostre isole. Sardegna e Sicilia, ricche tutte due d'antiche memorie, d'antiche libertà, e di popoli, non comparativamente numerosi, ma arditi e desiderosi di tutte le civiltà, si son mossi quasi contemporaneamente negli ultimi giorni di novembre. Tutti i popoli isolani, e tanto più quelli meridionali, seglono recare ne' fatti loro una vivacità, una peculiarità, un amore provinciale naturalissimo. I isolati dalla natura, s'isolano facilmente in politica. Ma noi lo diremo subito e francamente, in questa identità, in questa universalità politica che si svolge così felicemente in Italia, ogni isolamento politico è par pericolo, anzi danno grave. — Veggiamo i fatti sommari; perciocchè i particolari, nè ci sono noti esattamente, nè importano essenzialmente.

Quando giunsero in Cagliari e Sassari le notizie delle riforme pubblicate addì 29 ottobre in Torino, que' popoli si destarono alle speranze, comprese in quella pubblicazione e forse in altre notizie particolari, che la Sardegna parteciperebbe alle riforme, e sarebbe unita compiutamente agli Stati continentali di S. M. Tuttavia, non essendo ciò detto esplicitamente, in pochi dubitarono; e, fosse effetto di titubanza o di compressione governativa, ad ogni modo non vi furono dapprima nè feste, nè dimostrazioni. Queste scoppiarono solamente (non sappiamo qual giorno in Sassari) addì 19 novembre in Cagliari.

Principiarono dalla gioventù, dagli studenti dell'Università; e colla grida savie, felici, italianissime di viva il Re, viva Carlo Alberto, viva Pio IX, viva l'Unione. Vi si aggiunsero in brev'ora popolo, magistrati, clero, arcivescovo e viceré. Continuarono ne' giorni 20, 21, 22, 23 e 24, sempre unanimi; ed all'ultimo di quei dì fu imbarcata una deputazione di dieci membri principali dei tre principali ordini ecclesiastico, militare (cioè nobile), e reale (cioè popolano), degli antichi stamenti (cioè parlamento) di Sardegna. Tutti questi ebber carico di portare a Genova ai piedi del Re, il voto unanime, pronunciatissimo, chiaro: che la Sardegna fosse, secondo le speranze già date dal Re, assimilata in tutto, e uso col rimanente degli Stati. E quando si considera, che in questo voto era implicata la rinunzia di quel popolo, di tutte le classi di quel popolo, dei membri più interessati in quelle

leisure. The theatre was spreading in the new cities, and seat prices were dropping dramatically, widening the public for comment and criticism. Above all, cities were growing, cities which created news as well as provided audiences for it: there were fires, rapes, crimes, corruption, insurrection, all ready to become the raw material of the press. A huge social space exists within the city: suburbs and neighbourhoods develop which are utterly unconnected except through administration and the spread of information.

With the introduction in 1820 of the new paper-making process developed by Henry and Sealy Fourdrinier, paper dropped in price by a quarter; by 1860 newspapers were being produced from rolls of paper instead of single stamped sheets, and this was an important element in the great economies of scale which were to bring prices down to one penny (or one cent or one sou). Four thousand copies were run off without stopping from rolls of paper $3\frac{1}{2}$ miles in length. Chlorine had been used for bleaching from the turn of the century, making it possible for coloured rags to be used in the manufacture of paper, but shortages resulted from the expansion of the press, and gradually cotton came to be added to cheaper paper. Indeed, one enterprising English publisher printed his whole newspaper on pure cotton, thus evading the Stamp Act, which referred specifically to 'paper'. In 1772 a German experimenter had discovered that paper could be made from seventy-two known substances, but not until the American Civil War cut off supplies of cotton during a particularly severe shortage of rags did European presses start a serious search for a new method of producing newsprint. In 1865 the cost of paper went up to 30 cents a pound; England had already abolished the duty on paper of a penny-halfpenny per pound as a result of the final bout of the campaign against newspaper taxation ('the taxes on knowledge'), but it was still very difficult to keep paper down to a price which would guarantee a cheap newspaper industry. First esparto grass, then wood pulp replaced rags as the raw material of paper in the course of the 1860s and 1870s; in the 1860s America alone saw the foundation of 5,429 new journals. (Between 1850 and 1870 newspaper circulation in America increased by 250 per cent.) By 1880 paper in America had come down again to 5 cents a pound, and newspapers could get bulk discounts. In England the halfpenny paper was in sight at last.

Advances in printing during this period paralleled those in paper-making. In 1820 the Koenig press was producing 1,000 copies per hour; seven years later the New Press of Applegath and Cowper quintupled that figure, enabling *The Times* to be printed in its entirety from a single machine, where previously rows of Stanhope presses had been employed. The new machines were exported to various countries, including France. Circulations were much larger in Paris at that time than in London: the *Journal des Débats* printed 15,000 a day in 1825 to *The Times*'s 10,000. The French engineer Gaveaux in 1831 constructed a two-cylinder version of the press which handled the paper more easily and increased production further. The American Richard Hoe's revolving press of 1840 turned out 20,000 impressions per hour, as compared with the Napier double-cylinder press which American papers had bought in the 1830s to get their circulations up to 4,000. In 1846 Hoe developed the first version of the rotary press and sold it to the Paris paper *La Patrie*: he found a way to fit the type itself round the cylinder, which was then inked by automatic rollers, while four smaller cylinders brought the sheets of paper into contact with it. More cylinders were added later, until on the eve of the Civil War 20,000 newspapers per hour could be produced. In 1863 William Bullock perfected a method by which the paper was fed into the machine continuously instead of in sheets; the English Walter press, which used this 'web perfecting' process, was widely used in America after the Civil War.

Bullock's machine also included another device which had been the subject of several sporadic pioneering experiments carried out in Scotland and France since the previous century in the field of book-printing. Publishers found that their type became worn after a few months of use, occasioning expensive replacement. Claude Genoux and Nicolas Serrière had by 1852 invented the system of *clichage* for making page-moulds or 'flongs', the idea of using papier mâché for this purpose having been conceived by an Italian. In 1854 James Gordon Bennett in his *New York Herald* had experimented successfully with a method which involved using a metal plate impression of the type rather than the type itself. Other newspapers had imitated him, and Bullock now incorporated the idea into his 1863 machine, though commercial success arrived only with an improved version in 1871. Henceforth printing could be conducted from a series of these 'stereotypes', removing the necessity to set a paper in type more than once. Circulations now became merely a function of the number of machines employed. In 1865 the *Petit Journal* was being turned out at the rate of 250,000 per day.

Still lacking, however, were methods for improving the business of type-setting, which had scarcely changed in two centuries, and also for printing on both sides of a sheet continuously and simultaneously. Between 1815 and 1871 seventy attempts were made to create and patent a machine able to set type and adjust the spacing of the words at speed. The Paris Exhibitions of 1855 and 1889 both contained examples. In the 1860s the Hattersly machine introduced keyboard operation. Then Ottmar Mergenthaler, a Württem-berger who emigrated to America in 1872, built upon the idea of an American contemporary for a keyboard which set not type but matrices of letters which formed the mould of a line; molten metal was then used to set the line of type, hence the name 'Linotype'. Afterwards the original matrices could be redistributed for re-use. The machine was finally on sale in 1892, but in London the compositors, always powerfully organized, greatly retarded its application. The second problem, that of printing continuously and simultaneously, was eventually solved by Hippolyte Marinoni, who had been producing advanced rotary presses in Paris since the 1860s; in the 1889 Paris Exhibition he demonstrated a model which turned the roll of paper back on its path, enabling successive sheets of large or small size to be printed on both sides and then cut and folded into piles of completed newspapers, all at great speed. There was still enormous room for improvement in the quality of the product, but by 1890 an intending publisher had a wide choice of machines, according to the scope and nature of his newspaper. Each separate newspaper form had its own specialized technology.

The invention which demanded the greatest ingenuity and necessitated overturning the most entrenched working habits was not mechanical, but legal and social. The era struggled for an appropriate means by which the newspaper industry could be regulated. The newspaper had become the technology of revolution, but each successful revolution had a keen interest in staving off further upheaval. The Napoleonic totalitarian style was no longer in demand; the British system of a free press was widely feared and frequently scorned. What legal system was to be adopted?

It was probably in France that this problem caused the greatest argument and agony. By 1875 the new republican administration had to settle down to revise no fewer than forty-two laws containing 325 separate clauses, passed over seventy-five years by ten different régimes, and it still took five years of discussion to create the new system enshrined in a single law which opened with the words 'La presse est libre . . .'.

Kastenbein setting and distributing machines in use at *The Times*.

In 1820 France had acquired a system of caution money which was to remain in force until 1881: one named proprietor of every newspaper was made responsible for the entirety of the contents, and was obliged to deposit a large sum of money against the possibility of fines. The intention was to keep newspaper ownership within the middle class, rather as the stamp duty did in England, and the device forced the French newspaper, with certain exceptions, to keep to tiny circulations, as low as 500 in the provinces. Newspapers were found in clubs and reading-rooms. The typical investors in Paris newspapers were groups of politically minded men who put up the minimum capital necessary for what was never likely to become a profitable enterprise; old presses were used, with larger numbers of employees than necessary, and advertising was a laggard activity. Then the authorities adopted the practice of *amortissement*, or the surreptitious buying up of opposition papers to bend their editorial policy. The *Gazette de France* was

made to pretend that it was 'advising ministers' rather than reveal that it was in their pocket. The *Journal de Paris* made great play of criticizing less important officials of the government as a front for its total subservience. The owners of the *Quotidienne* refused to sell, but La Rochefoucauld, the mastermind of the policy of *amortissement*, infiltrated an accomplice as editor of the paper and acquired some of the shares under cover. When the plot was discovered by the publisher Michaud, his 'editor' arrived and tried to evict him, but a court action enabled Michaud to expose the whole truth and discredit the Ministry. Interference in the press contributed to the Revolution of 1830, which began when groups of liberal journalists protested against Charles X's abrogation of press freedom; in town after town, printers and journalists barricaded themselves inside their newspaper offices surrounded by police and troops, and revolutionary leaflets were flung down upon the crowds.

Newspapers of the 1830s and 1840s in France were weighed down with petty regulations, for breaches of which fines of some thousands of francs could be imposed; the more serious offences could result in the imprisonment of an editor for anything up to five years. The name and address of the printer had to be subscribed; the birth certificate of the responsible editor had to be lodged at the prefecture; the full title of the newspaper had to be presented at the Ministry of the Interior, and copies of every edition had to be supplied to the office of the Public Prosecutor. One of the most serious penalties which a court could impose was the prohibition of further reporting by a newspaper of trials, which effectively deprived it of much of its potential copy. After 1835 the libel laws were rewritten; all caricatures had to be submitted to the local prefect or the Ministry of the Interior; caution money was quadrupled to 100,000 francs, and fines doubled. Editors were encouraged to publish all announcements and corrections sent to them by public officials. But the papers were still kept from a formal 'censorship'.

The Revolution in March 1848 was redolent of 1789. Four hundred and fifty publications appeared overnight, some lasting a few days, some a few weeks. Their names were familiar – *Ami du Peuple, Tocsin, Robespierre, Bonnet rouge, Guillotine* – and they were printed on coloured newsprint, red, pink, yellow or green. In Paris and the provinces, republican papers now turned themselves into 'official' organs and the old 'official' papers adopted a tone of liberal disapproval. When the insurrection of June was put down by General Cavaignac, many of the Paris papers were closed down, and the old press laws reimposed. After Louis Napoleon's *coup d'état* all newspapers were closed down and allowed to reappear only when they agreed not to comment. Then came the 'Organic Decree' of February 1852, which combined all of the crippling restrictions attempted over the previous thirty years: newspapers now had to reacquire permission every time they underwent a change of staff; no foreign papers were allowed in France; huge caution moneys were imposed on all political papers; stamp taxes and postage rates were raised; publication of 'false news' was forbidden; it was forbidden to print the name of a suspended journal; two offences within two years led to automatic suspension, and all trials relating to these laws were held without juries; for good measure, officials had power to prosecute journalists who wrote material

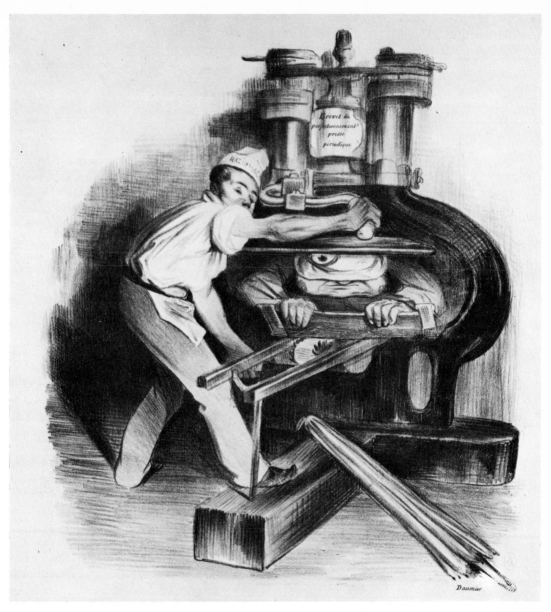

displeasing to the authorities even if it was not indictable under the law. The decree remained in force for sixteen years, mitigated only by sporadic imperial amnesties. Further layers of controls were spun like a web round the main enactments. All hawkers had to have licences, renewed by positive application every year, and railway stations were made to count as 'streets' for the purposes of hawking. All officials, central and local, had power to oblige editors to print public statements free of charge. A system of formal administrative 'warnings' was instituted which would lead to suspension and suppression on an accumulating scale. Fourteen newspapers remained in Paris out of the hundreds which had existed in March 1848.

'So you want to meddle with the press!' says this cartoon by Daumier, in which the 'citizen king', Louis Philippe, comes off worst.

In May 1868 another press law was passed – though too little and too late – which abolished the hated preliminary authorization, reduced stamp duty and curbed the egregious administrative powers. Within a year there were 88 newspapers in Paris alone and 150 in the provinces. Among the newcomers the most successful were a new group of satirical papers: *Figaro* sold 40,000 a day, *Gaulois*, *Cloche* ('the bell') and *Diable à quatre* ('rumpus') over 12,000. Satire emerged from the ghetto of the literary journals into the daily political press. Despite decades of repressive laws, France had a very lively journalism awaiting its chance.

The *Lanterne* of Henri Rochefort, printed on flame-coloured paper, was startling in every way: it had a tone of accusatory banter, ridiculing every public figure in the land, including the Emperor, and its audacity won the reward of occasionally selling half a million copies in a single day. Within three months Rochefort took flight abroad and continued the paper from exile. As Prussian troops closed in on Paris in 1871 and the Empire approached its demise, Napoleon III authorized further changes, including trial by jury and the abolition of stamp duties. Only the system of *délits d'opinion* (libel) remained, and it seemed inevitable, when the Republic was proclaimed in September 1870, that real press freedom would now arrive; the social upheaval which ensued after military defeat, however, and the months of civil war, resulted in the reimposition of the old press controls.

Only in 1876, when the state of siege was finally lifted, did French politicians settle down to plan new press legislation. The resulting law laid before the Deputies by Eugène Lisbonne appeared in July 1880. The Deputies had toiled through various proposals to amend the labyrinth of press laws before realizing that the only way to proceed was to scrap them all and start again. The new law was to be the most liberal ever devised, more liberal even than the English system. The Chamber decided in the event to retain a limited concept of 'press offences'; libel was severely reduced in scope, and fair reporting of all parliamentary or legal proceedings was exempted from libel prosecution; incitement by the press to commit offences was no longer indictable if the offences were not actually committed, except in the cases of murder, theft or arson. Prior authorization, caution money, etc. were removed, but all publishers had to present their names to the authorities and deposit two copies of every edition; hawkers and newsagents also had to register. A small list of offences was left, including outrage to public morals and defamation of the courts, the armed forces, members of the government, public officials, ministers of religion (who were public officials), members of juries and witnesses. It was forbidden to insult the President of the Republic, the memory of the dead, heads of foreign states or ambassadors. *The Times* of London congratulated the French on the reform: 'Newspapers without resources try to make a name by scandal and calumny; prosecutions serve to advertise them, and they seem to study how to provoke prosecutions not serious enough to destroy them . . . a better press makes exceptional laws needless.'

The new legal position made it possible for a mass press to take root in Paris and throughout France earlier than in any other country of Europe. Moïse Millaud had founded the *Petit Journal* in 1863, and its great rival the

Opposite The 1860s saw a flowering of satirical journalism in France, led by Henri Rochefort's *Lanterne*. A rival paper caricatured him as Don Quixote.

Première année — Nº 20   Un numéro : 10 centimes   7 Juin 1868

RÉDACTEUR EN CHEF
F. POLO
—
ABONNEMENTS
PARIS
Un an .... 8 fr.
Six mois .... 5 »
Trois mois 1 50
—
BUREAUX 6, CITÉ BERGÈRE

DIRECTEUR
F. POLO
—
ABONNEMENTS
DÉPARTEMENTS
Un an .... 8 fr.
Six mois 3 50
Trois mois ...... 2 »
—
BUREAUX, 6, CITÉ BERGÈRE

HENRI ROCHEFORT — par GILL

Louis Kossuth, Hungarian patriot, editor and leader-writer.

Petit Parisien arrived in 1876, followed by *Le Matin* in 1882 and *Le Journal* in 1889. Such large-circulation papers depended on large quantities of capital, controlled by finance houses and industrial concerns; doubts were soon raised concerning their true level of journalistic independence. It was an era of corruption scandals (Dreyfus, the Panama Canal), and the press itself gave rise to scandal as it grew in circulation and in scope. By the turn of the century Paris had acquired 139 daily papers, with a further 334 in the provinces.

Across Europe, the spread of the Revolution which had begun in February 1848 in Paris brought about a transformation in the world of the press. The newspaper was the carrier of insurrection, and established the basis for political activity for the rest of the century. In Hungary, for example, the struggle for freedom had been organized until 1848 by well-to-do supporters outside the country, while political clubs in Budapest grouped themselves round illegal newspapers. In the summer of 1848, fifty-nine contrasting political groups emerged. Louis Kossuth, who led the fight against Austria, made himself editor-in-chief of the *Pesti Hirlap* ('Pest newspaper') and wrote most of the fiery leading articles himself. Sandor Petöfi and his circle of admirers occupied the printing-presses of the city, and the first of the 'Twelve Points' which they demanded was press freedom. One important group of

Prince Alfred zu
Windischgrätz, who put
an end to Vienna's brief
outburst of journalistic
freedom in 1838.

papers was created by General Joseph Bem, who equipped his troops with
portable printing-presses and encouraged them to start newspapers as they
moved across the country. The *Budapesti Hiradó* ('Budapest intelligencer')
founded a few years before as *Világ* ('the world') was turned into a daily in
1848 and continued to put the conservative case. The victory of the Russian
troops put an end to the whole of this activity, and it was twenty years before
the newspaper rose again, but by the end of the century Hungary had over a
thousand newspapers and periodicals.

In Vienna, the post-1815 censorship virtually eliminated political
reporting, although the city supported a thriving literary and theatrical press,
including Adolf Bauerles's *Allgemeine Theaterzeitung* ('general theatre news');
it was the heyday of the feuilleton. When Metternich's political system
collapsed, all restrictions disappeared overnight, and editors trained in Paris
and London suddenly reappeared in Vienna. August Zang and Leopold
Landsteiner laid the foundations of an elegant new journalism, led by the
former's *Die Presse*, which began life on 3 July 1848. Between May and
October of that year a vast number of new titles appeared in a kind of
journalistic saturnalia which was then brusquely ended by the siege of
Vienna and the victory of Prince Alfred zu Windischgrätz, who put an end

to every journal except the *Wiener Zeitung*; all the old controls returned, with caution money, licensing, preventive censorship. The struggle against this absolutism became the training ground for a new liberal press in the 1860s.

Between 1864 and 1890 three new groups of papers emerged in Austria, liberal, conservative (including the Catholic and literary papers which had existed before the March events) and governmental. The Fundamental Law of 1867 created a new political system with a parliament, parties and press freedom and from then until 1918 Vienna was the leading European centre for newspapers of every kind – sensational, entertaining, informative, satirical, local, national, international. The city became a magnet for the talented in German-language journalism.

The basis of this upsurge was capital made by Viennese banks and credit institutions in the boom of the 1860s; until then newspapers had been small one-man businesses, but now an era of industrialized publishing began, with vertical cartels being created by paper-manufacturers and other related industrialists moving into magazines and newspapers. In 1848, for example, the book-publisher Leopold Sommer took over the Guggenbacher paper business, and by the 1870s large combines were beginning to dominate the printed media, each based on a string of paper concerns. Fashion magazines and other illustrated papers flourished under the same impetus.

The German press of the mid-nineteenth century developed along rather different lines from its neighbours. Few papers were based upon political parties, apart from certain Catholic and socialist journals. In fact, very few papers were in the possession of companies at all; most remained one-man or one-family businesses, with circulations of little more than a thousand. Even in 1926 a fifth of all Germany's papers were still family businesses, and only a fifth were party papers.

An important group was formed by the commercial papers. The *Börsenhalle* of Hamburg, started in 1805, appeared every day on which the Bourse opened; in the middle decades of the century it was joined by the *Berliner Börsen-Zeitung* and *Börsen-Courier*. The *Frankfurter Handelszeitung* ('Frankfurt commercial news') started up in 1856. Under the strict censorship which prevailed until 1848 there was little critical material in German papers, apart from those which concentrated on literary matters. In the middle-sized cities there evolved a new-style local paper, the *Heimat-Zeitung*, but this still did not have a mass readership.

In the year 1848 all controls on the German press, including the Carlsbad decrees, were swept away, but by 1850 publishers' licences, stamp taxes and caution money were all back again, although the right of press freedom was not formally revoked. A new Imperial Press Law of 1874 replaced the former regulations of individual German states, but all attempts at political papers were steadily thwarted by interference. In 1878, for example, all forty-two socialist papers were closed down. In the course of the *Kulturkampf* the ultra-Catholic *Germania*, edited by Paul Majunke, was banned over six hundred times. But the experience of 1848 increased interest in newspapers: in 1847, in Prussia, less than 100,000 newspapers were sold per day, but by 1856 this had leapt to 3 million and by 1870 to 9 million, by which time there were individual circulations of over 50,000.

The Promethean figure of Karl Marx chained to the *Rheinische Zeitung* press. Towns of the Rhineland hold up imploring hands to the censors, but in vain.

Another factor contributing to this growth was the abrogation of the state monopoly of advertising in Prussia and various other German states after the 1848 upheaval. At first, revenue from advertising still constituted only a small proportion of the income of the average paper. The first German publicity agency was founded in Altona by Ferdinand Hasenstein in 1855. A decade later Rudolf Mosse started his *Annoncen-Expedition* ('advertising dispatch'), a paper with highly organized advertising; gradually advertising space in the papers of the larger cities began to rise in price, and the prices of newspapers began to fall. New readers were found in their thousands, eager to buy the papers and the mass-produced goods which they advertised. A transformation took place in the German newspaper industry. Rudolf Mosse went on to found the *Berliner Tageblatt* ('Berlin daily news') in 1871, and a productive rivalry broke out in the Berlin press between him, Leopold Ullstein and August Scherl which brought forth a dozen new papers, all fiercely competitive, and made Berlin the home of an entertaining and lucrative newspaper industry for several decades.

Karl Marx was one of the German journalists whose fate was greatly influenced by the events of 1848. In Cologne in 1842 a well-to-do bourgeois publisher had founded the *Rheinische Zeitung für Politick, Handel und Gewerbe* ('Rhineland newspaper of politics, trade and commerce'); a year later the paper published, under the signature 'a Rhinelander', an article by the 24-year-old Marx arguing the case for press freedom. This and other articles in a similar vein led to his leaving the paper a year later, shortly before the censors banned it. Marx and Friedrich Engels were among the German journalists who edited papers in Switzerland, Strasbourg and Paris, in the months before the March uprising, which brought all the emigrant editors and publishers rushing back to their homeland. By 31 March Marx had brought out the first edition of the *Neue Rheinische Zeitung, Organ der Demokratie*, but his permission to reside was shortly revoked, leaving his colleagues to continue editing the journal until the whole enterprise was closed down after its 301st issue (May 1849). By March 1850 Marx was editing a German paper from London, but this *Neue Rheinische Zeitung, Politisch-Oekonomische Revue* lasted only a few issues.

Elsewhere in Germany, the new papers of March 1848 survived, a prominent example being Julius Knorr's *Münchner Neueste Nachrichten* ('latest news from Munich') an important liberal paper of the south. But increasingly the authorities played a part in the running of these papers, often by placing their own officials on the staff. Bismarck was thus not remarkable in editing personally, in the years before 1876, the *Norddeutsche Allgemeine Zeitung* ('north German general news'), which continued as a government paper until 1890. In power, Bismarck cracked down heavily on the socialist press. The next generation of socialist propagandists, August Bebel and Wilhelm Liebknecht, made Leipzig a journalistic centre of the left: the left wing of the German socialists (the Lassalleans) grouped behind the journal *Sozialdemokrat*, while Liebknecht ran *Volksstaat*, but the two merged in 1876 into the new paper *Vorwärts*, which flourished until the great Bismarckian crackdown of 1878.

In the Anglo-Saxon world the pattern of development in the nineteenth century was rather different, although based on the same evolving technology. Advertising developed earlier in England and America, where changes in form occurred more rapidly, and where the legal and political systems adapted themselves more readily to the needs of the newspaper industry. The leading light of the new London editors after Waterloo was Thomas Barnes, who took over at *The Times* in 1817, at the age of thirty-two, when John Walter II took the unconventional step of handing over complete control of his enterprise to another man while he himself entered politics. Barnes held the position until his death in 1841. He saw his role as that of interpreting and leading middle-class opinion; he selected the causes and the attitudes of a class and wagered the newspaper's circulation against his editorial judgment. *The Times* was *for* Catholic Emancipation, Queen Caroline and the Great Reform Bill, and *against* the Six Acts and the repression at Peterloo. Barnes's successor John Thaddeus Delane continued to mould the opinion of the same class for a further thirty-six years, but concentrated his energies on developing his contacts throughout the world of power until he found himself arguably the most knowledgeable single man in British public life. One of his obituarists wrote: '. . . the paper every morning

LORD BROUGHAM'S RAILWAY NIGHTMARE.

The boom in railway shares of the 1840s, and in Parliamentary Bills for the establishment of more and more new railway companies, was a nightmare to the Lord Chancellor. It also meant £6,000 a week for *The Times* in advertising.

was not a mere collection of pieces of news from all parts of the world, of various opinions, and of more or less valuable essays. It was Mr Delane's report to the public of the news of the day, interpreted by Mr Delane's opinions, and directed throughout by Mr Delane's principles and purposes.' Like most editors of the time, Delane believed fervently in the principle of journalistic anonymity. An editor's name was never mentioned in the paper. When Nicholas Byrne, editor of the *Morning Post*, was stabbed in his own office and died later of his wounds, his newspaper merely gave his name, age and address.

The successful London papers derived a great deal of income from all forms of advertising, and in the era of industrial growth played an important role in the raising of capital for new ventures. *The Times* drew over £6,000 a week at the height of the railway fever in 1845, though its editorial columns warned readers of the economic madness in which they were engaged. Each newspaper's personality was formed by its circle of readers, with whose attitudes it kept closely in touch. The abolition of the newspaper taxes was one of the great issues on which Victorian society divided: to abolish them would place the press in the hands of the uneducated classes, but to retain them prevented the newspaper from acting according to the *laissez-faire* precepts of the time. *The Times* equivocated and pressed upon the authorities the great loss in revenue which would follow from repeal. Thomas Milner-Gibson, MP, a former Vice-President of the Board of Trade, became the first President of the Association for Promoting the Repeal of the Taxes on Knowledge (APRTK), the leading pressure group in the field. He kept legislation constantly before the House, with Cobden fighting brilliantly in debates, until, one by one, the taxes disappeared. In 1836 the stamp was reduced from fourpence to one penny; in 1853 the tax on advertisements was dropped, and in 1855 the final penny stamp was made optional – paying it provided free distribution. In 1861 the taxes on paper were dropped, partly to reduce its price during the crisis caused by the American Civil War. The campaign against the taxes was a key cause of social reformers. Lord John Russell, Prime Minister, opposed the abolition of the stamp on the grounds that it would encourage popular newspapers and popular education and therefore tend towards anarchy. Feargus O'Connor in his *Northern Star: or Leeds General Advertiser*, the most powerful Chartist journal, was typical of the abolitionists: 'Reader, behold that little red spot in the corner of my newspaper: That is the Stamp; the Whig beauty spot; your plague spot.' Gladstone described the campaign as 'the severest parliamentary struggle in which I have ever been engaged'.

Despite the rapid growth of the market, newspapers were risky undertakings. John Murray, publisher of the *Quarterly Review*, was persuaded by Benjamin Disraeli in 1826 to start the *Representative*, a Tory morning paper which collapsed within six months and cost him £26,000. The *Constitutional*, a Radical daily boasting Thackeray as its Paris correspondent, failed in 1836, despite a host of eminent writers. A near failure was Charles Dickens's *Daily News*, which he brought out in partnership with Joseph Paxton, the builder of the Crystal Palace; its purpose was to press for 'principles of progress and improvement . . . the bodily comfort, mental elevation and general contentment of the British people'. Among its galaxy of distinguished contributors was Harriet Martineau, the first female leader-writer in Britain, who joined the staff in 1852 at the age of fifty. It narrowly survived, to become, as the *News Chronicle*, one of the most important English newspapers of the last hundred years.

There were frequent attempts at penny papers in London and the provinces, but the most important of the new foundings after abolition of the stamp was the *Daily Telegraph*, which ran heavily into debt after a few months and was taken over by its chief creditor, Joseph Moses Levy, editor and proprietor of the *Sunday Times*. The price was reduced from twopence to a penny, and the circulation shot up to 27,000 – nearly half the daily sale of *The Times* itself – within a few months. The real energy behind the *Telegraph*, however, came from Levy's son, Edward Levy Lawson (who adopted the

Edward Levy Lawson of the *Daily Telegraph*. From his head (here caricatured by Phil May) sprang numerous circulation-boosting stunts.

surname of an uncle whose fortune he had inherited); Lawson greatly increased the range of the paper, borrowed many new techniques from America, and developed classified advertising through the invention of the box number. From America he took the many-layered headline for the big story: the *New York Herald*, which specialized in these multiple layers of encapsulated information, would sometimes use a dozen or more lines, running to a foot in depth at the head of a story. The day after the assassination of Lincoln, the *Herald* carried seventeen headlines where *The Times* had three and Lawson four. After three years in business, the *Telegraph*'s circulation was larger than that of all its London rivals combined. It engaged in daring exploits to push its sales still higher, sharing with the *New York Herald*, for example, the sponsorship of Stanley's trip to Africa in search of Livingstone in 1871. On the staff of the paper was the most famous

THE NEW YORK H

WHOLE NO. 10,456. NEW YORK, SATURDAY, APRIL 15, 1865.

IMPORTANT.

ASSASSINATION OF PRESIDENT LINCOLN.

The President Shot at the Theatre Last Evening.

SECRETARY SEWARD DAGGERED IN HIS BED, BUT NOT MORTALLY WOUNDED.

Carence and Frederick Seward Badly Hurt.

ESCAPE OF THE ASSASSINS.

Intense Excitement in Washington.

Scene at the Deathbed of Mr. Lincoln.

J. Wilkes Booth, the Actor, the Alleged Assassin of the President.

THE OFFICIAL DESPATCH.

WAR DEPARTMENT,
WASHINGTON, April 15—1:30 A. M.

Major General Dix, New York:—

This evening at about 9:30 P. M., at Ford's Theatre, the President, while sitting in his private box with Mrs. Lincoln, Mrs. Harris and Major Rathburn, was shot by an assassin, who suddenly entered the box and approached behind the President.

The assassin then leaped upon the stage, brandishing a large dagger or knife, and made his escape in the rear of the theatre.

The pistol ball entered the back of the President's head and penetrated nearly through the head. The wound is mortal.

The President has been insensible ever since it was inflicted, and is now dying.

About the same hour an assassin, whether the same or not, entered Mr. Seward's apartments and under pretence of having a prescription, was shown to the Secretary's sick chamber. The assassin immediately rushed to the bed and inflicted two or three stabs on the throat and two on the face.

It is hoped the wounds may not be mortal. My apprehension is that they will prove fatal.

The nurse alarmed Mr. Frederick Seward, who was in an adjoining room, and he hastened to the door of his father's room, when he met the assassin, who inflicted upon him one or more dangerous wounds. The recovery of Frederick Seward is doubtful.

It is not probable that the President will live through the night.

General Grant and wife were advertised to be at the theatre this evening, but he started to Burlington at six o'clock this evening.

At a Cabinet meeting, at which General Grant was present, the subject of the state of the country and the prospect of a speedy peace were discussed. The President was very cheerful and

At the close of the third act a person entered the box occupied by the President, and shot Mr. Lincoln in the head. The shot entered the back of his head, and came out above the temple.

The assassin then jumped from the box upon the stage and ran across to the other side, exhibiting a dagger in his hand, flourishing it in a tragical manner, shouting the same words repeated by the desperado at Mr. Seward's house, adding to it, "The South is avenged," and then escaped from the back entrance to the stage, but in his passage dropped his pistol and his hat.

Mr. Lincoln fell forward from his seat, and Mrs. Lincoln fainted.

The moment the astonished audience could realize what had happened, the President was taken and carried to Mr. Peterson's house in Tenth street, opposite to the theatre. Medical aid was immediately sent for, and the wound was at first supposed to be fatal, and it was announced that he could not live; but at half-past twelve he is still alive, though in a precarious condition.

As the assassin ran across the stage, Colonel J. B. Stewart, of this city, who was occupying one of the front seats in the orchestra, on the same side of the house as the box occupied by Mr. Lincoln, sprang to the stage and followed him; but he was obstructed in his passage across the stage by the fright of the actors, and reached the back door about three seconds after the assassin had passed out. Colonel Stewart got to the street just in time to see him mount his horse and ride away.

This operation shows that the whole thing was a preconcerted plan. The person who fired the pistol was a man about thirty years of age, about five feet nine, spare built, fair skin, dark hair, apparently bushy, with a large mustache. Laura Keene and the leader of the orchestra declare that they recognized him as J. Wilkes Booth the actor and a rabid secessionist. Whoever he was, it is plainly evident that he thoroughly understood the theatre and all the approaches and modes of escape to the stage. A person not familiar with the theatre could not have possibly made his escape so well and quickly.

The alarm was sounded in every quarter. Mr. Stanton was notified and immediately left his house.

All the other members of the Cabinet escaped attack.

Cavalrymen were sent out in all directions, and dispatches sent to all the fortifications, and it is thought they will be captured.

About half-past ten o'clock this evening a tall, well-dressed man made his appearance at Secretary Seward's residence, and applied for admission. He was refused admission by the servant, when the desperado stated that he had a prescription from the Surgeon General, and that he was ordered to deliver it in person. He was still refused, except upon the written order of the physician. This he pretended to show, and pushed by the servant and rushed up stairs to Mr. Seward's room. He was met at the door by Mr. Fred Seward, who notified him that he was master of the house and would take charge of the medicine. After a few words had passed between them, he dodged by Fred Seward and rushed to the Secretary's bed, and drawing a large knife, plunged it in the breast.

It was supposed at first that Mr. Seward was killed instantly, but it was found afterwards that the wound was not mortal.

Major Wm. H. Seward, Jr., paymaster, was in the room, and rushed to the defence of his father, and was badly cut in the *mele* with the assassin, but not fatally.

The desperado managed to escape from the house, and was prepared for escape by having a horse at the door. He immediately mounted his horse, and sung out the motto of the State of Virginia, "*Sic Semper Tyrannis!*" and rode off.

Surgeon General Barnes was immediately sent for, and he *examined Mr. Seward and pronounced him safe.* His wounds were not fatal. The jugular vein was not cut, nor the wound in the breast deep enough to be fatal.

WASHINGTON, April 15—1 A. M.

The streets in the vicinity of Ford's Theatre are densely crowded by an anxious and excited crowd. A guard has been placed across Tenth street and F and E streets, and only official persons and particular friends of the President are allowed to pass.

The popular heart is deeply stirred, and the deepest indignation against leading rebels is freely expressed.

The scene at the house where the President lies *in extremis* is very affecting. Even Secretary Stanton is affected to tears.

When the news spread through the city that the President had been shot, the people, with pale faces and compressed lips, crowded every place where there was the slightest chance of obtaining information in regard to the affair.

After the President was shot, Lieutenant Rathbun caught the assassin by the arm, who immediately struck him with a knife, and jumped from the box, as before stated.

The popular affection for Mr. Lincoln has been shown by this diabolical assassination, which will bring eternal infamy, not only upon its authors, but upon the hellish cause which they desire to avenge.

Vice-President Johnson arrived at the White House where the President lies, about one o'clock, and will remain with him to the last.

The President's family are in attendance upon him also.

As soon as intelligence could be got to the War Department the electric telegraph and the Signal

THE PRESS DESPATCHES.

WASHINGTON, April 15—12:30 A. M.

The President was shot in a theatre to-night, and is perhaps mortally wounded.

SECOND DESPATCH.

WASHINGTON, April 15—1 A. M.

The President is not expected to live through the night. He was shot at a theatre.

Secretary Seward was also assassinated. No arteries were cut.

Additional Details of the Assassination.

WASHINGTON, April 15—1:30 A. M.

President Lincoln and wife, with other friends, this evening visited Ford's theatre, for the purpose of witnessing the performance of the American Cousin.

It was announced that General Grant would also be present; but that gentleman took the late train of cars for New Jersey.

The theatre was densely crowded, and all seemed delighted with the scene before them. During the third act, and while there was a temporary pause for one of the actors to enter, a sharp report of a pistol was heard, which merely attracted attention, but suggested nothing serious, until a man rushed to the front of the President's box, waving a large dagger in his right hand, and exclaiming "*Sic semper tyrannis!*" and immediately leaped from the box, which was in the second tier, to the stage beneath, and ran across to the opposite side, making his escape amid the bewilderment of the audience, from the rear of the theatre, and, mounting, a horse, fled.

The screams of Mrs. Lincoln first disclosed the fact to the audience that the President had been shot, when all present rose to their feet, rushing towards the stage, many exclaiming "Hang him! Hang him!"

The excitement was of the wildest possible description, and of course there was an abrupt termination of the theatrical performance.

There was a rush towards the President's box, where cries were heard:—"Stand back and give him air!" "Has any one any stimulants?"

On a hasty examination it was found that the President had been shot through the head, above and back of the temporal bone, and that some of the brain was oozing out.

He was removed to a private house opposite to the theatre, and the Surgeon General of the army was immediately sent for to attend to his condition.

On an examination of the private box blood was discovered on the back of the cushioned rocking chair on which the President had been sitting, also on the partition and on the floor. A common, single-barreled pocket pistol was found on the carpet.

A military guard was placed in front of the private residence to which the President had been conveyed. An immense crowd was in front of it, all deeply anxious to learn the condition of the President. It had been previously announced that the wound was mortal, but all hoped otherwise. The shock to the community was terrible.

At midnight the Cabinet, with Messrs. Sumner, Colfax and Farnsworth, Judge Curtis, Governor Oglesby, General Meigs, Colonel Day, and a few personal friends, with Surgeon General Barnes and his immediate assistant, were around his bedside.

The President was in a state of syncope, totally insensible, and breathing slowly. The blood oozed from the wound at the back of his head.

The surgeons exhausted every possible effort of medical skill; but all hope was gone.

The parting of his family with the dying President is too sad for description.

The President and Mrs. Lincoln did not start for the theatre until fifteen minutes after eight o'clock. Speaker Colfax was at the White House at the time, and the President stated to him that he was going. Mrs. Lincoln had not been well, because the papers had announced that General Grant and they were to be present, and, as General Grant had gone North, he did not wish the audience to be disappointed.

He went with apparent reluctance, and urged Mr. Colfax to go with him; but that gentleman had made other engagements, and, with Mr. Ashmun, of Massachusetts, bid him goodby.

When the excitement at the theatre was at its wildest height reports were circulated that Secretary Seward had also been assassinated.

On reaching this gentleman's residence a crowd and a military guard were found at the door, and on entering it was ascertained that the reports were based on truth.

Everybody there was so excited that scarcely an intelligible word could be gathered. But the facts are substantially as follows:—

About ten o'clock a man rang the bell, and the call having been answered by a colored servant, he said he had come from Dr. Verdi, Secretary Seward's family physician, with a prescription, at the same time holding in his hand a small piece of folded paper, and saying, in answer to a refusal, that he must see the Secretary, as he was entrusted with particular directions concerning the medicine.

He still insisted on going up, although repeatedly informed that no one could enter the chamber. The man pushed the servant aside, and walked hastily towards the Secretary's room, and was then met by Mr. Frederick Seward, of whom he demanded to see the Secretary, making the same representation which he did to the servant.

What further passed in the way of colloquy

LATEST EXTRA!

8:10 A. M.

New York, Saturday, April 15, 1865.

DEATH OF THE PRESIDENT.

Further Details of the Great Crime.

Additional Despatches from the Secretary of War.

What is Known of the Assassins.

THE OFFICIAL DESPATCHES.

WAR DEPARTMENT,
WASHINGTON, April 15—6:10 A. M.

Major General Dix, New York:—

The President continues insensible and sinking.

Secretary Seward remains without change; Frederick Seward's skull is fractured in two places, besides a severe cut upon the head. The attendant is still alive but hopeless. Major Seward's wounds are not dangerous.

It is now ascertained, with reasonable certainty, that two assassins were engaged in the horrible crime. Wilkes Booth being the one that shot the President, and the other an accomplice, whose name is not known, but whose description is so clear that he can hardly escape.

It appears from papers found in Booth's trunk that the murder was planned before the 4th of March, but fell through then, because the accomplice backed out until "Richmond could be heard from."

Booth and his accomplice were at the livery stable at 6 o'clock last evening, and left here with their horses at 10 o'clock, or shortly before that hour.

It would appear that they had for several days been seeking their chance, but for some unknown reason it was not carried into effect until last night.

One of the assassins has evidently made his way to Baltimore; the other has not yet been traced.

EDWIN M. STANTON,
Secretary of War.

THE PRESIDENT DEAD.

WAR DEPARTMENT,
WASHINGTON, April 15—7:30 A. M.

Major General Dix, New York:—

Abraham Lincoln died this morning at twenty-two minutes past 7 o'clock.

TH
JEF.
His
He Thi
Blessi
the
He Va
Virg
Lee
p
Breckin
Cab
The Orga
lina, Ad
to
Jef
VIRGINIA
The Gene
such move
capital. I
and materi
occupation
equally un
own energ
relaxed un
may be. I
army of t
leader who
in the tro
trammelle
watch over
been thus
tunity for
countryme
verses how
of those w
misfortune
dangers w
We have
struggle.
particular
from point
far from h
free.
Animated
That was
ow count
tain your c
and I will ne
one foot of t
confederacy
ancient his
more glorio
been bared t
whose sons
so sublime
to come—t
people and
held and defe
the infamou
If by the
compelled t
limits, or t
and again w
hausted ene
less and imp
people resol
Let us, the
relying on G
and with un
The Eva
THE FIRST R
[From the
Persons w
Monday mor
followed the
beggars desc
tect the prop
remained th
teenth Virgi
placed on po
ing of the
failed to ren
whatever. C
classes of th

William Howard Russell, the best-known war correspondent since Xenophon.

journalist of the day, George Augustus Sala, noted for his seismic quarrels with his many editors. His heavy circumlocutory writing – a style which completely vanished with the coming of the mass press – filled the imaginations of Victorians with vivid pictures of great events.

Completely new kinds of adventuristic journalism were emerging. The newspaper of this period often required the fuel of eccentric genius like that of Dr Emile Joseph Dillon, an eminent philologist who gave the impression of carrying all the secrets of the world about his person. This multilingual ex-priest had edited a paper in Odessa and held a Chair at Kharkov University. Several times expelled from countries in whose affairs he was interested, he sometimes re-entered them disguised as a monk. He was present at rebellions, massacres, invasions and stirring events of all kinds, in China, Turkey, Greece, Berlin. During his days on the *Telegraph* in the 1870s the paper's circulation reached 200,000, the highest in the world.

Two important personalities who both, in different ways, brought vivid description into the reporting of international news were Henry de Blowitz and William Howard Russell. Russell's reports from the Crimea enabled

Opposite The *New York Herald* reports the assassination of President Lincoln. The rash of headlines in 'steps' was characteristic of American journalism.

Delane to bring down one government and reconstruct another through the exposure of the appalling mismanagement of the War Department. After Russell the system of 'gentlemen travellers', by which reporters simply hitched themselves to a moving army, bringing their own tents and sharing provisions, was gradually terminated, but journalists could be officially accredited and admitted to the battlefield. Archibald Forbes gained the journalistic honours of the Franco-Prussian War of 1870–71; he argued that war reporting should be freely permitted, while the War Office insisted on the right to censor and alter despatches, which, in Forbes's words, 'made the position of a war correspondent untenable by a gentleman'. The newspaper was taking on the role of brokerage between authority and the middle class in Victorian society: 'Independent war correspondence has become a necessity to the contentment of a nation. It placates the just uneasiness that is occasioned by meagre, unexhaustive and not always wholly candid communications from official sources.' But Forbes did accept that the reporters should wear special badges and accept military discipline. A kind of half-conscious concordat was worked out between the reformed bureaucracies of late Victorian Britain and the newspaper profession.

In a totally different style De Blowitz, 'the prince of journalists', operated as the chief Paris correspondent of *The Times*, producing for his paper diplomatic scoops which chilled the spines of statesmen. His most famous *coup* was the revelation of the whole of the Berlin Treaty of 1878, seized from beneath the noses of the signatories while the ink was barely dry. De Blowitz was unrivalled for speed, tactics and subterfuge. Like Dillon, he carried with him an air of mystery which stimulated newspaper sales and baffled Ministers.

The provincial press at this time was in the midst of mushroom growth. The telegraph had brought an end to the London papers' monopoly of national, and especially parliamentary, news, and in 1868 the Press Association was founded as a limited company by provincial papers to furnish them with the same news as was available to the London press. Stereotypes or even partly printed papers could also be sent out daily to local printers, who had merely to supply a page of local material and an evening title; a dozen columns of stereotype, containing leaders, news, parliamentary sketches could be had anywhere in the provinces by the afternoon for £5. Filling a new weekly out-of-London newspaper was rendered very simple and very cheap by the new journalistic services available by wire: the Press Association, for an annual subscription of £7.5s., would send a weekly summary of general news, while a résumé of Reuter's telegrams could be obtained from them for £1 a week. The Central Press, which specialized in parliamentary reporting, would ensure that the speeches of all Members reached their local papers, though it did favour the Conservative interest; the National Press Agency functioned similarly in the Liberal interest. There were, in all, twenty press agencies in London offering material on competitive terms to the provinces.

By 1880 London had 18 dailies, the English provinces 96, Wales 4, Scotland 21 and Ireland 17. In 1821 there had been 267 newspapers in the kingdom as a whole, including weeklies; the tally had risen slowly until the

Charles Havas, founder of the famous French news agency.

abolition of the taxes and then leapt up to 1,102 by 1861, after which new foundings became rare. The introduction of special newspaper trains in 1876 meant that the London papers could circulate throughout the country, rivalling the major provincial papers in their own territory. Specialist papers abounded: in 1880 there were 44 religious newspapers, 35 temperance papers, 33 humorous publications, 24 fashion papers and 21 sporting journals.

The telegraph brought about a tremendous change in the business of reporting. No longer did a crowd of reporters have to work through their notes in a shaking train carriage or stage-coach as they brought back the details of a great speech or a dramatic event to their editorial offices in London. Nor was it necessary for every paper to keep a string of correspondents in all the important news centres, each haphazardly gathering what scraps of information he could. At first each London paper which could afford it used a system of private wires to reach its chief correspondents, the resulting nuggets of news frequently sending the Stock Exchange rocketing upwards and downwards. In 1851 Paul Julius de Reuter opened his London office and reporting became 'scientifically' organized; his agents forwarded their material to Reuter's offices, freed as far as possible from every suspicion of bias. In Paris the Havas bureau had existed since 1832, founded,

In the early days of Sunday papers, trumpet-blowing newsboys desecrated the Sabbath morning.

like Reuters, as a pigeon service; Charles Havas's enterprise grew rapidly in the following decades, though it remained very much in the pocket of the French government. In Prussia, in 1849, the War Ministry granted control of the telegraph to the General Post Office, which was then a section of the Ministry of Trade and Industry. Bernhard Wolff, director of the publishing company which owned the *National-Zeitung*, saw the opportunity to construct a telegraphic news agency serving the interests of Berlin newspapers and finance houses, and thus founded the Telegraphisches Correspondenz Bureau, which later, after various financial reconstructions, became Wolff's Telegraphisches Bureau AG (WTB), the third of the great European news agencies of the century.

In eighteenth-century London a number of enterprising printers had cautiously braved the cold winds of Sabbatarian disapproval and published Sunday papers containing a good deal of moral and religious material. Their market at this time was confined to the capital, there being no mail-coach service on Sundays; the distribution system was based on the hiring of small boys to call the name of the paper through a speaking-trumpet in the very early hours of the morning. Each boy wore a cap bearing the name of his paper. In the nineteenth century, the audience for Sunday papers came increasingly to consist of the newly literate who could not afford six papers a week and who were interested in non-political news. The Sunday journals traded in horrible murders, ghastly seductions and lurid rapes, but these were combined with a distinct brand of radicalism. Robert Bell's *Weekly Dispatch* and *Bell's Weekly Messenger* exercised a considerable influence in the passage of the Reform Bill. Edward Lloyd's *Weekly News*, founded in 1842, was the first publication to reach a circulation of a million; it appealed to a growing section of readers who supported radical and libertarian causes, as did *Reynolds News*, founded in 1850. The *News of the World*, which began in

C. P. Scott of the *Manchester Guardian*.

1843, was very radical indeed in tone, and delighted the authorities by putting much illegal, unstamped radical journalism out of business. The *Observer*, a classic late-eighteenth-century Sunday, was taken over by one William Clement, who had tried to build up a newspaper chain between 1820 and 1840, burning his fingers badly over a misjudged purchase of the *Morning Chronicle*; he had great success, however, with the *Observer*, which he turned into a lucrative weekly dispenser of ghastly crime and a pioneering exponent of pictorial journalism.

Perhaps the most influential single journalist flourishing at this time was C. P. Scott, who became editor of the *Manchester Guardian* in 1872 at the age of twenty-five; he made the paper an engine of liberalism with a reputation around the globe. Scott is still known today for his apophthegms, all founded upon his unshakeable conviction that journalistic practice must entail the rigid separation of fact from comment. 'The newspaper is of necessity something of a monopoly, and its first duty is to shun the temptations of a monopoly.... Its purest office is the gathering of News. At the peril of its soul it must see that the supply is not tainted.' Scott opposed the imperialism of the Boer War; he opposed rising protectionism; he supported the miners. But all around him traditional pacifist liberalism was falling away into socialism, imperialism, tariff reform. Scott was a different kind of editor from Delane, standing for values rather than for a party or class interest – a distinction which was to be an essential element in the gradual redefinition of the role of the newspaper in the approaching twentieth century.

The patterns of the English press were stamped on new newspaper industries throughout the Anglo-Saxon and imperial world. After Catholic Emancipation, the Irish press was ready to develop around nationalist and religious interests. The *Nation* was founded in 1842 by Thomas David, Charles Gavan Duffy and John Blake Dillon to explain how Irish nationhood was relevant to contemporary events rather than simply to the country's vast and romantic history. Thirty papers were founded before 1850, including historically important journals such as the Catholic *Penny Magazine* of 1834, the *Catholic Guardian* of 1851 and Frederick Lucas's *Tablet* of 1840.

In India, the foundations of the press had been laid in the 1780s by James Hickey's *Bengal Gazette* and several papers published in Calcutta and Bombay. Some of the papers of the early nineteenth century lasted rather longer; these included the *Times of India*, founded in 1838 as the *Bombay Times and Journal of Commerce*. The Mutiny of 1857 brought severe official measures against the press, but in 1861 a certain freedom returned, enabling newspapers to build upon the new telegraph and railway system which was then being constructed. The Vernacular Press Act of 1878 placed a new series of restrictions on the 170 native-language papers which then existed. In 1875 the liberal weekly paper *Friend of India* moved to Calcutta, and later merged with the *Indian Statesman* to become a most important instrument in the struggle for independence which began in the mid 1880s with the founding of Congress.

Although a printing-press had arrived in Australia in 1787 with the very first fleet, it was not used for newspapers. News (and, more important, critical comment) was confined at first to 'pipes' – handwritten sheets which passed from person to person. The *Sydney Gazette and New South Wales Advertiser* was founded in 1803, and this was followed by other papers in Hobart and Derwent; all were official journals, created by the administration. In the 1830s a more normal form of newspaper began to emerge, although occasionally, as in the case of the *South Australian Gazette and Colonial Register* of 1836, the first number was printed in London and shipped out. Victoria's first paper was actually handwritten in its earlier editions and its contemporaries were censored papers, issued only on licence from the authorities. A struggle developed for press freedom in the 1820s which

The Sydney Morning [Herald]

"IN MODERATION PLACING ALL MY GLORY, WHILE TORIES CALL ME WHIG—AND WHIGS A TORY."

VOL. XIV.   WEDNESDAY, AUGUST 3, 1842.   No. 1625.

embittered relations between settlers and officialdom. None the less, foundings were frequent: New South Wales by 1835 had seven competing papers, and fifty more were founded between 1840 and 1860, all with tiny circulations of a few hundred. The *Sydney Morning Herald*, started in 1831 and published daily from 1840, has survived until today. By 1848 there were eleven dailies in Australia, and by 1886 forty-eight, with a large group of other periodicals growing up around them. Much of the content at first consisted of reprints from London papers, but the connection of Melbourne, Sydney and Brisbane by cable in 1861 created a more realistic internal news market. Illiteracy was widespread in Australia until the 1870s, but after that educational reform, as in England, introduced a large new group of readers.

First things first for the *Sydney Morning Herald* in 1842: fast steamboats leaving every morning for the Parramatta races.

The *Montreal Herald*'s front page, heavy with advertising, reflects the great increase in mid-nineteenth-century Canada's population.

New Zealand's first paper was founded within three months of the docking of the first immigrant ship in 1839. A rash of new papers appeared in the 1850s, nearly all of them of brief duration. The modern press structure really dates from the period 1860–80, with such titles as *The Press* (Christchurch) and the *Otago Daily Times* (Dunedin) both being founded in 1861, the year of the establishment of the cable; in the North Island the *New Zealand Herald* (Auckland) and the *Evening Post* (Wellington) emerged in the same decade, together with a clutch of other papers, all concentrating on news from England and Europe rather than on New Zealand's own news.

In the colony of Hong Kong, administration and trade combined to create the first newspapers. The *Government Gazette* appeared in 1841 in Macao to print proclamations by the new British authorities. With the founding of the colony itself a year later a printing-press was brought to Hong Kong and a new paper, the *Friend of China and Hong Kong Gazette*, was created, alongside a Chinese-language coeval, the *Wha Tse Yat Pao* ('Chinese mail').

The press of Canada was having a far more troublesome time than its colleagues in the Antipodes in dealing with the London authorities. The total circulation of the Canadian press during the Napoleonic Wars was as little as 2,000, spread among 20 journals. But industrialization started very soon after, and massive population increases took place some decades earlier than in Australia. By the middle of the century there were nearly three hundred papers of varying periodicity, all of them heavy with advertising. A vigorous factionalism broke out between pro-government papers and reformists. In Montreal the *Minerve* (founded in 1826) fought against the francophone *Montreal Gazette* and the more extreme *Montreal Herald* (1811). There were frequent conflicts with the authorities, and many papers ceased after their staff were prosecuted. In 1835, in Halifax, Joseph Howe fell foul of the government after a blistering attack, and his case constituted an important step towards press freedom. The *Canadian* of Etienne Parat advocated reconciliation, and many papers realigned their politics to the new issues of the mid-century. In 1850 the cable finally reached the coastal provinces and made possible a flow of news concerning Canadian internal affairs; a series of new solid city papers were following in its wake, including the *Toronto Globe* and the *Ottawa Bytown Packet* (both renamed later). By 1850 every population centre either had its own newspaper or was within reach of one, although the extremely high cost of postage kept circulations relatively low. By 1900 there were 121 dailies and nearly a thousand weeklies; Manitoba had started its *Nor' Wester* in 1859 and Edmonton its *Bulletin* in 1880. Nevertheless, Canadian newspapers remained 'small-town' affairs until the great era of capital investment and industrialization at the end of the century.

In America, as we have already seen, the newspaper had become a crucial tool in building the nation. By 1830 there were still only 26 towns with more than 8,000 inhabitants, but there were 65 daily newspapers and another 630 weeklies. As political turbulence subsided, it became evident that commerce rather than politics provided the most stable basis for newspaper enterprise; a large group of 'advertisers' came into existence, bringing information to the new mercantile aristocracy of the larger cities. Arthur Tappan's *New York Journal of Commerce* (1827) adopted a rather lofty moralistic tone, adapting itself to the more sober and religious outlook of this class; his paper rejected advertisements for alcohol and for the theatres. The *New York Courier* (1826) was completely different: its proprietor, Mordecai M. Noah, both wrote and advertised plays, and used his paper to display his flair for the more theatrical kind of politics: he once tried to found a homeland for the Jews on Grand Island near Buffalo, renamed Ararat, of which he proclaimed himself the first governor. His fellow Jews, however, declined his offer to settle, and Noah contented himself with a succession of other, more practical posts as sheriff and judge in New York County. The commercial papers did not eschew political news, nor did the political papers completely avoid commercial information; but gradually, all papers were drawn into the task of national and local administration. They printed gubernatorial messages, the

Gordon's Children............ { Master Gallott
                                { La Petit Gallo t
betrothed to Donald Leslie..Miss Fanny Herring
Daughter to Gen. Wheeler. ....Miss Hathaway
Wife of Col. Gordon....... Miss N. Ferguson
Dancing Girls of the Rajah's Zenani. Scottish and
ish Soldiers Sepoys, Women, Children
British Soldiers, Sepoys, Gorkas, Mahrat'as, Fe-
Brahmins, by a well-trained and numerous army

SHNU IN THE GRAND SQUARE OF BENARES—Feast
  Procession of Hindoo Dancing Girls—Sepoys and
  Fakeers.

rahma Dance by Sig Felix and W. Carlo.
Hail hail! all hail to India's God !"
disguised; the Pass Word, "It is the Maharajah,"
by the unsuspecting British residents; Song by

"There's nae Land like Scotland !"
lot discovered to Havelock by Donald Leslie; the
pped; the Assassin's Doom—Instant Death; the
own from the Muzzles of the Guns; Grand Tableau
he Punishment inflicted on the Sepoy Murderers.
GHT VIEW OF RUINED HINDOO TEMPLES.
ie,
A Highland Laddie Heard o' War !"
ted with wine, attempts to insult Jessie: "I want
when I do, I'll e'en tak it frae Donald Leslie !"
our sword."
        HAVELOCK'S QUARTERS.
risoner ; Jessie Brown, disguised as a Goorka
er lover to escape.
TERIOR OF THE FORT AT CAWNPORE.
of the Fort by the English troops ; Miss Wheeler
he Zenani ; the American Missionary Protects the
Tableau of Horror Illustrating the
MASSACRE of the AMERICAN MISSIONARIES
        and the
WOMEN and CHILDREN at CAWNPORE.
eral Havelock ; "I struck in the defence of vir-
hat I was a soldier, and remembered only that
;" affecting interview between Jessie and her

ahib's Zenani ; Hindoo Spear and Shield Dance
n'le CARLINE and ELOISE CARLO.
fought against the ion of the Sea ; they fought
hen their wars ended, turned their bright blades
ooks, and gave Heaven thanks that brother had
he brother's blood ; "The Red Cross Flag of
he Starry Banner of my loved America, side by
ed float, and sweep t rauny from the world."
        MOUNTAIN PASS.
surrounded and defeated by the British High-
d Standard Fight by Leslie and A'canor ; Donald
s the sword and standard to the Hero Have-
Boys, Cheer ;"
ORY and TRIUMPH at BUDDAPORE
        TENT OF HAVELOCK.
THE WELL OF CAWNPORE ;
ct of General Wheeler's Daughter ; the Scot
ance on the dead body of the innocent, "for
fe." Thrilling ableau.
NEAR LUCKNOW—The Bivouac ; Song and Cho-
d Highlander.
"Caledonians, Wake to Glory !"
he Bungalow ; Heroic defence of Gordon, Stuart
lon ; Gordon, to save the honor of his wife,
nd slays himself.
AY IN THE TRENCHES."—Sergeant Magraw and
pedition; "Women and children want the bite

SCENE—THE RAMPARTS AT LUCKNOW.
ce of the Garrison, aided by the Women, who
uns; Arrival of the Sergeant with provisions—
r one meal anyway;" Death but no dishonor;
held! "'tis the Macgregors, the grandest o' them
ed !"
        "THE LAST ATTACK."
over the Ramparts; the
        RELIEF OF LUCKNOW
ders; Grand and Imposing Tableau of
HAVELOCK'S LAST VICTORY !

ed by the nautical drama of
        BEN BOLT.
....Mr. D. Harkins
        (Late of Burton's Theatre.)
.....................Mr. G. L. Fox
.....................Mrs. H. F. Nichols
t.....................Miss Fanny Herring
with the comedietta of
HE MAID WITH THE MILKING PAIL.
.....................Mr G. Brookes
.....................Miss Julia Daly

T'S MINSTRELS, MECHAN-
LL, 472 BROADWAY, ABOVE GRAND STREET.
March 15th, 1858, and every night this week.

Who would wish to go FREE when they can be INDEPEN-
DENT, and see and hear so much for 25 cents ? Children under ten, 13 cents.

ACADEMY OF MUSIC.—THE HU-
GUENOTS,
        ON MONDAY, MARCH 15, at 7½.
Fourth nights of Meyerbeer's
        HUGUENOTS.
        CARD TO THE PUBLIC.
The "Huguenots" has three times filled the Academy, and
has produced that sensation which a composition of such magnitude is entitled. The public have had ample opportunity to
convince themselves that the large promises held out before
its production have been strictly fulfilled. In consequence of
the approaching departure of MR. FORMES, the daily expected arrival from Paris of Monsieur MUSARD, there will be
given only
THREE MORE PERFORMANCES of the HUGUENOTS.
They will be succeeded by Mr. Fry's opera of
        LEONORA,
fter which the long and brilliant season of 1857-'8 will defini-
tively close.

BOWERY THEATRE.—
Lessee and Manager.....................Mr. E. Eddy
Boxes and Parquette.....................25 cents
Pit.....................12 cents
        MONDAY EVENING, March 15th,
First appearance of
        MR. McKEAN BUCHANAN,
who is engaged for six nights only.
        KING LEAR.
King Lear.....................Mr. McKean Buchanan
Edgar.......Mr. R. Johnston | Cordelia......Miss Alice Grey
And the drama, of
        MARY, QUEEN OF SCOTS.
With a powerful cast—and the farce of
        STATE SECRETS.

SANTA CLAUS CONCERT, BILLIARD
        AND REFRESHMENT SALOON.
APOLLO AND TERPSICHORE ! THALIA AND MELPHOMEME !
Unite every evening to please the admiring thousands who
will visit the
        SANTA CLAUS, 596 BROADWAY.
Charming Singing ! Pretty Dancing ! Sweet Music !
        Grace ! Beauty ! Talent !
        One door above Metropolitan Hotel.
R. Williams.....................Manager and Proprietor.
G. Rae.....................Stage Manager
        Admission. 12 cents.
R. WILLIAMS takes the pleasure of presenting to the pa-
trons of his establishment the finest assortment of Liquors,
Wines and Cigars, and pledges himself to make everything
agreeable to the tastes of the most fastidious. The Refreshment Department will be most promptly attended to by his
punctual attendants, and he is determined to prevent the neg-
ligence so visible in the Concert Room.
DODWORTH'S Band will give a Sacred Concert this (Sunday) evening.
Don't forget the Santa Claus, 596 Broadway, (formerly Empire Hall,) a few doors above Niblo's.

NOTICE EXTRAORDINARY !—
        BROOKLYN ATHENEUM.
        BY DESIRE,
GEORGE CHRISTY & WOOD'S MINSTRELS,
from 561 and 563 BROADWAY, will give their
        FIRST EVENING ENTERTAINMENT,
as above, on MONDAY EVENING, March 15th, when they will
present a
        GALAXY OF ETHIOPIAN STARS
and give selections from their
        CHOICEST GEMS OF MINSTRELSY.
GEO. CHRISTY and GEO. HOLLAND
will appear together.
This Company will produce, in a few days, at their
        NEW HALL IN BROADWAY
AN ENTIRELY NEW GRAND PANORAMA,
descriptive of the incidents in a
        NEW YORK SLEIGHING CARNIVAL,
painted on upwards of
        1000 FEET OF CANVASS !
Tickets 25 cents.
Doors open at 6½; to commence at 7½.

NEW YORKER STADT THEATRE.—
        GERMAN THEATRE.
Nos 37 and 39 Bowery, opposite the Bowery Theatre.
        THURSDAY EVENING, March 18,
the new play, entitled
        LOLA MONTEZ IN BAVARIA.
Mrs. HOYM as LOLA MONTEZ. After the play, Madame
LOLA MONTEZ will give a new Lecture (in English) entitled
THE COMIC HISTORY OF LOVE. Doors open at 7; Curtain

---

proceedings of State legislatures, election news and accounts of important trials and Supreme Court proceedings. Samuel Harrison Smith, friend of Jefferson and founder of the *National Intelligencer* of Washington, had handed his paper over in 1810 to two men who specialized in transcribing debates. The paper became a daily in 1813, and foreshadowed the *New York Times* of today in acting as a kind of newspaper of national record.

When John C. Calhoun broke up his political partnership with Andrew Jackson in 1830, Jackson found himself in need of a paper which would support his line on tariffs. Two tough Kentucky cotton men, Francis P. Blair and John C. Rives, started the *Washington Globe* to rally support and to provide political intelligence for Jackson and his party managers; the two men adopted the role of private advisers, watching for dangerous alliances, detecting discontent, flying kites, acting as political bargainers, suggesting the recipients of 'spoils'. Their causes were those of popular government: cheap lands and state banking. The *Globe* became the eye of the political storm; it supplied the machinery for wheeling and dealing, the bargain store of the administration.

Jackson was the first President to elevate the press to an actual means by which government was conducted. At one point there were fifty-seven journalists on the official payroll. One of them, Duff Green, had acquired Jackson's trust by printing a story before Jackson's election to the effect that President and Mrs Adams had had premarital sexual relations. It was when Green later defected to the Calhoun faction that Jackson decided to form an even stronger bond with Blair and his *Globe*, through which he was able to play public opinion like an orchestra. Editorials and pro-Jackson gossip would be spirited into the columns of rural papers and then triumphantly copied in the *Globe* as unassailable evidence of Jackson's popularity with the public. His enemies found themselves entangled in a network of influences which spread outwards from the *Globe*.

It was not until the establishment in 1860 of the Government Printing Office, which meant the end of patronage through printing contracts, that the party press of Washington was completely extinguished. Abraham Lincoln, who had himself been a secret correspondent during his time in the Illinois legislature, politely rejected all offers from editors to serve him, not because he eschewed direct patronage but because he had had relationships with so many journalists during his political career that he felt he could only lose by selecting a few to deal with. Joseph Medill of the *Chicago Tribune* had pushed Lincoln towards the Presidential candidature and persuaded the party leaders to hold the nomination convention in Chicago, handing out the best seats in the hall to Lincoln stalwarts. But Lincoln wanted the support of the other new men of the press also, men who could command much more popular support than a cabal of party hacks. He worked on getting information into a new generation of papers produced by journalists with a more common touch.

Even before the middle of the century, however, there were publishers who saw the potential of purely popular newspapers making their profits directly from their readers. Benjamin H. Day founded the first penny paper in New York, the *Sun*, in 1833. Instead of selling subscriptions on an annual basis,

Opposite Mordecai M. Noah's *New York Courier* carried advertising for drink, lotteries and even the theatre – anything from *King Lear* to the *Christy Minstrels*.

Newsboys picking up their wares in Union Square, New York, in 1878.

Opposite James Gordon Bennett.

according to the prevailing system, Day hired a squad of small boys, letting them have a hundred copies for 67 cents. The pavements thus became a publicity platform for his paper, which was filled with mass-appeal news of trials, suicides, fires or burglaries. It was easy to read: all the sentences were short. In New York, Day had concluded, there was a large potential public of maids and draymen, clerks, shopkeepers, barbers, people who occupied the streets and who fed the gossip of the city. The *Sun* addressed the restless, those without roots, but did not completely avoid politics, dealing only with those affairs which were meaningful to people who had no direct physical contact with the political world and who were not themselves affected by every shift and change of administration. By 1837, when he sold it, Day's paper had a circulation of 30,000.

James Gordon Bennett, in 1835, founded the *New York Herald* with the intention of reaching an audience very similar to that of the *Sun*. However, Bennett's innovation was to bring into his pages the specialized material of the other existing forms of journalism: political essays, foreign news, commercial intelligence. He was more catholic in his own tastes and skills than Day, more literary, but his tongue was sharper and his confidence in his own views greater. 'A newspaper can be made to take the lead ... in the great movements of human thought, and human civilisation. A newspaper can send more souls to Heaven, and save more from Hell, than all the churches or chapels in New York.' Bennett worked at every element of his extremely variegated paper himself, building his circulation to 20,000 in a single year

137

and then doubling the price to 2 cents. He approached the world of New York events like a tornado; his paper was like himself, high-blown, self-publicizing, pungently witty, egotistic. By 1860 60,000 people bought it every day.

The *New York Tribune* of Horace Greeley, founded in 1841, was in a rather different genre. Greeley adopted the stance of journalistic messiah, prophesying against the sins of the era, preaching to his readers against slavery, alcohol and war, enjoining them to adopt uncomfortable reforms such as women's rights, scientific agriculture or trades unions. One of his causes was associationism: he wanted to divide America into small co-operative communities. For thirty years he absorbed vast quantities of contemporary information – statistics, politics, science, reports of government – and made it the raw material of his crusades. Although his influence in political circles grew with the years, Democratic party leaders were nervous of giving him office lest they be stained with the ridicule which his restless earnestness aroused. On his staff was a group of similarly determined and convinced reformers – travellers, poets, philosophers – all intent on examining and expounding the condition of their time. Karl Marx was among his occasional contributors. Greeley snatched at every available idealism, however untried, impractical or self-righteous.

By 1850 the New York newspaper was the repository of a large quantity of solid capital, and the time was ripe for the advent of journalism as a major business. Where Bennett had founded the *Herald* with $300 and Greeley the *Tribune* with $3,000, Henry J. Raymond started the *New York Times* in 1851 with $10,000, and reached 45,000 purchasers by 1860 at a price of 2 cents. It was a stylish paper, with none of the hysteria or ballyhoo of its rivals; it was professionally managed and drew its material from local, national and international affairs, from finance, literature and politics, on the basis of judicious selection. Its investment was too large for recklessness. In New York alone 200,000 people were now buying daily newspapers, with a similar number in Boston and Philadelphia, and newspaper-owners were accepted as part of the commercial élite. They were able to cope with the libel laws more easily because they could afford the risks and could even benefit from the publicity of a major libel trial. However, the majority of American papers were still country weeklies, of which there were over 3,000 compared with only 400 dailies, all benefiting from the postal privileges which effectively subsidized country publishing.

Within the newsroom, a revolution was taking place. The editing of papers was ceasing to be a matter of clipping pieces from letters and other papers. There were specialist agencies springing up which provided comprehensive services of clipped news from all the English or European papers; these private agencies supplied large groups of customers, who could thus provide their readers with a far better service than that of their smaller rivals. The telegraph improved the speed and competitiveness of these services after the late 1840s. Groups of newspapers would sometimes pool their resources to speed the flow of information from an important single event such as the Mexican War or, later, the American Civil War. In 1848 six New York papers allied themselves into the Associated Press, which

Opposite Horace Greeley, earnest journalistic messiah.

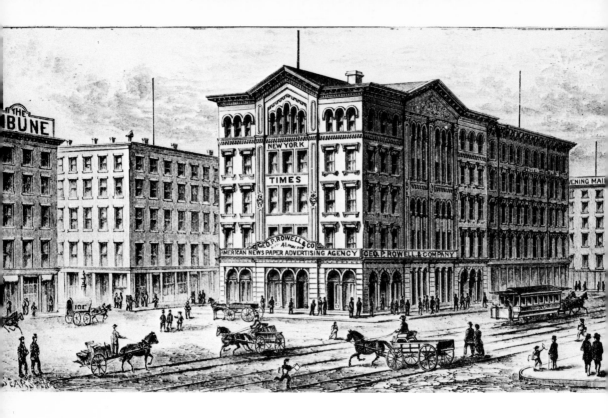

Times Square, about 1872.
By now, newspapers were
becoming big business.

arranged for an agent in Boston to collect news from steamships and
telegraph it to New York at the rate of thirty words for a dollar. Any paper
joining the AP service had to agree to use no other agency, and in the 1860s
there was little choice for the papers of provincial cities but to subscribe to a
service which was run by New York papers for the benefit of New York
papers; the growth of the agency was an important factor in the decline of
political, religious and other specialist papers, who were cut off from the kind
of information on which their links with their special-interest audiences
depended. The more successful papers were creating their own networks of
correspondents in Europe to make their coverage more colourful and
personal. The same applied to the coverage of affairs in Washington, where
scores of papers soon had their own specialist correspondents.

The larger of the owner-editors were being forced further into
management and away from day-to-day control. The *New York Times* alone
spent half a million dollars on the coverage of the Civil War, and had to
deploy enormous organizational skill to assemble horses and wagons,
steamboats and special trains to ferry correspondents and copy. Reporting
became highly specialized, its very logistics demanding knowledge and high
energy. With the arrival of advertising agencies in the 1840s, the manager
and the editor became even further removed from control of their advertising
material. There were now professionalized intermediaries everywhere, new
centres of inaccessible and expensive expertise. Nevertheless, the great
publishers were still something more than investors; they had to push the

journalistic revolution from stage to stage, aware of their role as links between local administration and great geographical blocks of population.

In the 1880s, all over the world, the newspaper was ready for a new formula. The market was now large enough for the old loyalties between a newspaper and a tiny social group to have lost their meaning; the technology of the industry was such as to make further expansion essential, and this in turn required investment on a large scale. A wholly new audience was waiting to be catered for, but it needed completely different treatment at the hands of editors and journalists. The newly literate would not read the long ribbons of type reporting hour-long political speeches verbatim without cross-headings. The new gadgetry of the period – from organized pigeons for sports reporting to the telephone – was waiting to fulfil a new journalistic design.

A war correspondent's bivouac in the Civil War: photograph by Matthew Brady.

6

'The Demon of Sensationalism'
1880–1980

In the view of the writers and owners of newspapers in most of the countries we have mentioned so far, the 1880s and 1890s were a golden age of journalism. One English provincial editor, Charles Pebody, wrote a sort of hymn to the press in his book *English Journalism and the Men Who Have Made It* (1882): the press, he said, 'had renewed the youth of the State ... purified the public service; raised the tone of our public life; made bribery and corruption ... impossible'. Ella Wheeler Wilcox, in *The Worlds and I* (1919), described America's popular 'yellow press' as 'a newspaper which glows with the colour of sunshine and throws light into dark places'. Public opinion appeared to have become the primary force by which modern society moved, and its miraculous dynamism was the end-product of the newspaper. W.T. Stead, who as editor of the *Pall Mall Gazette* (so titled after Thackeray's fictitious newspaper in *Pendennis*, 1849) pioneered the 'new journalism' of England in the 1880s and prepared the way for the mass newspaper of the twentieth century, wrote that the telegraph and the printing-press together 'had converted Britain into a vast agora, or assembly of the whole community, in which the discussion of the affairs of State is carried on from day to day in the hearing of the whole people'. The combined operations of a broad electorate, a free platform and a cheap newspaper were widely deemed to have created a perfect mechanism for the governance of society. In *Physics and Politics* (1872), Walter Bagehot had characterized the period as an 'age of discussion' in which social conflict had finally been transferred to a mental realm.

This bout of self-confidence was more than a journalistic spasm; in many countries the last generation of the nineteenth century experienced a press which had taken over a major part of the representation of large sections of opinion and of the scrutiny of government. 'The true Church of England, at this moment,' wrote Carlyle in his essay 'Signs of the Times' (1829), 'lies in the Editors of its newspapers'; and Stead was doing no more than exaggerate when he said that the newspaper 'is the great court in which all grievances are heard and all abuses brought to the light of open criticism'. The press was finally able to perform functions of this kind, where it wished to, as a matter of policy. But golden ages quickly pass, and while the newspaper has retained something of the aura which it acquired so widely in the late nineteenth century, it has accumulated more in the way of self-scepticism and crisis-stricken concern in the course of the present century, and in the 1980s it will, without doubt, undergo a major historical convulsion. Its production technology is changing under the impact of a changing economic role and a shifting position within a new range of information industries. The roots of

Opposite Midnight: the sub-editors' room.

these late-twentieth-century changes are discernible in the circumstances which brought the new newspaper forms of the late nineteenth century into being.

The improvements in reporting and production methods in the middle of the nineteenth century meant that very large amounts of capital had to be injected into new titles; £100,000 was raised to start Charles Dickens's *Daily News* in 1846, and a similar sum was spent over the course of ten years to bring its circulation up to a profitable size. A newspaper needed a dozen parliamentary reporters, six court reporters, a string of correspondents in European capitals and a small squad of leader-writers, plus provincial reporters and 'penny-a-liners' by the dozen. Sixty men were required to print a daily paper. Profits also were high: *The Times* made £30,000 in 1845, and a well-run provincial paper selling a thousand a day should make its owner between £1,500 and £3,000 a year in profit. The *Manchester Guardian* made nearly £7,000 a year. Clearly, the newspaper in Victorian society was no

W. T. Stead, pioneer of the 'new journalism'.

MR. W. T. STEAD.

THE MAN WITH THE MUCK-RAKE.

Opposite The press gallery in the House of Commons, above the Speaker's chair.

144

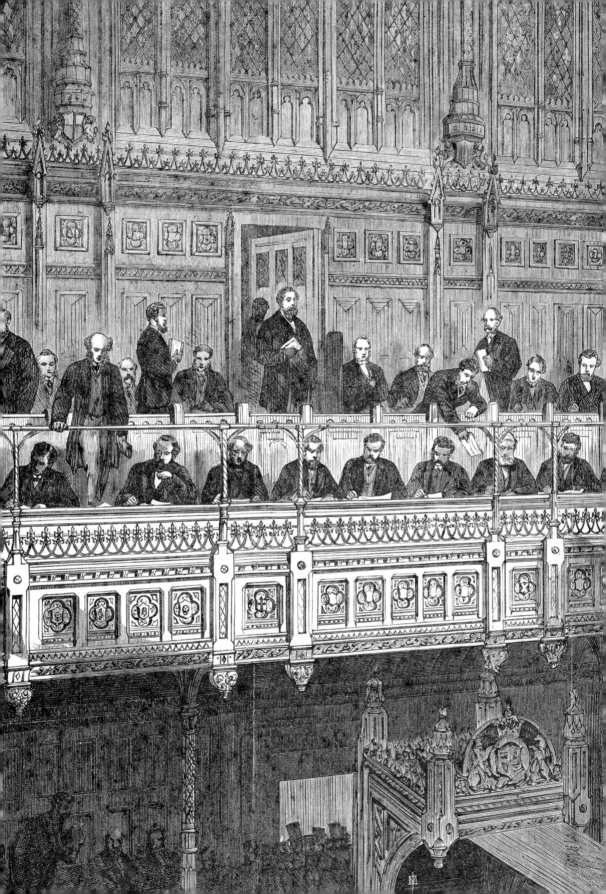

Advertisement for Lipton's Teas, about 1893 – the high noon of empire.

longer merely an appendage of the printing industry, but had become an important industry in its own right, its machinery, capital and management belonging primarily to itself. It had also added to its special political role an important role in the shaping of the economy, making possible new forms of social and economic activity which came to depend upon it for their continued existence. Mr Lipton's groceries could be marketed only through an advertising medium which reached right out into and through society, down to the poorest sections of the community. The great new departmental stores needed to get customers to the city centres in their tens of thousands. Before the coming of the cinema, radio and television, the advertising industry was largely dependent upon the newspaper.

Indeed, the newspaper became inextricable from all those other industries and activities which were directed at the same vast public. Mr Lipton's packaged tea was wrapped in paper made cheap by the same processes which created halfpenny newspapers. The public which flocked to football matches and other sporting events had been created by the sports reporters in the newspapers. A new fashion industry offered designs to suit the pockets of the women who read the new women's journalism. What was good for the newspaper was good for a series of other industries whose commercial success was based upon regular supplies of public information. Gradually, the management of the newspaper came to accommodate itself to a new situation in which advertising regulated the whole shape, size and general design of its product. Newspapers had always, as we have seen, drawn a large proportion of their revenue from advertising; what happened in the twentieth century was that newspapers came to look upon their potential readers as segments of consumerdom. In some countries, the population was divided into great demographic slabs and newspapers tailored their contents and their advertising policy to the needs and presumed attitudes of specific social groups or carefully delineated sections of social classes. In others, newspaper markets operated geographically, each community supporting a group of newspapers which has tended since the Second World War in most places to shrink into a local monopoly. The opinion-leading functions of the newspaper have shrivelled as its economic functions have become better and more scientifically organized. Where it saw itself in its heyday as a medium competing for the attention of voting groups and interest groups, it has now come to concentrate on making itself indispensable to consumers of goods.

A further constraint has developed from this. Where a newspaper sees that it has a monopoly over the flow of advertising to a given group of consumers, it can afford to add pages, supplying them with editorial material to accompany the quantities of advertising available; where it competes within the same market of readers with other newspapers, it is constantly in danger of losing large sections of its advertising revenue, since advertisers always like to go to the largest audience in a given region. The iron laws of modern newspaper management have, therefore, transformed the whole economic context in which the newspaper operates. Monopoly means safety and in many ways a better service for the reader; competition means serious uncertainty, with the danger that the loss of a small number of readers could cause the loss of a large amount of advertising. Newspapers seek to grasp and hold on to coherent sections of the population, growing up with them, growing old with them until their spending power withers away.

In the United States, the total amount spent on advertising in 1880 was just under 40 million dollars; by 1904 it was over 140 million. Although other media gradually started to absorb large sections of the rapidly growing volume of advertising, and newspapers found that their proportion of the total was declining, in classified advertising the newspaper continued to exercise a quasi-monopoly. In the late 1970s, America generated over 3 billion dollars' worth of classified advertising out of 6 billions in total advertising, with the prospect of that doubling or even tripling by 1985.

As soon as the newspaper became the supplier of large amounts of non-political information, the political line of the paper, while still important, ceased to be the main reason why its readers took it. Such has been the great transformation wrought in the last hundred years, and many of the other changes in the newspaper as a form follow from it.

In technological terms the twentieth century added only in speed and quantity to the production capacity of the newspaper until the development

of offset printing and photo-composition in the 1970s. At the turn of the century American newspapers were able to produce editions of well over a hundred pages; unit-type presses came into use by which a number of machines carrying duplicate stereotypes were linked for large circulations, while smaller local papers used just one or two units. From 1910 onwards various forms of colour printing were possible, and were used extensively in display advertising. Rotogravure illustration – etched on the cylinder – started in England in 1895, but became a regular feature of the American newspaper only after the First World War. Automatic devices were invented for making stereotypes, replacing the manual pouring of molten lead; improved folding mechanisms appeared, with stuffing devices for carrying extra supplements; and, of course, electricity replaced steam everywhere after 1900 to provide the energy for this improved gadgetry. The teletype machine enabled news to pour forth simultaneously in newspapers across the globe at hundreds of words per minute, where previously slower dot-and-dash telegraph signals had been used. In 1927 a method was developed by which perforated tape, punched out on a keyboard, was used to drive type-setting machines in the composing rooms of newspapers; this secured great economies of time and energy, and meant that composing work

Opposite Various forms of colour printing became possible in magazines in the early 1900s.

In the 1920s came the teletype machine.

could be spaced out through the day, with fewer peaks and troughs. In 1924 the first pictures were transmitted over wires, and a decade later the Associated Press was operating the first Wirephoto service, its competitors starting similar services within a year or two.

In 1859 Firmin Gillot, a French lithographer, had developed an improved method for etching on metal plates, and in 1872 his son invented zincography, which combined photography with etching so that the resulting picture could be sized up or down as required. *The Times* in 1877 boldly introduced the zincographic weather map. This technique, however, was limited to a uniform black on white. In 1880 the *Daily Graphic* announced a method of producing intermediate tones directly from a photographic plate 'without the intervention of drawing'. Other photographers, such as Frederic Ives of Cornell University, perfected this system of half-tones, representing lighter and darker areas by dots of differing sizes, and by the end of the century photography had become a new subdivision of the journalistic profession.

The telephone brought about a further subdivision among journalists: there were 'legmen' who went about the city collecting news and phoning it in, and 'rewrite men' who stayed in the office and tailored the news to fit the personality of the paper. Copyreaders then wrote the headlines. Women's news brought in the first groups of female reporters, while sports news demanded illustrators and photographers.

The real technological revolution in newspaper production of the twentieth century was based on a technique, conceived during a printing strike in 1919 but not developed until after the Second World War, for making a photo-engraving of typewritten material instead of setting it on line-casting machines. In 1947 an engineer working with a string of newspapers in Florida began experimenting with various photographic processes and adapting them to conventional letterpress printing; at the same time a number of book and magazine printers started examining ways to cut production costs with the use of photo-composition. A page-sized film was used for 'composing' the typewritten material and then employed to create an engraved plate which could be fixed on the existing press. Such plates, however, are expensive to make, and their use entails the wastage of a certain number of copies as each new roll of paper is introduced; it took many years before these 'offset' methods became economical, and even by 1960 they were usable only in small newspapers with small printing runs. Papers with many pages found it cheaper to use conventional stereotypes, but as production costs began to mount with the great inflation of the 1970s, further improvements were made and offset printing became viable for larger and larger publications. Cold type gradually replaced hot metal, and the whole atmosphere of newspaper production changed.

In the 1970s cheap computers became available, and ways were found to introduce them in the production of newspapers; the most wasteful aspect of newspaper work has always been the endless checking and retyping of material between journalist and pressroom by editors, secretaries, sub-editors, compositors. With the use of video-display units instead of conventional typewriters, journalists can 'type' their material direct into a central

One of the first lady journalists was Flora Shaw, who wrote for *The Times* on colonial questions in the 1890s. Later she married Lord Lugard, the great colonial administrator.

computer, from which it is recalled for reading on a display screen by editors, sub-editors and the journalist himself, and is then sent, at the push of a button, direct into the composition process. The computer sets the material in the correct type-size and arranges it on the page according to programmed instructions. Proof-reading is eliminated, human error reduced. Corrections are made at video terminals; the original key-strokes of the journalist are never repeated. The photo-composed plate can be printed on a modern offset press or attached to a conventional letterpress printing machine.

In the late twentieth century the newspaper has ceased in most countries to be a Victorian mechanical industry and has become a silent electronic industry employing a fraction of its once huge work-force. The great newspaper entrepreneurs find themselves with acres of empty buildings and office space in the centre of cities where once thousands of printers and compositors heaved hot and heavy metal from foundry to workbench. The newspaper has become the subject of a new industrial revolution, one which has brought it – by a technical paradox – much closer in the manner of its production to its electronic rivals, radio and television.

Technical change has always tended to reach the newspaper later than other industries. The entry of mass-production, as of automation, was delayed in the newspaper industry; it is as if the press always waits for the rest of the economy to take on a new shape before it accepts the process. The newspaper form is slow to change. In appearance, a paper of the 1890s was a product substantially the same as our own. Quarter-, half- and full-page advertise-ments were for the same basic things – fashions, personal transport, cosmetics, home utensils. The publishers fought hard for this new type of advertising to offset their investment in the large presses of that time; the advertisers, of course, wanted newspapers to be cheap, as consumer goods moved down-wards through the economic pyramid. So large were the risks now entailed in publishing newspapers that firms running into difficulties could be bought up only by other industrialists: Henry Villard, the railroad promoter, acquired the *New York Post* in 1881, hoping no doubt to gain a voice in the public press as well as a profitable new enterprise.

Throughout much of the nineteenth century, the Stamp Acts had kept British newspapers dull in format; so anxious were editors to crowd available space that the headline stood no chance. The pages were a uniform grey and covered in type. There was little sport and less humour. Only when W.T. Stead took over the *Pall Mall Gazette* in 1881 did a new, visually arresting form of journalism develop in London, greatly influenced by new practices in the United States. Stead imposed heavy black headlines, introduced the interview as a way of bringing out the personalities of journalists and public figures, and brought in the gossip column. He refused to use his newspaper any longer for the ponderous dissection of political affairs in theoretical terms. He mounted great causes, such as his attempt to expose white slavery, which landed him in gaol when he himself purchased a young girl to prove to his readers how easy this had become in London. Perhaps his most influential innovation was the cross-head, rendering long stories accessible to those without the habit of reading them in full. *The Times* finally went over to the Americanized headline in 1887, heaping its stories with a string of headings in different type-sizes. Stead mocked the paper for its belated conversion to this 'demon of sensationalism', but *The Times* had already introduced the equally arresting innovation of display advertising.

The phrase 'new journalism' was first used by the poet Matthew Arnold of the lively work of the *Pall Mall Gazette* and its competitors in the late 1880s. This was indeed the seedbed of the twentieth-century commercial popular press. However, improved machinery and a diversifying market of readers have produced wave upon wave of 'new journalisms' in the last hundred years. In the time of Stead there were many 'firsts' in journalistic style still to be achieved, and the big readership was still to be established as the norm, in Britain at any rate.

HOTEL
MÉTROPOLE.
TABLE D'HOTE DINNER,
6.0 to 8.30 WEEKDAYS and SUNDAYS,
Price Five Shillings,
Is AVAILABLE for LADIES and GENTLEMEN NOT RESIDING in the HOTEL. SEPARATE TABLES for LARGE or SMALL PARTIES may be ENGAGED in ADVANCE. HIGHEST CLASS CUISINE, FINEST WINES, and VERY BEST ATTENDANCE.
Telegraphic Address, "Métropole, London."

THE PALL MALL GAZETTE

INVIGORATING. NOURISHING.
BOUILLON FLEET.
THE NEW BEEF TEA.
Of all Grocers, Chemists, Licensed Victuallers, &c. If you find difficulty in obtaining BOUILLON FLEET from your own Grocer or Dealer, please send Order and Remittance direct to FLEET and CO., 1, Fenchurch-avenue, E.C. (and Camberwell), who will deliver free.
BOTTLES, 2s. 3d., 1s. 3d., and 6d.

No. 7465.—Vol. XLIX. *TUESDAY EVENING, FEBRUARY 19, 1889.* *Price One Penny.*

TO-NIGHTS ENTERTAINMENTS.

DRURY LANE.
(Augustus Harris, Lessee and Manager.)
THIS EVENING, at 7.30, THE BABES IN THE WOOD. Messrs. Harry Nicholls, Herbert Campbell, C. Lauri, jun., Stevens, Leno Griffiths Bros., Andrews, Inch, Pleon, Henderson, Stanley, Derano, and Harry Payne; Mesdames Florence Dysart, Maggie Duggan, Mayer, ÆNEA, Grey, Charteris, Deering, and Harriet Vernon. Box-office open daily from 10 to 5.

HAYMARKET THEATRE.
(Lessee and Manager, Mr. H. Beerbohm Tree.)
TO-NIGHT, at 8.15, THE MERRY WIVES OF WINDSOR. Mr. Tree, Messrs. F. Macklin, Edward Righton, Fuller Mellish, C. Allan, H. Kemble, Percival-Clarke, F. Harrison, J. S. Blythe, Robert Harwood, Crisp, Legge, C. Dodsworth, and Charles Brookfield; Misses Rose Leclercq, Henrietta Lindley, Aylward, and Mrs. Phelps and Mrs. Tree. Preceded, at 7.45, by THAT DREADFUL DOCTOR. Box-office open daily, 10 till 5.
MATINEES.—TO-MORROW (Wednesday), and Wednesday, Feb. 27, at 2.30, MASKS AND FACES. Triplet, Mr. TREE; Peg Woffington, Mrs. BERNARD BEERE; Mabel Vane, Mrs. TREE. Seats can now be booked.
"CAPTAIN SWIFT."—MATINEE SATURDAY NEXT, at 2.30.

LYCEUM THEATRE.
(Sole Lessee and Manager, Mr. Henry Irving.)
MACBETH, TO-NIGHT, at 7.45. Overture 7.40. Macbeth, Mr. Henry Irving; Lady Macbeth, Miss Ellen Terry. Messrs. Alexander, Wenman, Tyars, Webster, Howe, Haviland, Harvey, Johnson, Raynor, Outram, Lacy, Archer, &c.; Misses Marriott, Seaman, Desborough, Coleridge, Ivor, &c. Box-office (Mr. J. Hurst) open 10 to 5. Seats can also be booked by letter or telegram. Carriages 11. —LYCEUM.

CRITERION THEATRE.
(Lessee and Manager, Mr. Charles Wyndham.)
THIS EVENING, at 8.50, STILL WATERS RUN DEEP. Mr. CHARLES WYNDHAM, Messrs. H. Standing, W. Blakeley, S. Valentine, E. Emery, E. Dagnall; Miss MARY MOORE and Mrs. BERNARD-BEERE. Preceded by at 8.10, A PRETTY PIECE OF BUSINESS. Doors open at 7.45. N.B.—MATINEE of STILL WATERS RUN DEEP, EVERY SATURDAY, at 3.

TOOLE'S THEATRE.
THE DON. Mr. J. L. TOOLE. EVERY EVENING, at 8.30, THE DON. 25th Time. MATINEE of ARTFUL CARDS and ICI ON PARLE FRANÇAIS, on SATURDAY NEXT.

SAVOY THEATRE.
(Proprietor and Manager, R. D'Oyly Carte.)
TO-NIGHT, at 8.15, the New and Original Opera, in Two Acts, by W. S. Gilbert and Arthur Sullivan, entitled THE YEOMEN OF THE GUARD: or, THE MERRYMAN AND HIS MAID. Preceded at 7.20 by MRS. JARRAMIE'S GENIE. Doors open at 7. MORNING PERFORMANCE EVERY SATURDAY, at 2.30. Doors open at 2. Box-office open continuously from 9 A.M. to 11 P.M.

ADELPHI THEATRE.
(A. and S. Gatti, Sole Proprietors and Managers.)
THIS EVENING, at 8.0, THE SILVER FALLS. Mr. William Terriss; Messrs. C. Cartwright, J. D. Beveridge, J. L. Shine, W. L. Abingdon, Eardley Turner, J. Carne, W. Erskine, James East, H. Russell; Mesdames Millward, O. Nethersole, A. Dairolles, and Clara Jecks. At 7.15, Farce.

VAUDEVILLE THEATRE.
(Mr. Thomas Thorne, Sole Lessee and Manager.)
THIS EVENING, at 8.50, THAT DOCTOR CUPID. At 7.50, THE POET. Mr. Thomas Thorne; Messrs. Cyril Maude, Frank Gillmore, Scott Buist, F. Grove, Pagden, J. Wheatman, and Fred Thorne; Misses Fanny Robertson, Dolores Drummond, Annie Irish, Marion Lea, Maunder, and Winifred Emery, &c. Doors open, 7.30. Box-office open, 10 to 6.30. MATINEE of THAT DOCTOR CUPID, SATURDAY NEXT, and EVERY SATURDAY. Overture at 2.30.

GAIETY THEATRE.
THIS EVENING, at 7.30, FIRST MATE. At 8.30, FAUST UP TO DATE. Miss Florence St. John, Miss Violet Cameron, Miss Marie Illington, Miss Fanny Robina, Miss Jenny M'Nulty, Miss Lillian Price, Miss M. Jones, Miss A. F. Levey, Miss Young, Miss E. Greville, Miss M. Wilmot, Miss M. Love; Mr. J. E. Lonnen, Mr. H. Parker, Mr. E. Haslem, and Mr. George Stone.

TERRY'S THEATRE.
(Sole Lessee and Manager, Mr. Edward Terry.)
The safest Theatre in the world, constructed entirely with concrete and iron absolutely fireproof, lighted throughout by electricity.
TO-NIGHT, at 8.30, SWEET LAVENDER, by A. W. Pinero. 340th Time. Messrs. Edward Terry, Alfred Bishop, Brandon Thomas, F. Kerr, H. Reeves Smith, Sant Matthews, Prince Miller; Mesdames M. A. Victor, Carlotta Addison, Maude Millett, and Blanche Horlock. Doors open at 8. Carriages 11. MATINEE EVERY SATURDAY, at 2.30. Box-office open from 10 to 5. Telephone 2,702.—Acting Manager, Mr. H. T. Brickwell.

GLOBE THEATRE.
(Sole Lessee, Mr. Richard Mansfield.)
TO-NIGHT, at 8, SCHOOL FOR SCANDAL. Miss Kate Vaughan (specially engaged) as Lady Teazle; Mr. James Fernandez as Sir Peter; Mr. Lionel Brough as Moses. In the second act Miss Vaughan will dance in a Minuet arranged by herself. RICHARD III., Shakespeare's Tragedy, will be played at this theatre EARLY NEXT MONTH, upon the return of Mr. Mansfield.

STRAND THEATRE.
(Proprietor, Mr. J. S. Clarke. Manager, Mr. W. Duck.)
EVERY EVENING, at 9.15, under the immediate supervision of Mr. Charles Wyndham, the Farcical Comedy entitled THE BALLOON, by J. H. Darnley and G. Manville Fenn. Preceded, at 8.15 by F. W. Broughton's Comedietta of RUTH'S ROMANCE. Box-office open 10 to 5. PROFESSIONAL MATINEE on MONDAY, the 25th inst., and FIRST SATURDAY MATINEE on the 23rd inst., at 3 P.M.

OPERA COMIQUE THEATRE, Strand.
(Lessee, F. J. Harris.)
UNDER THE MANAGEMENT OF MRS. OSCAR BERINGER.
EVERY EVENING at 8.30, TARES, a Play in Three Acts, by Mrs. Oscar Beringer. Mr. J. Forbes Robertson, Messrs. C. W. Somerset, G. Canninge, E. Hendrie, W. Guise, and J. G. Grahame; Miss Kate Rorke, Misses Mary Collette, Marie Hudspeth, Gracie Murielle, Miss Maria Saker, and Miss Gertrude Kingston. Preceded by, at 8.0, A REGULAR FIX. Mr. Charles Collette, Mr. E. Hendrie, &c.—Business Manager, Henry Ball.

COURT THEATRE.
(Proprietors, Mrs. John Wood and Mr. Arthur Chudleigh.)
(Under the management of Mrs. John Wood.)
EVERY EVENING, at 9.0, LES SURPRISES DU DIVORCE, adapted by Sydney Grundy, and entitled MAMMA. 135th Performance. Preceded at 8 by COX AND BOX. Doors open 7.45. Box-office open 10 to 10. Telephone 3,031. LAST THREE MATINEES of MAMMA SATURDAYS, Feb. 23, and March 2 and 9, at 3.

PRINCE OF WALES' THEATRE.
(Lessee and Manager, Mr. Horace Sedger.)
TO-NIGHT, at 8.15, PAUL JONES. Preceded by, at 7.30, JOHN SMITH. Misses Agnes Huntington, Phyllis Broughton, Annie Schuberth, St. Cyr, Jeanie Mills, and Miss Wadman; Messrs. Harry Monkhouse, Henry Ashley, Templer Saxe, Albert James, George Preston, and Frank Wyatt. MORNING PERFORMANCE EVERY SATURDAY at 2.30.

LYRIC THEATRE.
(Sole Proprietor and Manager, Henry J. Leslie.)
TO-NIGHT, at 8.15, DOROTHY. 884th Performance. Mesdames Effie Chapuy, C. Saumarez, H. Coveney, F. Neville, and Amy Augarde; Messrs. Ben Davies, Furneaux Cook, Arthur Williams, J. Le Hay, W. T. Hemsley, and C. Hayden Coffin. At 7.30, WARRANTED BURGLAR PROOF. MATINEE EVERY SATURDAY at 2.30. LAST WEEKS of DOROTHY.

AVENUE THEATRE.
(Manager, Mr. H. Watkin.)
EVERY EVENING, at 8.15, SATURDAY MATINEES at 2, NADGY. Mdlle. Vanoni, Mr. Arthur Roberts, and powerful company. Conducted by Mr. John Crook. Preceded at 7.30 by QUITS. Doors open at 7.15; box-office open daily from 10 to 5 o'clock. Telephone 3,241. MORNING PERFORMANCE EVERY SATURDAY at 2.—R. D'Albertson, Acting Manager.

NO GUNS!

WE commend to the respectful attention of the good people who met last night at Birmingham to protest against the proposal to spend more money upon the Defence of the Empire, the letter which Lord CARNARVON has addressed to the *Times*, and the article which Mr. BURDETT contributes to the *Universal Review*. Taken together, they constitute about as discreditable a picture of unpreparedness for defence as ever scandalized the world. The arming of our coaling stations is certainly not an aggressive measure. It is simply and solely for the protection of the gateways of our Empire. But here is what Lord CARNARVON, who knows what he is talking about, tells us of the condition of some of the most important naval positions in the British Empire:—

Gibraltar.—"Out of accord with the necessities of modern warfare."

Sierra Leone.—Forts built: neither guns nor gunners.

The Cape.—Forts built or building: one gun, if there be one.

Mauritius.—Only old muzzle-loaders.

Hong Kong.—Some modern guns, low calibre.

Singapore.—A few ditto; none as heavy as 9 in.

So far the Coaling Stations, now for the Navy. The following is Mr. BURDETT'S list of ships at present without guns:—

No. of Ships.	Class of Ship.	No. of Guns wanting.	Calibre in Inches.	Weight in Tons.	Value of Ship without Guns in £'s sterling.	Remarks.
1	Barbette	4	13.5	87	650,000	New ship
1	"	4	...	67	680,000	"
1	"	4	...	67	675,000	"
1	Not known	2	9.2	22	265,000	...
1	New turret	4	...	67	800,000	Guns wanted in June.
1	Old turret	4	10.	30	600,000	To be rearmed this next year.
1	" "	2	9.2	22	400,000	To be rearmed this year.
1	Turret	2 2	16.25 10.	111 29	750,000	New Ship
1	"	2 2	16.25 10.	111 29	750,000	"
5	Twin-screw belted cruisers	10 50	9.2 6. 4.	22	1,300,000	Average cost of each ship, £260,000.
Total 14	...	92	...	...	6,870,000	

In addition to the ships enumerated in the table, there are at least five twin-screw cruisers of the second class and one twin-screw sloop nearly finished, which will require between them thirty-eight more guns before the year is much older. The value of these ships without the guns may be put down as about £690,000. Fifty six-inch guns are required for the twin-screw belted cruisers. There would therefore be required, in addition to the guns enumerated, a great number of quick-firing and machine guns, which have not been included. What chance is there, then, with nearly a score of warships as useless as coal hulks for want of guns, that there will be any to spare for the defence of coaling stations and home ports?

This is a pretty state of things to find ourselves in. It is an Imperial danger, and a great administrative disgrace. Imagine for a moment that war broke out to-morrow or next week, or, for the matter of that, next year, and where should we be? Here in England, the very Vulcan among the nations, we have not got, and, what is more, under the utmost stress of war could not cast, cannon to arm our battle ships and defend the gates of our ocean highways until after the war was over! What the ordinary man fails to realize is that nowadays it takes almost as long to construct a big gun as it does to build a ship. If the order were given to-morrow for the construction of every gun that is required and every available furnace and factory in the country set a going night and day, we could not get them manufactured in twelve months. No modern war in Europe has lasted so long.

The fault is in the system which leaves us no one to hang. No one is responsible because every one is responsible. What we want is an authentic, live man who is charged by the country with the duty of seeing that we have guns and ships, and who if he cannot prove that he has publicly, and solemnly, and formally demanded the means for providing them, and has been as publicly, and solemnly, and formally refused, will, on the discovery of such a state of things as is here set forth, be punctually hanged.

THE SILLY STORY OF SIMPLE SIMON.

BEING A NURSERY RHYME ADAPTED TO THE TIMES.

Simple Simon met a Pieman, looking very sly,
Says Simple Simon to the Pieman, "Have you got a pie?"

Says the Pieman to Simple Simon, "I haven't one as yet;
But as many as you'll swallow, from the Baker I can get."

So the Pieman saw the Baker just across the way,
To the Baker said the Pieman, "Tell me, Baker, pray,

Can you bake some pies for me?" "Yes," said the Baker bold,
"I'll bake some pies if you will pay a Thousand Pounds in Gold."

CHIT-CHAT FROM THE CONTINENT.

One of the most interesting buildings at Berlin is the Reichskanzlerpalais, which is just about to celebrate its one hundred and fiftieth birthday. King Frederick William I. himself inaugurated it in 1739, having presented Count von der Schulenburg with the plot of ground on which it was built. The Count, who was a member of the King's famous tobacco club—although the poor man had a perfect horror of the fragrant weed—received also a concession to brew within the walls of his "palais" "white beer and brown, and to sell it wholesale and retail."

* * * * *

Since then the stately building has seen many changes. At the end of last century Countess Dönhoff, the morganatic wife of Frederick William II., mourned in it the loss of her Sovereign's affections; *littérateurs* have laid many a scene in comic plays or tragedies within its walls, and now the Bismarcks reign supreme in the *ci-devant* brewery which in 1791 was sold at the price of £1,500, while in 1875 the Crown bought it for its Iron Chancellor at £100,000, and is still proud of the bargain.

* * * * *

The bazaar in the old Palace over which Princess Bismarck annually presides, has just been held, and the Chancellor has not disappointed the ladies, who hoped that he would grace the occasion by his presence. For a whole hour he remained every afternoon while the bazaar was open, delighting everybody by his gallantry and suavity. Next to Prince Bismarck, his tiny granddaughter, aged three, was the *persona grata* of the bazaar, and a golden harvest poured into the lap of the graceful little flower-girl.

* * * * *

It is a pity the Moorish Ambassadors did not arrive at Berlin a fortnight later, for of all the sights of the carnival they would incontestably have been the most picturesque as well as the most popular. As it is, they have quite dazzled the Prussians. Like the wise men of old who came from the East to bring their gifts to the newborn Sovereign, they have overwhelmed the powers that be with gorgeous presents. The Emperor received quite a stud of Moorish ponies, richly caparisoned, and Prince Bismarck was endowed with cloths and shawls and gold-embroidered silken stuffs, such as only the East knows how to produce. A pair of Moorish shoes and a magnificent carpet were also among the presents to the Chancellor.

* * * * *

But the heart of the German Pharaoh was hardened in one respect towards the polite and cultured Orientals. For lo, and behold! when they received their first audience at the Imperial Palace, it appeared that they were excellent French linguists, while not a sound of the terse tongue of the Fatherland was familiar to them. At which discovery his Majesty frowned, thenceforth addressing his guests only through their interpreter, and not even when four of the white-robed attachés, returning from a visit to the Krupp establishment at Essen, stuck ignominiously in the snow—whereat the Prussian heart was touched—did one word come across his lips in the language in which the Emperor could personally have expressed his sympathy to his honoured guests.

* * * * *

Madame Louise von Schiller, who has just died at Stuttgart at the age of eighty-five years, was the daughter-in-law of the poet, and the wife of his eldest son, Karl von Schiller.

* * * * *

To the curiosities of Paris belongs a placard on the wooden shutter of a baker's shop in the Rue de Rennes. It was posted in 1871 at the time of the Commune, and exhorts the soldiers of the Versailles army on their return to Paris to throw their guns away and to come and sit down at the hospitable hearth of the Communists. The shutter being only put up for a few hours during the night, it has never been taken down, and the rain has only effaced a few words of the interesting document.

* * * * *

A great deal is being said about the desirability of improvement in men's dress, and a few Parisian dandies are in good earnest trying to "make a change." Here is a description of the costume worn by one of them at a recent fashionable soirée—"mauve coat, white waistcoat and knee-breeches, black stockings, and buckle shoes." This costume, say the prophets of *la mode*, is to be universally worn during the coming season.

* * * * *

Lovers of birds beware of parrots and other birds of gay plumage! especially of those which come to us from the fair shores of South America; for it has just been discovered at Marseilles that a cargo of birds has brought over the germs of yellow fever from the swamps and lagoons of Venezuela and other South American countries. The first to fall a prey to the murderous germ were a couple of lovers and an old lady who had bought some of the gay plumaged chatterers. M. Pasteur will have to come to the rescue, for the desolation in French ports would be great were the shrieking parrots to disappear from the streets.

* * * * *

General Boulanger has posed for many a character, but in none has he ever been more admired and successful than in that of "snow man," as which he has graced the squares and streets of Copenhagen during the recent snow. It is the custom in Northern Europe to erect gigantic snow men during the winter, which are modelled after some eminent personage, provided with collecting-boxes, and put up in various parts of the towns where the traffic is liveliest. Last winter one of these snow men collected no less than 10,000 kroner, but the snow man who owed his existence as "Boulanger" to the recent snow has beaten last year's favourite, and collected quite a fortune, which is to be devoted to some benevolent purpose.

* * * * *

Miss Bergliot Björnsen, the eldest daughter of the great Norwegian poet Björnstjerne Björnsen, has just made her début as opera singer at Paris, and French impresarios and artists are enthusiastic in the praise of the wonderful soprano and the great dramatic talent of the young lady. Miss Björnsen is nineteen years old, strikingly beautiful, with fair hair and a tall slender figure. For the next two years she is to continue her musical education and at the end of that time a "starring tour" to America will be undertaken.

* * * * *

The export of fresh fish from Sweden in the course of the year 1888 amounted to 76,500,000 lb., while Norway, chiefly on account of its inferior railway and steamer service, has exported less than half of the quantity. The Swedes are evidently much more on the *qui vive* where the "wealthy foreigner" is concerned than their Norwegian brethren, and even now a decree has gone forth at Stockholm that a large number of railway guards should, at the expense of the State, be taught the German language, at an Upsala institution, in order to facilitate matters for the increasing number of German tourists and travellers in Sweden.

The Times continued to limp along with a circulation of 60,000, just about where it had been at the time of the repeal of the newspaper taxes. By 1880, however, the *Telegraph* was over 300,000, and the *Standard* not far behind, though it soon fell back. Solid journals like the *Daily Chronicle* and *Daily News* had reached a comfortable plateau at 100,000. There was also a new group of evening papers circulating in London and going out aggressively for new readers. The 'clubby' *Pall Mall Gazette* and the radical *Echo* were refurbished papers of the 1860s, but the *Evening News* and the *Star* of the radical journalist T. P. O'Connor were newcomers, as was the *Westminster Gazette* of 1893.

It was these evening papers which first educated the morning papers into editorial policies suitable for the masses. Kennedy Jones and Alfred Harmsworth (later Lord Northcliffe) worked out their ideas for mass journalism after they had acquired and developed the *Evening News* in the 1880s. There was a new generation emerging in the years after the Great Exhibition of 1851 which had great curiosity but little education. It needed new journalism of its own.

The first morning papers to follow the new approach of the evenings were the *Morning Leader* and the *Morning*, both founded in 1892; the latter was edited by Chester Ives, formerly of the *New York Herald*. Both of these papers proved to be a little before their time; in adopting the new layout and features they neglected to ensure that they looked like morning papers. Kennedy Jones himself worked for a time on the ill-fated *Morning* and took great pains, when he and Harmsworth started the *Daily Mail*, to see that it continued to bear the external appearance of that model of morning journalism, *The Times*. Its main news page, therefore, was opposite the leader page inside, the front page being reserved for advertising. In content and format it only cautiously reflected the great changes and experiments which had been transforming evening journalism for fifteen years. Only occasionally was a headline allowed to sweep across two or three columns, although stirring events such as the Boer War and the death of Queen Victoria did provide opportunities for the *Mail* and other papers to break loose from their conservative bonds.

The 1890s produced a brace of halfpenny morning papers, of which the *Daily Mail* was the first and most important. By the time of the First World War it had reached its million and made a fortune for its owner, who in 1908 had bought *The Times* as a signal of his own political importance and symbolically, though temporarily, reduced its price to one penny. In every major city there existed at least two penny dailies, which were as a group biased towards the Liberal interest and could make a living within their respective cities at circulations below – sometimes well below – 40,000. Alongside them there were an equal number of halfpenny evening papers, which gradually came to seem more viable than the mornings as the new mass-audience London papers advanced into the provinces. By 1914 it was clear that the Liberal penny dailies, backbone of provincial journalism, were to be the victims of the Northcliffe revolution.

Mass circulations were not in themselves the product of this revolution; *Lloyd's Weekly News* had sold 100,000 copies even in the days of the taxes,

Opposite T. P. O'Connor, radical editor of the London evening *Star*.

Lord Northcliffe, the pioneer
of mass journalism.

and reached a million in 1896 when the *Daily Mail* was only struggling into
the world. The *News of the World* and *Reynolds News* both achieved very high
circulations among working-class readers long before the new mass press
existed, and the former actually sold 1½ million in 1909 when its owner,
George Riddell, was ennobled by Asquith.

The periodicals which set the new owners of mass newspapers up in
business were not dedicated to news at all, but to digestible snippets of
popular information. Alfred Harmsworth, George Newnes and C.A.
Pearson owned magazines called *Tit-Bits*, *Answers* and *Pearson's Weekly*
respectively, which reached circulations close to a million and helped to
finance the much more difficult ventures of their publishers in the field of
daily newspapers. The capital needed to nurse a national halfpenny paper
into solid existence was beyond the capacity of the family firm, still the basic
unit of ownership for British newspapers; the characteristic form of enterprise

which now came into use was the joint stock company. The profits were there if a publisher could hold on and build his circulation slowly out of the virgin territory of the newly educated. The advertisers would help, but not sufficiently to save several ventures in the field from collapse: Franklin Thomasson's *Tribune* cost him £300,000 in two years, and for nothing. The rewards of success, on the other hand, were tremendous, in terms of profits, social status and political influence.

The success of the *Mail* lay in its brilliant distribution. The original intention of Harmsworth and Kennedy Jones had been to start not a national newspaper but a chain of allied papers, sharing a certain amount of material, in a series of cities. Various American proprietors were endeavouring to profit from similar economies. There had been a desperate effort to do the same thing with the London evening *Echo*, but the Storey–Carnegie alliance failed to pull off the plan for a chain of provincial weeklies. Harmsworth reorganized his scheme, realizing that what his weekly magazines could do, a daily paper could also do, with the help of newspaper trains and careful organization. The *Daily Mail* of 1896 was the product of a series of journalistic developments which date back to W.T. Stead's editorship of the *Pall Mall Gazette*.

What the end of the newspaper taxes in Britain in 1861 meant in the long term was that economic forces took precedence over political ones. Newspaper-proprietors had become 'gentlemen', and the greatest fear of some of them was that the cheapening of the press would undermine their social status. On the other hand, there was a new case to be made for allowing the press to become a cheap and generally available medium: an educated democracy would emerge. In the decision to make government responsible for mass literacy, a gigantic market had been guaranteed; the question was not whether the resulting hunger for printed material should be satisfied, but how it should be satisfied, with 'sweetness and light', as Arnold demanded, echoing Bunyan, or with 'anarchy'.

Newspapers everywhere were now becoming such large investments that many editors shrank from narrowing their potential readership by clinging too closely to one political party. In America this process went further than in England. Charles Dana of the New York *Sun*, for example, gave scanty support to Democrat candidates, preferring to adopt a position of general scorn towards all politicians, foreigners, farmers, reformers and trades unions. A kind of non-partisan crusading cynicism became a standard tone in much American journalism; men like William Rockhill Nelson, with his *Kansas City Star*, concentrated on exposing the misdeeds of city officials, building their papers on local rather than national muckraking; Victor Lawson's *Chicago Daily News* was likewise built up on clever local reporting, political independence and populist crusades. Another element in this particular phase was the circulation-building 'stunt', the deliberate creation of an item of sensational news by the paper itself: perhaps the most notorious of these was the journey of H.M. Stanley of the *New York Herald* to Africa in 1871–2 to find the lost Dr Livingstone. The 'yellow press' of later years in America was part of this phase – a form of stuntmanship in which readers were shocked by revelations of political huckstering into buying more papers.

Was Ihr auch thut, laßt mich aus Eurem Rath!
Ich hab' mit meiner „World" mich abzuquälen;

Bedürft Ihr meiner zu bestimmter That,
Dann ruft den Joe, es soll an mir nicht fehlen.

In the United States the dynamic of the new popular journalism lay in the struggle between great city papers to be first with the news, in the pursuit of 'beats' and 'exclusives' to accompany the material provided by the co-operative news-gathering agencies. It was no longer necessary for the newspaper to provide a continuous history of the era. Long-term processes of society became relegated to 'background'; the rapidly accelerating pace of city life created the pace, the tense, in which news was sought, created and presented. The raw material of the modern newspaper had to be 'hot', earth-shaking; the world of the newspaperman seemed to consist of a succession of convulsive actions, autonomous, sudden, unanticipated, disconnected. The stunt and the crusade replaced the great liberal causes as the intellectual quest of journalism. Joseph Pulitzer came over to America from Hungary in 1864 to fight in the Union army, and entered mainstream journalism via the German ethnic press; in 1878 he merged two newspapers of St Louis, the *Post* and the *Dispatch*, into a paper which fought a series of crusades; then he moved to New York and in 1883 took over the *World*, intending to profit,

Opposite Joseph Pulitzer, whose crusading *World* captured a mass market in New York. Elected to Congress in 1884, he soon found, as this cartoon makes plain, that he could not find time for both careers, and resigned before his term was up.

The *World* was one of the first papers to have a women's page, in recognition of their growing economic 'pull'. This one is dated 6 February 1898.

through the paper's attitudes and also by the use of simple, accessible language, from the market of new immigrant readers. He called for curbs on the great commercial monopolies, defended the right to unionize, supported income tax and death duties; but his greatest contribution lay in his ability to incite the reader to purchase the paper through the skilful banner headline designed for the sidewalk: 'Did She Steal the Diamonds? A Hotel Maid Accused of Stealing Jewels'; 'A Brother on the War-Path – He Attacks his Sister's Dentist and Then Tries to Shoot Him'. Within a year of its change of ownership, the *World* was selling 100,000 copies, and by 1890 its Sunday edition was up to a quarter of a million; by 1892, the total circulation of the morning and a new evening edition had reached 374,000. Pulitzer sent a woman journalist to beat Phineas Fogg's fictitious journey round the world in eighty days. He raised the money from his readers in nickels and dimes to build the Statue of Liberty. The *World*, however, was far less easily identified with a conciously working-class readership than its imitators in France and Britain; the paper contained a good deal of hard financial, foreign and political news. When in 1898 the *World* advocated war with Spain, its circulation topped the million; it was the sense of excitement rather than any of the paper's actual political lines which produced its extraordinary rise in sales. What Pulitzer offered the public was a ringside seat at a great display, rather than the conscientious enlargement of their citizenship. The new, professional popular press of the twentieth century turned its reader into a consumer of excitement, sensation, pity and fear.

The 'opinion' press had been strengthened for a time during and after the Civil War, but rapidly faded away under the impact of the new forms of journalism striving for entertainment and information rather than political leadership. Mary Baker Eddy founded the *Christian Science Monitor* in 1908 as a protest against the practices of the mass press, and went on to combat the 'jazz journalism', the organized sensationalism of papers like the *Illustrated Daily News* (started 1919); even more shocking forms were to follow in the tabloids which began life in America in the aftermath of the First World War and later spread to Britain. The publishers of newspapers went to greater and greater lengths to meet the reader on his own ground.

Another strain which died away in the last decades of the nineteenth century was personal journalism – the writing of a newspaper in the name of its owner or editor. In its place came the syndicated column, often written by a Washington-based journalist such as Arthur Brisbane or, during the years of the New Deal, Ernest K. Lindley. Perhaps the most famous and longest serving in this now firmly established tradition were Walter Lippman and the brothers Joseph Wright A. Alsop and Stewart A. Alsop. From political syndicated columnist to gossip columnist was but one step. Walter Winchell was in his day the supreme scourer of the lives of the famous.

Among the new forms which developed in the era of the mass press was the comic strip, of which no fewer than 150 now exist in the United States. Pulitzer's *World* was the first paper to run a strip regularly, but in 1894 the coloured strip entitled 'Shantytown' established itself as a major source of new readers in scores of papers: it was the work of Richard F. Outcault, whose main character, the 'Yellow Kid' provided American journalism of the whole period between the Civil War and the First World War with its chief sobriquet, the 'yellow press'. The phrase conjures up the sensationalist competition between the New York papers of that period, jostling on the streets for readers, with headlines written in the language which immigrants could understand.

The new power of the press lay in its ability to conjure with the moods and minds of its massed readers. It tended to move several steps away from control by or adherence to political parties. In America in particular, the parties had become machines for delivering votes, precinct by precinct, and for obtaining jobs for prominent supporters. The newspaper had to collect its audience first before it could help deliver votes, and thus a subtle change came about in the relationship between newspaper and politician. The bid for mass circulation had made the newspaper into an industry inaccessible to crude political interference. In Britain, on the other hand, a press structure was developing which was dependent upon the loyalty of specific papers to specific social classes; increasingly, in the years between 1890 and 1930, newspapers which failed to fit into the new patterns of circulation had recourse to wealthy individuals and to political parties for hidden subsidies. Party activists continued to feel that it was vital to keep special 'ideological' papers alive, although the cost was high. Conservative Central Office provided nearly half of the money necessary to buy the *Observer* in 1914; during the First World War the *Pall Mall Gazette* was taken over and run as a party paper. Lloyd George organized a group of prominent men who took over the *Daily News* during the Boer War and made it an organ of anti-war Liberalism, while another wing of the same party took over the *Westminster Gazette*. The great barons of the cheap mass press themselves contributed to this activity; both Northcliffe and Beaverbrook acted as 'cover' for party acquisition of papers in the early decades of the century. The Unionists at Manchester had mixed feelings when Northcliffe generously came forward with £50,000 to save a local Tory paper in 1908.

Many journalists were ex-politicians (and vice versa). Eyebrows were raised by traditionalists when Gladstone, on retiring from office in 1895, handed out six knighthoods to journalists; when Lloyd George distributed twenty-three high honours to men connected with the press at the end of the First World War, the practice had ceased to seem improper. The press barons, especially in wartime, demanded direct political office for themselves, as if their command of the organs of public opinion constituted a qualification. Northcliffe, Beaverbrook, Reith of the BBC felt that the transition from public communication to public (or ministerial) office would be a natural one; yet when they got it, their exercise of office was mediocre. It was all a far cry from the 1850s, when Palmerston had difficulty in convincing Queen Victoria that it was impossible to exclude newspapermen from public functions, however regrettable this might be. Newspaper publishing was now one step from propaganda, and that but one step from politics.

When Stanley Baldwin denounced Northcliffe's brother Rothermere and Beaverbrook of the *Daily Express*, in a phrase supplied by his cousin, Rudyard Kipling, for seeking 'power without responsibility, the prerogative

The Times.

My dear Walter,

I am very sorry not to have seen you before I
start on my world tour. I should have liked to
discuss with you affairs at Printing House Square.
The Paper is coming satisfactorily through this
grave financial crisis in newspapers. I cannot
say more than that. At the present moment I believe
there are only three morning newspapers in London
that are paying expenses.

I am going partly for reasons of health, and partly
because I think we ought to know something of the
aims and work of the Japanese. You, I know, went
for health entirely, and I earnestly trust that you
will return completely restored.

Yours sincerely,

Northcliffe

John Walter, Esq.   15th July 1921.

Letter from the owner of the ailing *Times* to its Chairman, John Walter IV. Soon after this Northcliffe's mind gave way, and a year later he was dead.

of the harlot throughout the ages', he was expressing his indignation that the new mass papers were not buyable, not as easily manipulated as their predecessors had been. Baldwin, and other politicians since him, have feared the repercussions of the press falling into too few hands. Opposition to monopolies and chain ownership has been the occasion for official commissions of investigation in many countries. In Britain, allegations that control of papers lies in the hands of a tiny group are of long standing; since 1835 there has been a growth of small chains of papers, and it seemed even then that, as a result of the restrictive effects of stamp taxation on sales and of certain common practices among tradesmen in advertising, fifteen men could control the editorial policy of the whole of the London press. Certainly many owners at that time, including the Provincial Newspaper Society, were hostile to changes in taxation which would ease the entry of competitors into the market. The sheer monopolistic dominance of *The Times* over all other (legal) newspapers was a further deterrent to the starting up of rival publications.

The shrinking of the number of newspaper owners in control of large segments of readership was already in evidence, however, before the First World War. In 1910 Northcliffe, Cadbury and Pearson published papers which accounted for a third of all morning circulation and 80 per cent of all evening circulation. Northcliffe, together with three other publishers, also controlled 80 per cent of all Sunday paper sales. The owners of the more serious intellectual papers feared that the barons of popular journalism would simply go on scooping up paper after paper. Northcliffe had by now acquired

Opposite Beaverbrook: 'power without responsibility', complained Stanley Baldwin.

163

William Randolph Hearst depicted by the cartoonist Herford as a politically ambitious spider, with one hand on the Governorship of New York state, another on the Capitol. By his ear is a smaller insect, his leader-writer Arthur Brisbane.

control of the ailing *Times* itself, though it continued to ail. The *Observer*, the *Manchester Guardian* and the *Economist* all turned themselves into special trusts, by which they hoped – successfully as it turned out – to maintain the kind of editorial independence traditionally conferred by family ownership, now endangered by the iron laws of rising costs and taxation.

But in the newspaper business there are many, many ways of restricting pluralism. In their content, the newspapers of the 'new journalism' were basically trying to widen their market by adding more and more different kinds of information. They were attempting to consolidate the new audience through multiplication of the tastes which they served. It was impossible for many of the existing papers to adjust to the new competitive round, and syndicates soon formed in America for selling written work around small and medium-sized papers. The new American copyright laws of 1870 and 1874 had made it harder for such papers to 'lift' material as freely as they had in the past. A.N. Kellogg, after the Civil War, started sending editors half-made newspapers to which they added a side of news for themselves. The practice was adopted everywhere. Then thin stereotype plates were sent out ready for printing. Kellogg next offered his customers the choice of various specialist services, from agricultural information to serial fiction. Agencies like McClure's started signing up the most popular authors of the day – Kipling, Jack London, Conan Doyle – to supply new fiction in serial form. In England the Tillotsons of the *Bolton Evening News* had started a similar service in their Fiction Bureau. The Hungarian immigrant Edward Bok specialized in selling women's reading material to the American papers after his success with his *Ladies' Home Journal*. By the end of the century the American population was divided half and half between city and country, and these services helped the non-metropolitan reader to receive word of the fashions, attitudes and new interests of the great cities.

But the spirit of standardization, once stirred, did not rest. Country papers had started to lose their powerful hold on circulations after 1864, when the American News Company set up rapid delivery systems which got the metropolitan dailies out to the countryside early enough to compete with local dailies. While syndication grew and the wire services magnified their spread (by 1900 the AP was sending 50,000 words a day to 2,300 newspapers), the chain ownership of newspapers seemed to offer some newspaper entrepreneurs further scope for rationalization through uniformity. Edward W. Scripps, in his partnership with Milton Macrae, had established a 'League' of 23 newspapers by 1914; the group was large enough to run its own news service, which later developed into the United Press. The League's policy was to take an interest in a paper, invest in it, and pull out if it failed to develop. Meanwhile, William Randolph Hearst was acquiring an even larger chain, which soon after the end of the First World War comprised 31 papers (including Sundays), 6 magazines, various film interests and a pair of wire services. It may come as a surprise to many who decry the growth of chains in the late twentieth century to know that, as early as 1929, more than a third of America's total circulation was in the hands of 70 chains. By the late 1970s the 12 largest chains controlled 38 per cent of the total daily circulation of the United States (23 million out of just over 60 million newspapers). Sixty per cent of the 1,750 newspapers which remained in 1977 (down from 2,000 at their peak in 1919) were owned by chains, and observers expected that within a decade or so five or six chains would emerge to consolidate their grip on an industry which in 1979 employs 400,000 people. The only statistics which dismayed the controllers of this vast machinery of advertising and information were the decline after the Second World War in the number of newspapers taken per household (down from 1.25 to 0.92), and the number of young people who purchased daily newspapers, which seemed to sag badly in the 1960s. Total circulation still rose annually, but not nearly as much as population.

Changes in the patterns of marketing in consumer goods and rising costs in the newspaper industry itself made the 1960s the era of concentration and consolidation, not only in America but throughout the developed world. It quickly passed from the exception to the rule for the main (or only) morning paper in a given city to be the owner of the main (or only) evening paper. The merging in 1959 of the United Press with the International News Service (born in 1909 as a Hearst agency) was evidence of a trend which quickly spread through the news industry. Fears grew that radio and television, which were now the main interlopers in the newspapers' monopoly of news in medium-sized and small towns, were gradually slipping into the hands of the same companies which controlled local papers. Court decisions in the late 1970s started the process of breaking up local 'cross-ownership' of electronic and print media. Newspapers began to exchange their local radio and TV stations with those of newspapers in other cities.

Similar processes were under way in all those countries which had managed to maintain a traditional nineteenth-century 'opinion' press with hosts of tiny papers. On the eve of the Second World War, Switzerland still had 406 separate newspapers, but by the mid 1970s this had dropped to 290. At the end of the war France experienced a major upsurge in journalistic activity, with 206 papers in Paris and the provinces – a number which dropped steadily to little over 80 by 1975. Germany largely re-created her press industry in the 1940s and 1950s, possessing at the peak 225 separate 'editorial unities', with rather more in actual titles – some papers differed only in their front page and advertising; by 1976 this had fallen to 122. Sweden, which was determined to retain its politically differentiated press structure, was so anguished by the demise between 1920 and 1970 of 50 of its conservative papers, 30 of its liberal papers and a number of social democrat papers that it instituted a complex form of subsidy whereby any paper serving less than 40 per cent of the households in its region of distribution could claim a wide variety of benefits and grants, the aim being to guarantee that each town of reasonable size would continue to have ideological competition between locally produced newspapers. Norway has pursued a similar ideal, and both of these countries claim that the decline has been arrested, certainly for a decade or so. Perhaps the greatest tragedy of all can be seen in Vienna, where 7 daily newspapers remain; true, this is far more than most cities of Vienna's size can support, but it is a pale shadow of the *grand siècle* when Vienna was the glittering, multitudinous journalistic capital of the world. The country which has undergone the most severe panic over the loss of newspapers has been Denmark, where over 100 papers out of 150 have died since the end of the Second World War; Denmark, unlike its Nordic partners, has set its mind against direct subsidies to damaged papers and has placed its faith, like Germany and Britain, in the hope that economic forces will gradually cease to threaten the lives of newspapers which have survived so far. In fact, in the late 1970s hopes have risen in many parts of Europe and America that the next decade will be one of expansion, not merely in terms of pages and supplements, but in new foundings of papers. Paris and New York have seen new morning papers in the shape of *Le Quotidien, Le Matin* and the short-lived *Trib*, and in other cities and countries there are plans for weeklies to become dailies and projects for new evening and weekly papers. Newspapers concentrating on finance have done well in Britain, Italy, Canada, the United States and the Far East. The *Wall Street Journal* publishes all over the United States and also in Hong Kong. London's *Financial Times* publishes by facsimile in Frankfurt. A new prosperity has dawned for specialist papers, especially business papers, but it is increasingly difficult for any city to support more than one paper with the same specialism or approach.

Throughout the century, the main intellectual tension among newspapers has been between the ethic which demands 'independence' and an older ethic, surviving in many places, by which the newspaper is *supposed* to belong to one of several contending ideologies. A steady gulf has grown between American and European practice, the former dedicated to a journalism of neutral, 'factual' information, untainted by party, unblemished by influence,

167

the latter still clinging, half-contradictorily, to the view that journalists should carry their party affiliations open to view. When a new press structure was created for Germany after 1945, the differences between these two traditions became very clear: in the British zone the newspapers were 'licensed' only to groups of supporters of one of the new legal political parties, while in the American zone each paper had to have an editorial committee comprising representatives of all the available parties (including the communists in some instances). Both approaches were based upon the same intention – to re-establish a firm democratic system in Germany. The origins of the American ethic lie in the changeover from party to non-party newspapers in the late nineteenth century; editors established themselves in large cities or grew up with their respective communities, needing to remain in touch with the whole of their markets. The agencies and the local 'legmen' needed to cast all partisan bias from their minds as they supplied material to city papers. Even in Washington, the growing band of accredited journalists (110 in 1900, 1,200 by 1960) had to be able to form relationships with politicians of all groupings. Indeed, journalists became an important instrument within the political and constitutional life of America: they were rumour-mongers and story-planters; they mingled with politicians, collecting information from some to use against others; they were inseparable from the politics of spoils, supplying in publicity the coinage of the wheeling and dealing of Washington life. The Teapot Dome scandal of 1923 – the exemplar of all scandals laid bare by congressional committees, which brought out a series of shady dealings in naval oil supplies – consisted in politicians grilling officials amid a blaze of publicity. Senator Joseph McCarthy, in exposing 'communist' infiltration of American life in the 1950s, was acting in this same tradition. At the time of the Watergate scandal in 1972 the world saw very clearly how firmly ingrained in America was the notion that it was the business of journalists to perform certain kinds of police action which public authorities themselves, because of political involvements, were unable and frequently unwilling to undertake.

The First Amendment to the American Constitution, which guaranteed freedom of the press, became the basis of a constitutionally guaranteed flow of information from bureaucracy to public; it also became the means by which publishers and broadcasting entrepreneurs could run their newspapers and stations in whatever way brought most profit. Not only did the American press emerge as arbiter and inspector of the congressional and administrative worlds; it also had an important role to play as broker between Presidency and people. Andrew Jackson had relied upon the support of close political friends who owned helpful newspapers; Andrew Johnson was the first President to give interviews to reporters regularly. Theodore Roosevelt was the first to be seriously preoccupied with pursuing the 'politics of the image', providing a non-stop monologue for journalists, displaying his daily activities to the press in a kind of moral drama of American values. He liked to be seen in his nightly rambles through the streets (he had once been Police Commissioner of New York); he liked to make constant popular, 'human' news. Woodrow Wilson had established the press conference as an instrument of government, and in 1932 Franklin D. Roosevelt seized upon the idea, mastered it and transferred it to the new medium of radio, offering the people frequent personal, paternalistic homilies. Each subsequent President has altered the institution to suit his style or political situation. Kennedy introduced television regularly to the conference and, more than his immediate predecessors, used this direct link with the public as a tool in his political battles with Congress. The press conference brought the Presidency into more subtle contact with the ebb and flow of public moods and sentiments; the press coverage reacting to a televised Presidential statement or interview became a means by which the competence of men in high office could be assessed.

Even the politics of the image, however, has its roots visible in the last part of the last century. The professionalization of newspaper reporting occurred in the context of a general professionalization of all the processes of information handling. Alongside the reporting of news there grew up a kind of counter-activity, the professional supplying of news. In the 1870s American political parties set up 'press bureaux' to ensure that editors received suitable information about their candidates and office-holders. Big-time actors and showmen, fashion houses, railway companies, all who required publicity to pursue their livelihood, rapidly saw the advantages of cultivating the friendship of press people. Ivy Lee, who had gained experience as Democratic Party press agent, in 1905 set up a 'literary bureau' available 'frankly and openly, on behalf of business concerns and public institutions, to supply the press and public of the United States prompt and accurate information'.

Public relations grew up as the *alter ego* of twentieth-century journalism. No longer did respectable people attempt to purchase favourable reputations

The presidential press conference in the White House, invented by Woodrow Wilson and mastered by Franklin D. Roosevelt (below).

for themselves in newspapers; instead, they employed specialists to promote the better understanding of their products and personalities. In 1910 Congress itself had taken on a press agent to send press handouts to the newspapers in Washington. A vast trade in manufactured news developed, the handling of which is the principal activity of a large proportion of the journalistic profession today; in Washington alone there are two press agents for every accredited journalist. At the very moment when the newspaper had achieved, in economics and in ethics, a realistic independence from government and party, and was able to pose as a free arbiter of fact, it found itself confronted with another complete industry founded on the assumption that information could itself be 'managed', that facts could create an impression. Journalists trained to distinguish fact from fiction were apt to be baffled by the subtleties and complexities of the new situation; the old rules of checking names and dates, discovering authentic sources, no longer measured up to the task. Where politicians no longer instructed reporters or editors what to say, they employed – or became – publicity experts dedicated to catching headlines and deadlines, to grooming away harsh realities. The journalist stood at the middle of the process by which powerful social forces constructed the effective 'realities' of society.

The journalistic practices worked out in Europe and America between 1865 and 1900 have been copied or exported throughout the world. It was evident to political groups in Africa, Asia and South America that newspapers were an intrinsic element in waging social revolution or campaigning for changes in social structure; only in very recent times has terrorism appeared to offer a serious substitute or an additional tool. Dr Nnamdi Azikiwe, later Governor-General and President of Nigeria, founded the *West African Pilot* in 1937 and followed it with six sister papers constituting the Zik Press, which replaced the Christian-moralistic tone of existing newspapers with a nationalist-revolutionary one. In China Sun Yat-sen, the 'Father of the Republic', established a revolutionary party press round the *Chung-kuo Jih-pao* ('Chinese daily paper') of 1899, and used this and other papers to spread knowledge of his three principles (nationalism, democracy and the people's welfare). Mao Tse-tung was also active in journalism, through the *Kung-ch'an tang-jen* ('the Communist') of 1939 and the *Chung-kuo kung-jen* ('the Chinese worker') of 1940. Only for a brief period after the Revolution of 1911 did China ever experience a free press in the European manner: 500 papers sprang up within a few months, run mainly by Chinese journalists who had learned their craft abroad, and the spirit of radicalism spread so fast that soon most papers were closed apart from those dedicated to the modernization of the economy and business. In South America, too, the same influences were felt: José Baille y Ordonez, later President of Uruguay, founded *El Día* ('the day') as a reforming political paper in 1886, when the modern state was being consolidated after a period of upheaval; within a couple of decades a European-style press structure began to develop, with two competing chains of papers, the Blanco and Colorado groups.

One of the few non-Anglo-Saxon countries whose press is powerful enough to have any impact outside its own borders is Japan. There a

newspaper press was founded in the 1860s by expatriate Englishmen, one of the earliest being A. W. Hansard, whose *Nagasaki Shipping List and Advertiser* of 1861 ranks as the first newspaper of the country. Japanese papers soon followed, and on the seizure of power from the Shogunate by the Emperor in 1868 ten newspapers sprang up, which were quickly suppressed for rashly supporting the ousted ruling group. However, after the opening of a parliament in 1881 competing parties came into existence, and with them party papers, the Tokyo *Nichi-Nichi Shimbun* for the Imperial Party, the *Yubi Hochi-Shimbun* for the Progressives and the *Jiyu Shimbun* for the Liberals. Even this second flowering soon withered under the impact of a fresh law which came to be known, not without reason, as the 'Law of Newspaper Extermination'. The Meiji Constitution of 1890 again permitted new foundings of newspapers, and a commercial press began to develop alongside the political papers, with the *Asahi Shimbun* ('morning sun') linked to Reuters and its main rival, the *Mainichi Shimbun* ('daily paper'), creating its own news agency. In 1890, too, the first Marinoni press was imported, making mass-production of newspapers possible. By 1910, 250 papers flourished in Japan, and it was largely due to their pressure that general suffrage was granted in 1925. With the beginning of the Manchurian conflict in 1931, government pressure began to 'bend' the editorials of all Japanese papers. In 1936 the Cabinet set up its own Information Committee, and this, together with Domei, the state news agency, manipulated the press until the end of the Second World War; a large number of papers were suppressed altogether. In 1937 there were 1,200 papers, with a combined circulation of 19 million per day; by 1945 there were 57, reduced in size to two pages each, with a total circulation of 14 million.

In the immediate aftermath of the war the occupation administration (SCAP) tried to purge from the press all those deemed to have been responsible for the conflict; hundreds of 'war criminals' were expelled from their jobs, only to be allowed back in 1950, after a reversal of occupation policies, in an attempt to reduce communist influence in the press. Seven hundred communist sympathizers were then fired, but by this time much of the Japanese press had irrevocably acquired a highly radical line – which was not what had been intended by SCAP. The occupation had also, in 1948, modified its censorship system to a post-publication scrutiny, pushing newspaper deadlines forwards and inducing an extremely aggressive form of competition between the tiny two- and four-page papers, even though they shared a joint distribution service and were restricted in size due to newsprint rationing.

The controls were not removed altogether until the San Francisco Peace Treaty of 1952, but within a decade the Japanese economy was in a 'mass' phase. Total circulation of morning and evening papers rose to well above 50 million, second only to that of the United States. Today, 400,000 people are employed in the production and distribution of newspapers in Japan.

As radio and television took a larger and larger share of advertising, and as circulation reached saturation level, new forms of competition began to appear in the Japanese press. The new goal of newspaper managers is to increase profit margins rather than circulation, to curb aggressive competition and to moderate the editorial tone at the same time. In fact, after the political upheaval which took place in 1960 at the time of the signing of the US – Japan Security Treaty, the press decidedly reduced its almost institutionalized anti-government line. Still, however, the Japanese press refuses to participate in the distribution of national honours, and declines to co-operate with the government's attempts to set up a special consultative agency between the industry and the administration. On the other hand, the flow of information from government to press is organized on an extremely cosy basis: each Minister, including the Prime Minister, has a private 'Reporters' Club' which admits specialist correspondents who remain attached to that particular individual while he continues in office; only members may attend its sessions and share its reporting facilities. The Reporters' Clubs are in some ways similar to the parliamentary lobby in the British legislature. While information is handed out through these closely knit agencies, the editorial policies of papers tend to be extremely critical.

The Japanese press has a tendency towards sudden 'crazes'. It went into an anti-pollution, anti-petroleum phase in the early 1970s to the point at which the advertising policies of several papers were placed at hazard, so hostile had the advertisers become and so sceptical were the public of the advertisers' claims. A year or two later the newspapers became extremely preoccupied with the Lockheed affair and other political scandals, indulging in an almost frantic competitive search for further information on misdeeds in high places.

One major problem faced by the Japanese press is the feeling that the structure has developed as far as it can go. On the one hand, there are five national newspapers with vast circulations (between 1.5 and 6 million) printing in many cities and supporting scores of local editions: one national paper has 140 daily sub-editions containing local news and advertising. On the other hand, there is a spread of local papers, one in each prefecture, which mop up the bulk of local circulation and local advertising. There is no further room for expansion unless papers move into the new electronic media, which several already are doing. Japan is, therefore, building its future hopes upon such phenomena as facsimile newspapers printed in the home, or various new teletext services sent out from broadcasting transmitters. (A large number of newspapers in Japan own controlling interests in radio and TV stations whose installations may be used for this purpose.) Japan is in the forefront of virtually all of the new developments in the printing and distribution of information, partly in order to find work for personnel displaced by other new techniques, since Japanese companies have to guarantee employment throughout the working lives of employees, but partly also to find uses for additional capital which cannot be used for expansion in the normal way.

One heritage of the occupation days is the fact that most of the capital in Japanese newspapers is owned by the employees; 60 per cent of the newspaper-owning companies have a majority of their shares in the hands of their workers. The bigger the paper, the bigger the ratio of shares held in this way. Unlike the countries of the West, Japan has no fears that its press will pass into the hands of outside interests. When the *Mainichi Shimbun* went bankrupt in 1976, the banks agreed to keep it going throughout its period of restructuring; despite the many financial problems from which certain of the

田中前首相を逮捕

毎日新聞
夕刊
毎日新聞東京本社
東京貿易
取締役社長 松宮慶夫
1976

ロッキード事件 一挙に頂上作戦

檜山から五億円受領

外為法違反「ピーナツ」「ピーシズ」分

東京地検

榎本秘書も逮捕

政治責任を痛感

自民の体質改善に全力

三木首相会見

離党届、自民が受理

LIBÉRATION

ORGANE DES MOUVEMENTS DE RÉSISTANCE UNIS

Un seul chef : DE GAULLE
Une seule lutte : pour nos Libertés

Notre seul but est de rendre la parole au Peuple Français Général DE GAULLE

1ᵉʳ Mai 1943 : Fête Nationale du sabotage contre l'Ennemi

Vive le 1ᵉʳ Mai

Le 1ᵉʳ Mai est traditionnellement un jour de fête et de lutte pour la classe ouvrière. Que ce quatrième premier mai de guerre manifeste clairement à nos amis et à nos ennemis que le peuple français — loin d'être abattu — est plus que jamais à la pointe du combat.

Le 1ᵉʳ mai 1942 fut un jour de manifestations impressionnantes. Il faut faire mieux encore. L'ennemi est au bord de la défaite. Que ce dernier premier mai avant la Libération soit marqué dans les Annales de la Résistance française par une recrudescence du sabotage et des coups de main contre l'ennemi et ses valets, que la résis-

vos organisations de résistance. Le 1ᵉʳ mai 1943, vous manifesterez par tous les moyens contre l'oppression nazie, contre la déportation de vos frères en Allemagne, pour vos droits humains les plus élémentaires.

Il ne suffit pas d'être de cœur avec les Alliés. Il ne suffit ni de détester les Allemands, ni d'écouter les bonnes nouvelles de la radio anglaise. Il faut participer à la guerre, il faut que le peuple français agisse et fasse la preuve de sa force, s'il veut un jour se faire entendre. Un peuple qui attend passivement est un peuple condamné par l'histoire.

large national papers suffer, the way is now open for great economies to be effected through the adoption of electronic devices in both production and distribution.

In other countries which, like Japan, have been the victims of invasion and occupation in one or other World War, the main trends of the century have been diverted or distorted. France, for example, developed its mass circulations very early, with individual papers topping a million well before Britain's *Daily Mail* was even launched. *Paris-Soir*, which was modelled by its owner Jean Prouvost on the Northcliffe/Beaverbrook/Rothermere press of Britain, achieved a circulation of 2 million in 1938, a little after the *Daily Herald* in London reached the same hotly competed-for sale. *Paris-Soir*'s very rapid success deeply affected the general state of the Paris newspaper market. Although France had been used to having several giants among its numerous papers (four *grands journaux* shared a combined circulation of 4½ million before the First World War), it began to seem impossible for a traditional press of information and serious opinion to survive alongside the new popular papers. The rise in costs brought on by the First World War had already resulted in the stagnation of the big circulations of the earlier part of the century. But the dilemma was resolved by a further war and an occupation which swept away most of the existing papers; a large number co-operated with the Vichy régime, while others were turned into propaganda sheets. A group of new papers of the Resistance started up clandestinely, although *Libération*, *Combat* and *Défense de la France* all managed to distribute over 100,000 copies apiece, even in secret.

Libération, organ of the French Resistance, clandestinely and rather smudgily printed.

Opposite Front page from the land where headlines are vertical. This is the *Mainichi Shimbun* of 27 July 1976, reporting the arrest of former Prime Minister Tanaka in connection with the Lockheed scandal.

Lundi 22 decembre 1941

DIRECTION-REDACTION
85 Fleet Street, Londres,
E.C.4 Tel. : CENtral 8467

ADMINISTRATION et PUBLICITE
Practical Press Ltd., I Dorset
Buildings, Salisbury Square,
Fleet Street, Londres, E.C.4
Tel. : CENtral 1555

Journal quotidien paraissant
à Londres avec le patronage
de l'Association des Français de
Grande-Bretagne.

Tous les jours UN PENNY

2ème année Nº 412

BLACK-OUT
à Londres : 17.24

ABONNEMENTS

Registered at the G.P.O.
as a newspaper.

FRANCE

Dernière
Edition

LIBERTE • EGALITE • FRATERNITE

CRISE EN ALLEMAGNE

HITLER ECARTE SES GENERAUX ET PREND LE COMMANDEMENT SUPRÈME DES FORCES ARMEES DU REICH

DERNIER ACTE

EN Allemagne, la crise décisive est ouverte. Ecartant de son poste le maréchal von Brauchitsch, Hitler a fait annoncer hier soir qu'il prenait le commandement direct de toutes les forces armées allemandes.

Que signifie ce geste? Pour en apprécier la portée, il faut, en remontant de plusieurs années en arrière, se souvenir des rapports de l'état-major allemand avec Hitler; l'homme nouveau. Au début, en 1933, ce furent des relations de méfiance. Puis, voyant que ce dictateur rendait le

HITLER A ANNONCE HIER SOIR QU'IL A DECIDE DE PRENDRE PERSONNELLEMENT LE COMMANDE-MENT SUPRÊME DES FORCES ARMEES ALLEMANDES.

Dans une proclamation au peuple, il rappelle qu'il détenait, depuis 1938, le commandement théorique des trois services armés, mais ajoute que, devant "les proportions énormes" de la campagne de Russie, il prend maintenant le commandement direct et effectif des forces allemandes. Voici cette proclamation:

"Le 4 février 1938, quand le Führer prit le commandement de toutes les forces armées, ce fut en raison de la bataille qui menaçait déjà de s'engager pour la liberté du peuple allemand.

"La 'raison d'état' exigeait impérieusement que tous les pouvoirs fussent concentrés en une seule main. Ce n'est qu'ainsi que les pré-

HITLER LANCE A L'ARMEE UN APPEL DESESPERE

APRÈS LA PRISE DE DERNA ET DE MEKILI, ROMMEL PRIVÉ de chars, tente de fuir vers l'ouest

LES Britanniques parachèvent leur victoire de Libye. D'ores et déjà, on le sait, les forces blindées du général Rommel ont été presque entièrement détruites:

TROIS CROISEURS JAPONAIS TOUCHES par des bombes hollandaises

Débarquement japonais dans le sud des Philippines

La garnison de Hong

Le dernier effort du général allemand se produisit, la semaine dernière, au sud de Gazala. Mais les troupes indiennes subirent le choc assez longtemps pour permettre aux chars anglais de déborder l'ennemi par l'ouest et de disloquer sa résistance. Vendredi, Rommel était obligé d'abandonner Derna sur la côte et aussi Mekili dans l'intérieur, qui est la clé du golfe de Syrte. Il essaya alors en vain de sauver les quelques tanks qui lui restaient, en accélérant sa fuite vers l'ouest en direction de Benghazi.

N'ayant pas réussi, à occuper une ligne défensive entre ces deux localités, l'ennemi se retire rapidement, à l'ouest.

France was printed under somewhat easier conditions in London and secretly distributed.

The Liberation gave an enormous new impetus to the press: it was possible, in the conditions of stringent paper rationing and an enormous hunger for information, for new papers to start up with very little capital, and 175 papers circulated in Paris and the provinces in a very short-lived information boom. As interest in news subsided and the economy stagnated, the new papers were forced gradually either out of business or into the hands of people willing to apply new capital to their development. In 1947 a month-long printers' strike led to the loss of scores of papers, and the sudden miracle of a 'decapitalized' press was over, together with much of the spirit of the Resistance. Many of the pre-war press-owners, including Prouvost, who had been banned from owning papers at the Liberation, returned to their businesses, and France ceased to be among the major newspaper-consuming countries of the world. By 1970 it had a total daily circulation of 11 million, which means that every thousand people in France purchase little more than 200 papers, compared with 500 in Japan and 440 in Britain. In order to reach the level achieved by a comparable European country like Holland, with 300 newspapers sold per thousand people, the publishers of France would have to raise their daily circulation to 16 million.

Yet Paris has remained a city producing a constant flow of political news, and for every newspaper lost during the 1960s a new one has sprung up, usually having a small circulation within a specific political community. The phenomenal rise of the white-collar worker in France is symbolized by the growth of *Le Monde*, a post-war foundation, to a circulation of half a million, rivalling that of the largest mass paper of the period, *France-Soir*. A complicated set of subsidies helps papers dedicated to political and ideological activity rather than to high circulation to stay in business, even though new press barons such as Robert Hersant have emerged, moving into the Paris press from success in the provinces, in search of journals with prosperous advertising and political influence.

The German press, paradoxically, has shared a number of characteristics with that of France. Although it retained a large number of family-owned papers right into the Weimar period – some of them, indeed, have survived to the present day – there grew up in the 1890s a group of sizeable publishing houses which started acquiring a large number of papers. Rudolf Mosse bought the old *Vossische Zeitung* (known for decades as Berlin's 'Aunt Voss') to sit beside his *Berliner Volkszeitung*, and Leopold Ullstein acquired the *Berliner Allgemeine Zeitung* in 1909 and after the war founded the *Montagspost* ('Monday post'). Several of the papers in these new chains became major city journals; others turned into a new brand of boulevard paper. Alongside them there began a newspaper war between two new groups of ideological journals of the far right and the far left respectively. The communists' *Rote Fahne* ('red flag') started as soon as hostilities had ceased, and a while later Joseph Goebbels started the *Deutsche Montagsblatt* (later called *Der Angriff* or 'attack'), a major Nazi organ until 1944. Both the Mosse and Ullstein empires were taken over by the Nazis together with all their fixed property. A third large chain had belonged to August Scherl, whose papers had been involved in the intense competition inside Berlin in the 1890s. In the middle of the First World War these were taken over by Alfred Hugenberg, who had been President of the Friedrich Krupp concern in Essen and whose propaganda against the Weimar régime in the 1920s played an important role in the destruction of democracy and the rise of the Nazis.

With the Nazi 'Co-ordination Measures' of 1933, a large proportion of papers were forced into the ownership of a few firms sympathetic to the National Socialist cause. Communist and socialist publishing houses were confiscated or closed, as were a number of right-wing ones. In 1935 a new Reich Press Chamber was created under Max Amann which systematically dismantled all the *Generalanzeiger* papers in Germany by means of a stream of repressive decrees. By 1944, over 82 per cent of all newspapers had come by gradual stages to be controlled by a single Press Trust. One interesting aspect of the Nazi system was that it imposed from the start a state monopoly of newspaper advertising, exactly as the Prussian kings had done over a hundred years before. All advertising was encouraged to assist in the propagation of Nazi ideals, although a normal advertising industry did manage to survive until the end of the war.

The Nazi period brought about the only real transformation in the content of the newspapers which had occurred for a generation. Foreign reporting was truncated and criticism of any kind forbidden. The Reich Propaganda Minister dictated the scope of each publication, its intended audience and the nature of the content. The traditional divisions and demarcations within the German press between the *Anzeiger*, the *Heimatzeitung*, the opinion papers and the popular and financial papers was thrown into confusion. Germany had had a wartime Press Office overseeing newspapers in the First World War, and only in 1919 had a new and painfully acquired press freedom begun again, enshrined in Article 118 of the Weimar Constitution. However, the new régime contained various provisions 'for the protection of the republic' under which radical newspapers were prosecuted even before the Nazis seized power. In 1931 and 1932 emergency regulations closed down both Nazi and communist papers, but within a year Goebbels's new Ministry of Public Education and Propaganda was supervising the process of crippling the newspaper industry. The entire profession of journalism was placed under standing orders and obliged to carry out its work 'in the interests of the state'. Certain aspects of Germany's nineteenth-century press survived, however, including the small circulations of the majority of papers. At the turn of the century 90 per cent of all German papers had sold less than 5,000 per issue; at the end of the war over half still had circulations below 8,000.

As in Japan, the victorious powers in Germany in the 1940s systematically removed all the former press-owners from the newspaper world, and constructed a new set of papers in their respective zones of occupation. Each zone contained one paper of major importance: *Die Welt* in the British zone, the *Neue Zeitung* in the American, *Nouvelles de France* in the French and the *Tägliche Rundschau* ('daily review') in the Russian. Within four years these 'licensed' papers were 170 in number, and with the ending of newsprint rationing Germany quickly reacquired an extremely lively and enterprising press. The Basic Law of May 1949 granted a wide set of press freedoms, slightly complicated in their administration through the division of functions, in the new federal structure of West Germany, between state and federal governments. Within one year 600 papers came into being, although the majority of circulation remained with the papers established by the occupying powers. The distinction between these 'licensed' papers and the rest has been maintained ever since, and most German households tend to take one of the former plus a *Heimatzeitung* with local news and local advertising. Many of the smaller papers are really one paper with different titles for its various local editions; in 1954, therefore, it was possible to claim that Germany had either 1,500 papers or 225 separate 'editorial entities'. As mentioned earlier, a process of concentration has set in during more recent years, and a quarter of the population now lives in an area of local newspaper monopoly; the individual German household does not in practice have a very wide daily choice. One very large firm, the Springer concern, based in Hamburg and Berlin, has acquired a huge and worrying influence within the German press. In parts of Germany this one firm has control of 60 per cent of the circulation; on Sundays, when few papers are published, Springer has a total monopoly. He owns the powerful *Die Welt*, plus the country's largest circulating paper, the tabloid *Bild-Zeitung* ('picture post') with its four million copies per day, in addition to a host of magazines. The German authorities have instituted several inquiries into general press concentration and the growth of local monopolies; it is now impossible for papers of any size to merge without an investigation by the Kartelamt (anti-trust administration) in Berlin, although this of course has little power to force collapsing companies to continue in existence. It is expected, however, that a

programme of technical investment and the introduction of electronics into production will cut costs and keep most of the existing papers going in the foreseeable future. The panic of the late 1960s appears to have subsided.

Italy and Austria have passed through similar stages of occupation and reorganization from outside. In July 1924 Mussolini promulgated a decree by which the directors of all newspapers, who until then had carried legal responsibility for the political content of the papers, were placed under the supervision of the local prefects; without a formal censorship, therefore, press freedom disappeared and non-fascist papers could not exist. Mussolini's party, however, found the cost of this operation, which entailed taking financial control of many papers, too much to bear, and a large number of papers were merged or closed. The general control was later taken over by a Ministry of Popular Culture, while the allocation of paper was placed under a separate department of state. Journalists were enrolled in their own *ordine* – a kind of guild still operating today – which guaranteed them enormous privileges and high pay while restricting entry into the profession.

As Italy gradually collapsed during the war, German troops moving into the north closed down a number of publications, Catholic ones in particular, while the Allies set up a licensing system in the south and partisan groups started up their own clandestine papers. The Communist Party had seized the presses of the Fascist Party and proceeded to publish its own papers on them. In the new republic many of the old large papers were permitted to reappear, but with the word *nuovo* in their title, e.g. *Il Nuovo Corriere della Sera* ('new evening mail'). A new 'information' press was born, emerging from the licensed papers and competing with a host of party political papers. What Italy finally acquired, therefore, was a patchwork structure of papers operating within a system by which official bodies continue to control the supply and price of paper, the salaries and conditions of journalists and, in addition, the selling price of the newspaper itself.

The daily newspaper has never taken root as a mass phenomenon in Italy, where fewer papers are purchased daily than in any other European country. The press has become the property of powerful interests with ulterior motives for sustaining often rather costly burdens. Newspapers are owned by political interests or parties, or by large companies who need them to perform favours or make trouble for one group of politicians or another. Very few indeed make a profit, and the government provides an elaborate set of subsidies, based on the quantity of newsprint consumed, partly as compensation for its insistence on controlling the selling price. Italy's newspaper industry is like a very lively cripple, performing many of the critical functions of the nineteenth-century newspaper, investigative, vituperative, informative, but in a state of constant emergency.

In every country of Europe the most pressing phenomenon in the newspaper business since 1950 has been the steady loss of titles. It has become common for national inquiries to be held and for subsidies to be granted. Italy, France, Austria and the Scandinavian countries (apart from Denmark) have tried through subsidies to hold on to a late-nineteenth-century heritage of political papers, even though the role of the newspaper in general has changed everywhere during the present century: it is much larger

today, with more functions to perform and with a considerably greater amount of advertising. Editors, in order to keep this revenue, have had to widen the appeal of their papers, to the point at which the old political readerships have become inconvenient. This paradox is at its most extreme in Britain, where the Labour Party laments bitterly the loss of all the papers which supported it through thick and thin and has to rely upon papers which support it only on economic grounds, i.e. because their readers tend to vote Labour rather than Conservative. The *Daily Mirror*, with its very large circulation – despite the loss of a million or two in recent years to rivals including the *Sun*, now belonging to the Australian Rupert Murdoch – supports the Labour Party out of its own economic interests rather than out of real ideological preference. The *Sun*, on the other hand, circulating at a very similar level of the population (perhaps including the less educated section of the working class), is far less concerned to wave a political flag. The other mass papers, the *Daily Express* and the *Daily Mail*, are avowedly Conservative. Among the quality papers there is a better balance, with one right-wing (the *Telegraph*), one leftish (the *Guardian*) and one independent (*The Times*). The problem of the decline of political papers in Britain is buried inside the question of class structure and income distribution. It is many years since it has seemed sensible for anyone to attempt to create a new mass political paper. The *News Chronicle* and the *Daily Herald* both

Death of a newspaper. This was the scene in the news room of the London *News Chronicle* on Monday, 16 October 1960, shortly after it was announced that the paper was to cease publication. The first issue of the *Daily News* had been brought out 114 years before by Charles Dickens.

disappeared because, though they had huge circulations (above two million), they appealed only to less well-off sections of the population. Their readership was ageing. The middle class spends enough money, whatever its political persuasions, to support a variety of papers; the working class, reader for reader, can support only papers which circulate right across ideological groupings. The market can no longer support a minority paper within the working class, and fears continue to exist about the viability of all the national papers presently existing. A similar set of problems applies to the Sunday papers.

The great press baronies established before or between the wars continue to exist, but most of the original barons, who tended to enjoy very long lives, have died. The *Daily Express* has passed into the control of a large commercial company, and the spirit of 'personal ownership' which it had retained ever since the Canadian immigrant Max Aitken (later Lord Beaverbrook) acquired the paper early in the century has evaporated. Lord Thomson, with his enormous influence among the quality papers as owner of both *The Times* and *Sunday Times*, has died, his huge international press empire conjoined with valuable oil interests. The Astors have given up control of the *Observer*, also to oil interests, this time American. It seems that the only secure homes available for papers which used to depend upon the whim and genius of extremely wealthy and sometimes politically motivated individuals are large corporations whose primary interests lie outside the press. A similar dilemma exists in other countries, though in many of the most successful press enterprises ownership of newspapers by other than newspaper interests is regarded as unacceptable.

In the course of four hundred years the newspaper press has not finally dealt with the issues into which it was born. Its methods of production and distribution are always inadequate to the ideals and purposes which appear to

Composing room of the future: electronic composition and making-up of advertisements at the *Minneapolis Star and Tribune*.

rise from the activity of collecting news. Every century or so they undergo a major alteration, and the 1980s, as we are beginning to realize, will certainly see the end of molten lead as the main raw material for setting the pages of the press; with the end of 'hot metal' a large proportion of the work-force will disappear, and the great aggregations of capital and real estate on which the massive papers of the twentieth century have come to depend may no longer be necessary. It may become easier to enter into the market-place of newspapers in the next twenty years than it has been at any time in the last seventy. At the same time, the other great asset of established papers – the habit of purchasing them which exists among a given section of the population – may help to carry them through the current transformation into an even more complete monopoly. Newspapers are ceasing to be manufacturing concerns pure and simple, and are commencing a new existence as conduits for advertising and information transmitted by various electronic techniques or at least produced on paper by electronic means. Either way, the newspaper is coming to depend for its being upon a resource (telecommunications capacity) which is closely linked by its nature to government. The whole riddle out of which the newspaper was born, the paradox of how to acquire information affecting the control of the society while remaining separate from goverment, remains as clearly unanswered as in the days of the Habsburgs and the Tudors. The newspaper, whether it is trying to destroy a President or entertain the semi-literate, operates within a network of influences which run throughout society; in the last decades of the twentieth century it is moving from one sector of the economy to another, changing its appearance, reorganizing its lines of supply and distribution; but it cannot release itself from the field of forces set up by the highly charged phenomenon of public information.

Reading List

D'Ainvelle, V., *La Presse en France* (Presse universitaire de Grenoble, 1965)

Altick, R.D., *The English Common Reader* (University of Chicago Press, Chicago and London, 1963)

Altman, Albert A., 'Shinbushi – the early Meiji adaptation of the western-style newspaper' in W.G. Beasley (ed.), *Modern Japan* (Allen & Unwin, London, and University of California Press, 1975)

Archambault, F., and J.F. Lemoine, *4 Milliards de Journeaux* (Alain Moreau, Paris, 1977)

Ayerst, D., *The Guardian: Biography of a Newspaper* (Collins, London, and Cornell University Press, 1971)

Bellanger, C., *et al.* (eds), *Histoire Générale de la Presse Française*, 4 vols (Presses universitaires de France, Paris, 1969–)

Castronovo, V., and N. Tranfaglia, *Storia della Stampa Italiana*, 5 vols, 1 and 5 only completed (Laterza Editori, Bari, 1976)

Coleman, D.C., *The British Paper Industry, 1495–1860* (Oxford University Press, 1958)

Collins, Irene, *The Government and the Newspaper Press in France, 1814–1881* (Oxford University Press, 1959)

Cook, E.T., *Delane of The Times* (Constable, London, 1915)

Curran, James, George Boyce and Pauline Wingate (eds), *Newspaper History: Studies in the Evolution of the British Press* (Constable, London, 1978)

Ejiri, Susumu, *Characteristics of the Japanese Press* (Nihon Shinbun Kyokai, 1972)

Emery, E., and H.L. Smith, *The Press and America* (Prentice-Hall, Englewood Cliffs, N.J., 1954)

Escott, T.H.S., *Masters of English Journalism* (T. Fisher Unwin, London, 1911)

Filler, L., *The Muckrakers* (Pennsylvania State University Press, 1976)

Frank, Joseph, *The Beginnings of the English Newspaper, 1620–1660* (Oxford University Press and Harvard University Press, 1961)

Franklin, Benjamin, *Autobiography* (reprinted by Washington Square Press, New York, 1975)

Gustafsson, Karl Erik, and Stig Hadenius, *Swedish Press Policy* (Swedish Institute, Stockholm, 1976)

Hobson, H., *et al.*, *The Pearl of Days: An Intimate Memoir of The Sunday Times* (Hamish Hamilton, London, 1972)

Høyer, Svennik, Stig Hadenius and Lennart Weibull, *The Politics and Economics of the Press: A Developmental Perspective* (Sage Publications, Beverly Hills, California, 1975)

Kieve, J.L., *The Electric Telegraph* (David & Charles, Newton Abbot, and Harper & Row, New York, 1973)

Knightley, Philip, *The First Casualty – the War Correspondent as Hero, Propagandist and Myth Maker from Crimea to Vietnam* (André Deutsch, London, and Harcourt Brace Jovanovich, New York, 1975)

Kobre, S., *The Development of American Journalism* (Wm. C. Brown, Dubuque, Iowa, 1972)

Koszyk, K., *Die Deutsche Presse im 19. Jahrhundert* (Colloquium, Berlin, 1966)

—— *Die Deutsche Presse 1914–1945* (Colloquium, Berlin, 1972)

Lee, Alan J., *The Origins of the Popular Press, 1855–1914* (Croom Helm, London, and Rowman & Littlefield, Totowa, N.J., 1976)

Lindemann, M., *Die Deutsche Presse bis 1815* (Colloquium, Berlin, 1969)

Mayer, Henry, *The Press in Australia* (Angus & Robertson, London, Lansdowne Press, Melbourne, and Soccer Associates, New Rochelle, N.Y., 1964)

Mazedier, René, *Histoire de la Presse Parisienne* (Editions du Pavois, Paris, 1945)

Morison, S., *The English Newspaper, 1622–1932* (Cambridge University Press, and Macmillan, New York, 1932)

Mott, F.L., *American Journalism: A History, 1690–1960* (Macmillan, New York, 1969)

Padrutt, Christian, *Zur Lage der Schweitzer Presse* (Universität Zürich, 1975)

Pons, Dominique, *H.. comme Hersant* (Alain Moreau, Paris, 1977)

Pound, R., and G. Harmsworth, *Northcliffe* (Cassell, London, 1959; Praeger, New York, 1960)

Prakke, H., W.B. Lerg and M. Schmolke (eds), *Handbuch der Weltpresse* (Westdeutscher Verlag, Opladen, 1970)

Seymour-Ure, Colin, *The Political Impact of Mass Media* (Constable, London, and Sage Publications, Beverly Hills, California, 1974)

Shaaber, M.A., *Some Forerunners of the Newspaper in England, 1476–1622* (Frank Cass, London, and Octagon Books, New York, 1966)

Smith, A.C.H., *Paper Voices: The Popular Press and Social Change, 1935–1965* (Chatto & Windus, London, and Rowman & Littlefield, Totowa, N.J., 1975)

Smith, Anthony, *Subsidies and the Press in Europe* (Political and Economic Planning, London, 1976)

Taylor, A.J.P., *Beaverbrook* (Hamish Hamilton, London, and Simon & Schuster, New York, 1972)

Tebbel, John, *The Compact History of the American Newspaper* (Hawthorn Books, New York, 1963)

Thomas, P.W., *Sir John Berkenhead, 1617–1679* (Clarendon Press, Oxford, 1969)

History of The Times, 5 vols (The Times, London, 1935–52)

Webb, R.K., *The British Working-Class Reader, 1780–1848* (Chatto & Windus, London, and Columbia University Press, 1955)

Weisberger, Bernard A., *The American Newspaperman* (University of Chicago Press, 1961)

Wickwar, W., *The Struggle for Freedom of the Press, 1819–1832* (Allen & Unwin, London, 1928)

Williams, Raymond, *The Long Revolution* (Chatto & Windus, London, and Columbia University Press, 1961)

List of Illustrations

The publisher gratefully acknowledges the help and advice given by Mr Gordon Phillips of the Archives of *The Times*.

Index

Where the definite article is an integral part of a newspaper's title (*Die Welt, The Times*), this determines its place in the alphabetical order. Page numbers in italics refer to illustrations.